Regional Security

Regional organizations are an inescapable feature of global politics. Virtually all countries in the world are members of at least one regional or other intergovernmental organization.

The involvement of international organizations in the realm of regional peace and security, and their cooperation in this domain with the United Nations, has reached an unprecedented level. Regional organizations have traditionally been formed around economic, political, or environmental objectives; however, over the last decades these organizations have gradually penetrated into the security sphere and developed their capacities in conflict prevention, peacekeeping, or post-war reconstruction.

In Europe, Africa, Asia, or the Americas, regional and other intergovernmental organizations have been concurrently empowered by the UN and their own member states to maintain peace and security. Despite suffering from important discrepancies in both their mandates and capacities, regional organizations have become indisputable actors that play a role from the outbreak of a crisis to the reconstruction efforts in the aftermath of a conflict.

Presenting the most up-to-date critical and comparative analysis of the major regional security institutions, assessing a wide range of regional organizations, and providing an accessible and comprehensive guide to 11 key organizations, this book is the first systematic study of the capacities of the most recognized intergovernmental organizations with a security mandate. *Regional Security* is essential reading for all students of international organizations, peace and security studies, and global governance.

Rodrigo Tavares is Research Fellow at United Nations University (UNU-CRIS), Belgium and the School of Global Studies, University of Gothenburg, Sweden. He also served as a consultant to national governments and several UN agencies.

Routledge Global Institutions

Edited by Thomas G. Weiss
The CUNY Graduate Center, New York, USA
and Rorden Wilkinson
University of Manchester, UK

About the Series

The "Global Institutions Series" is designed to provide readers with comprehensive, accessible, and informative guides to the history, structure, and activities of key international organizations. Every volume stands on its own as a thorough and insightful treatment of a particular topic, but the series as a whole contributes to a coherent and complementary portrait of the phenomenon of global institutions at the dawn of the millennium.

Books are written by recognized experts, conform to a similar structure, and cover a range of themes and debates common to the series. These areas of shared concern include the general purpose and rationale for organizations, developments over time, membership, structure, decision-making procedures, and key functions. Moreover, current debates are placed in historical perspective alongside informed analysis and critique. Each book also contains an annotated bibliography and guide to electronic information as well as any annexes appropriate to the subject matter at hand.

The volumes currently published include:

The International Labour Organization
by Steve Hughes (University of Newcastle) and Nigel Haworth (University of Auckland Business School)

The Regional Development Banks
Lending with a regional flavor
by Jonathan R. Strand (University of Nevada)

Multilateral Cooperation Against Terrorism
by Peter Romaniuk (John Jay College of Criminal Justice, CUNY)

Peacebuilding
From concept to commission
by Robert Jenkins (The CUNY Graduate Center)

Governing Climate Change
by Peter Newell (University of East Anglia) and Harriet A. Bulkeley (Durham University)

Millennium Development Goals (MDGs)
For a people-centered development agenda?
by Sakiko Fukada-Parr (The New School)

Human Security
by Don Hubert (University of Ottawa)

Global Poverty
by David Hulme (University of Manchester)

UNESCO
by J. P. Singh (Georgetown University)

UNICEF
by Richard Jolly (University of Sussex)

Organization of American States (OAS)
by Mônica Herz (Instituto de Relações Internacionais)

The UN Secretary-General and Secretariat, 2nd edition
by Leon Gordenker (Princeton University)

FIFA
by Alan Tomlinson (University of Brighton)

International Law, International Relations, and Global Governance
by Charlotte Ku (University of Illinois, College of Law)

Preventive Human Rights Strategies in a World of New Threats and Challenges
by Bertrand G. Ramcharan (Geneva Graduate Institute of International and Development Studies)

Humanitarianism Contested
by Michael Barnett (University of Minnesota) and Thomas G. Weiss (The CUNY Graduate Center)

Forum on China-Africa Cooperation (FOCAC)
by Ian Taylor (University of St. Andrews)

The Bank for International Settlements
The politics of global financial supervision in the age of high finance
by Kevin Ozgercin (SUNY College at Old Westbury)

For further information regarding the series, please contact:

Craig Fowlie, Senior Publisher, Politics & International Studies
Taylor & Francis
2 Park Square, Milton Park, Abingdon
Oxford OX14 4RN, UK

+44 (0)207 842 2057 Tel
+44 (0)207 842 2302 Fax

Craig.Fowlie@tandf.co.uk
www.routledge.com

Regional Security

The capacity of international organizations

Rodrigo Tavares

Routledge
Taylor & Francis Group

LONDON AND NEW YORK

First published 2010
by Routledge
2 Park Square, Milton Park, Abingdon, Oxon OX14 4RN

Simultaneously published in the USA and Canada
by Routledge
711 Third Avenue, New York, NY 10017

Routledge is an imprint of the Taylor & Francis Group, an informa business

© 2010 Rodrigo Tavares

Typeset in Times New Roman by
Taylor & Francis Books

British Library Cataloguing in Publication Data
A catalogue record for this book is available from the British Library

Library of Congress Cataloging in Publication Data
Tavares, Rodrigo.
  Regional security : the capacity of international organizations / Rodrigo
  Tavares.
    p. cm.
  Includes bibliographical references and index.
  1. Regionalism (International organization) 2. Security, International.
  I. Title.
  JZ5330.T37 2009
  355'.033—dc22   2009002436

ISBN 978-0-415-48340-7 (hbk)
ISBN 978-0-415-48341-4 (pbk)
ISBN 978-0-203-87405-9 (ebk)

To Mirna
Queres casar-te comigo?

Contents

Illustrations

Tables

Boxes

Foreword by the series editors

The current volume is the thirty-sixth new title—several have already gone into second editions—in a dynamic series on "global institutions." The series strives (and, based on the volumes published to date, succeeds) to provide readers with definitive guides to the most visible aspects of what many of us know as "global governance." Remarkable as it may seem, there exist relatively few books that offer in-depth treatments of prominent global bodies, processes, and associated issues, much less an entire series of concise and complementary volumes. Those that do exist are either out of date, inaccessible to the non-specialist reader, or seek to develop a specialized understanding of particular aspects of an institution or process rather than offer an overall account of its functioning. Similarly, existing books have often been written in highly technical language or have been crafted "in-house" and are notoriously self-serving and narrow.

The advent of electronic media has undoubtedly helped research and teaching by making data and primary documents of international organizations more widely available, but it has also complicated matters. The growing reliance on the Internet and other electronic methods of finding information about key international organizations and processes has served, ironically, to limit the educational and analytical materials to which most readers have ready access—namely, books. Public relations documents, raw data, and loosely refereed web sites do not make for intelligent analysis. Official publications compete with a vast amount of electronically available information, much of which is suspect because of its ideological or self-promoting slant. Paradoxically, a growing range of purportedly independent web sites offering analyses of the activities of particular organizations has emerged, but one inadvertent consequence has been to frustrate access to basic, authoritative, readable, critical, and well researched texts. The market for such has actually been reduced by the ready availability of varying quality electronic materials.

For those of us who teach, research, and practice in the area, such limited access to information has been particularly frustrating. We were delighted when Routledge saw the value of a series that bucks this trend and provides key reference points to the most significant global institutions and issues. They are betting that serious students and professionals will want serious analyses. We have assembled a first-rate line-up of authors to address that market. Our intention, then, is to provide one-stop shopping for all readers—students (both undergraduate and postgraduate), negotiators, diplomats, practitioners from nongovernmental and intergovernmental organizations, and interested parties alike—seeking information about the most prominent institutional aspects of global governance.

Regional security organizations

In thinking about which organizations are best-designed to carry out the important task of maintaining global peace and security, readers will most likely think of the UN Security Council and the UN's own peacekeeping forces or a regional organization like the most powerful and well equipped North Atlantic Treaty Organization (NATO), which is why we have previously commissioned books about these two.[1] In a world with an increasing number of conflicts, however, the UN with its approximately 100,000 soldiers, and NATO due to its operations in Afghanistan and the Balkans, are nearly at capacity. Other options, especially regional ones, have to be considered when the UN's security apparatus is "in crisis" according to another title in this series.[2]

This leaves the unexplored and essential task of finding other possible sources, which is why NATO set up the Partnership for Peace (PfP). In looking toward the future, many other regional actors undoubtedly will be involved in peacekeeping and peace enforcement, and in fact, the last two decades have witnessed high levels of action from regional organizations such as the Economic Community of West African States (ECOWAS) and the African Union (AU).[3]

Because of the increasing importance and involvement of regional organizations in security operations, we were eager to include a book in the series on this topic and were delighted when Rodrigo Tavares agreed to author it. Rodrigo is a research fellow at the United Nations University Centre for Comparative Regional Integration Studies (UNU-CRIS), which serves as a research and policy-advising branch of several UN agencies. In 2008, Rodrigo coordinated a team of researchers who conducted the first-ever global survey of the capacities of regional organizations in the field of peace and security (conflict prevention, peacemaking, peacekeeping, enforcement, and peacebuilding). The comprehensive results of the survey were presented to the UN secretariat and were the basis of this current volume.[4]

Rodrigo has done a highly commendable job of translating the raw research data into a book that is both accessible to a general audience and engaging. It undoubtedly should be required reading for anyone interested in global governance. As always, we look forward to comments from first-time or veteran readers of the Global Institutions Series.

Thomas G. Weiss, The CUNY Graduate Center, New York, USA
Rorden Wilkinson, University of Manchester, UK
June 2009

Foreword by B. Lynn Pascoe

The increasing depth and breadth of the role played by regional and sub-regional organizations in the realm of peace and security has been one of the most noteworthy developments in this field of late. The framers of the Charter of the United Nations had in mind a global collective security architecture with a clear role for regional arrangements and agencies under Chapter VIII. They could scarcely have dreamed of the landscape we have today, however. The number of such agencies and arrangements has grown significantly, and so has the magnitude and complexity of the challenges that we collectively face.

In addressing these challenges, one of the key emerging principles is the concept of a "global-regional partnership" between the United Nations and regional bodies. The intention is to maximize our comparative advantages and capabilities and therefore make a decisive and positive difference on the ground. Such a partnership is all the more critical in the present context. In light of the overlapping global crises currently unfolding before our eyes, Secretary-General Ban Ki-moon has consistently drawn attention to the importance of multilateralism as indispensable for finding answers that are collective and global in nature.

Our work on peacemaking, peacekeeping and peacebuilding has in many ways improved our understanding of how this partnership could be realized and made effective. The United Nations has worked with regional partners in a variety of permutations: in a lead role, a supporting role, a burden-sharing role, in sequential deployments and indeed in several joint operations. These models of working together have proved particularly valuable in mediation and peacekeeping contexts, and have yielded important lessons on how to structure and improve our relationships so we can respond as quickly, comprehensively and effectively as possible to urgent needs on the ground.

Of course, a number of challenges remain. As Rodrigo Tavares rightly points out, we still need to address a number of open questions, including our distinct political and operational environments as well as bridging mandates, capacities and structures.

Any solution to these dilemmas should be practical and operational. It should ensure that we achieve results whenever called to support the prevention, management and resolution of armed conflict. We know from experience, however, that there is no one-size-fits-all answer; clarity and predictability should not come at the expense of flexibility. Finding the right balance will be key to realizing the full potential of this partnership, and the answers will ultimately depend on the political will and creativity of all Member States.

Just as the problems we face are real and tangible, this book is both timely and welcome. If we are to achieve such results, fresh and broad thinking of the kind that the present book provides is essential. Rodrigo Tavares's work will provide a much-needed contribution at a time when peace and security challenges are multiple and pressing, and will require our full collaboration, persistence and commitment.

B. Lynn Pascoe
Under-Secretary-General for Political Affairs
United Nations

Acknowledgments

I have always been intrigued by the limitations of the modern state as a provider of welfare and security and I have always been interested in studying what alternative modes of governance have the aptitude to complement or substitute traditional state-thinking. Given the great attention that regional organizations have received over the last decade, and the proclivity of the policy community in sharing the burden of security and conflict management with them, writing this book became almost a necessity. But a book is rarely the product of only one person, and this one is no exception. In part, the book is a natural offspring of the research environment where it was produced, the United Nations University (UNU-CRIS) in Belgium, which over the years has gained the status of a leading institution on the topic of regionalism. As stated in the foreword, in the genealogy of this book, its ancestor is a Capacity Survey on the capacity of regional and other intergovernmental organizations produced by UNU-CRIS for the UN secretariat. The Survey, which I had the privilege to coordinate, was produced by a team of researchers that included my colleagues Maximilian B. Rasch, Emmanuel Fanta, Francis Baert, and Tânia Felício, with research assistance from Lucia Husenicova.

This book takes a step away from the Survey and provides a more analytical and critical perspective on the role of regional organizations. During the writing, I visited the headquarters of several organizations and interviewed a very large number of policy-makers and academics with an expertise in a wide range of organizations. I am sincerely grateful to Fredrik Söderbaum, Sofia Moreira de Sousa, Helene Gandois, Naison Ngoma, Stephen Kingah, Linnea Bergholm, and Zewdineh Haile Beyene for their logistical help and/or proof-reading. At UNU-CRIS I am particularly thankful to Emmanuel Fanta, Francis Baert, Tiziana Scaramagli, and Daniele Marchesi for providing valuable assistance in the writing of some chapters; to the Director Luk Van Langenhove for the unceasing dedication to his staff; to Kennedy Graham for inspiration; and to Liesbeth Martens for her splendid work with the style formatting. Writing a book is also a sailing trip and the family is the best astrolabe to help us face the predicaments. I thank my larger family in Portugal and my smaller family in São Paulo, Mirna and Gabriel, for reiterating my conviction that love is still the best creation.

Abbreviations

ACDS	African Chiefs of Defense Staff
ACP	African-Caribbean-Pacific Group of States
ACSP	Arab Collective Security Pact
AMU	Arab Maghreb Union
ANZUS	Australia, New Zealand, United States Security Treaty
ARF	ASEAN Regional Forum
ASA	Association of Southeast Asia
ASEAN	Association of Southeast Asian Nations
ASEM	Asia-Europe Meeting
ASF	African Standby Force
ASPAC	Asian and Pacific Council
AU	African Union
BSECC	Black Sea Economic Cooperation Council
CAN	Andean Community
CARICOM	Caribbean Community
CDC	Community of Democratic Choice
CEAO	West African Economic Community
CEMAC	Economic and Monetary Community of Central African States
CEN-SAD	Community of Sahelo-Saharan States
CEWARN	Conflict Early Warning and Response Mechanism (IGAD)
CFSP	Common Foreign and Security Policy
CICA	Conference on Interaction and Confidence-Building Measures in Asia
CIS	Commonwealth of Independent States
COE	Council of Europe
COMESA	Common Market for Eastern and Southern Africa
COMSEC	Commonwealth Secretariat
COPAZ	co-prosperity zone

CPLP	Community of Portuguese-Speaking Countries
CST	Collective Security Treaty
CSTO	Collective Security Treaty Organization
DDR	Disarmament, demobilization, and reintegration
DPA	Department of Political Affairs (United Nations)
DRC	Democratic Republic of Congo
EAC	East African Community
EASBRICOM	African Standby Brigade Coordination Mechanism
EASBRIG	East Brigade
EC	European Commission
ECC	European Economic Community
ECCAS	Economic Community of Central African States
ECOMOG	ECOWAS Monitoring Group
ECOWARN	ECOWAS Early Warning
ECOWAS	Economic Community of West African States
EDC	European Defense Community
EPC	External Policy Cooperation
ERRF	European Union Rapid Reaction Force
ESDI	European Security and Defense Identity
ESDP	European Security and Defense Policy
ESF	ECOWAS Standby Force
EU	European Union
EURATOM	European Atomic Energy Community
FLS	frontline states
GCC	Gulf Cooperation Council
GUAM	GUAM Organization for Democracy and Economic Development
HLM	High-Level Meeting
IC-GLR	International Conference on the Great Lakes Region
ICPAT	IGAD Capacity-Building Program Against Terrorism
IGAD	Intergovernmental Authority on Development
IGADD	Intergovernmental Authority on Drought and Development
IOF	International Organization of Francophonie
ISDSC	Inter-State Defense and Security Committee
ISPDC	Inter-state Politics and Diplomacy Committee
KFOR	Kosovo Force
LAS	League of Arab States
LCD	Lesotho Congress for Democracy
LHWP	Lesotho Highlands Water Project
LURD	Liberians United for Reconciliation and Democracy
MAPHILINDO	Malaya, the Philippines, and Indonesia

MERCOSUR	Mercado Común del Sur
MICIVIH	International Civilian Mission in Haïti
MODEL	Movement for Democracy in Liberia
MoU	memorandum of understanding
MRU	Mano River Union
NATO	North Atlantic Treaty Organization
NCP	National Congress Party (Sudan)
NGO	non-governmental organization
NRF	NATO Response Force
OAS	Organization of American States
OAU	Organization of African Unity
ODA	Official Development Assistance
OECS	Organization of East Caribbean States
OIC	Organization of Islamic Conference
OPEC	Organization of the Petroleum Exporting Countries
OSCE	Organization for Security and Cooperation in Europe
PALIPEHUTU-FNL	Party for the Liberation of the Hutu People-National Forces of Liberation
PCRD	Policy Framework on Post-Conflict Reconstruction and Development
PDD	Presidential Decision Directive
PIF	Pacific Islands Forum
PNG	Papua New Guinea
PRAN	Pacific Regional Assistance to Nauru
PSC	Peace and Security Council (African Union)
RECAMP	Renforcement des Capacités Africaines de Maintien de la Paix
RENAMO	Resistência Nacional Moçambicana (Mozambique)
REWS	Regional Early Warning System (SADC)
RLDF	Royal Lesotho Defense Force
SAARC	South Asian Association for Regional Cooperation
SADC	Southern African Development Community
SADCBRIG	SADC Standby Brigade
SADCC	Southern African Development Coordinating Conference
SCO	Shanghai Cooperation Organization
SEAC	South East Asia Command
SEATO	Southeast Asia Treaty Organization
SPC	South Pacific Commission
RAMSI	Regional Assistance Mission to the Solomon Islands
SPLM/A	Sudan People's Liberation Movement/Army
TAC	Treaty of Amity and Cooperation in Southeast Asia
UNAMID	United Nations African Union Mission in Darfur

UNEP	United Nations Environment Programme
UNMIK	United Nations Interim Administration Mission in Kosovo
UNOSOM	United Nations Operation in Somalia
UNOWA	United Nations Office for West Africa
UNPROFOR	United Nations Protection Force
WACSOF	West African Civil Society Forum
WANESP	West Africa Network for Peacebuilding
WMD	weapons of mass destruction
WTO	World Trade Organization
ZOPFAN	Zone of Peace, Freedom and Neutrality

Introduction

We all know that the end of the Cold War led to an important paradox. On the one hand, the end of bilateralism resurrected the confidence in universalism and in the United Nations, but on the other it paved the way for the emergence of a sole great power, the United States, that often acts unilaterally and only according to national prerogatives. In addition, both agents have shown considerable limitations in shaping a global order that can bring about security and development to individuals. Hence, over the last years, the academic and the policy communities have gone back to the drawing board and have invested significant resources in identifying new agents and methodologies in international relations. This book contributes to this debate by analyzing the capacity of international organizations to serve as providers of regional peace and security.

By doing so it does not question the cardinal idea that the United Nations has primary responsiblity in the maintenance of international peace and security. Even if the UN Charter embodies an obsolete configuration of power, the central parameters, postulates, and principles of the UN are as relevant today as they were in the 1940s. But for a host of reasons that will be enumerated in the book, regional organizations have emerged to provide similar services to those of the UN and often to supplant it. Aware of its own operational limitations, the global body even encourages the delegation of responsibilities to international organizations and underlines that this process is in line with the UN Charter (chapter VIII). Needless to say, this raises fundamental legal, operational, and political questions. Is a division of labor between the global and regional bodies desirable? What are the major assets and shortcomings of international institutions?

Although we conceptually tend to use the terms "regional organizations" or "international institutions," the empirical reality is more complex, and several types of organizations might fit under that designation. As will be discussed in Chapter 1, the UN Charter hints only at a distinction between "agencies" and "arrangements," without providing any guidelines as to their difference. But in practice the group of institutions that are able and willing to partner with the UN is much more comprehensive and involves an impressive array of institutions with very distinct mandates, capacities, and experiences.

Presently, there are approximately 38 organizations that have a regional peace and security mandate, but because of its economy of space this book cannot provide a critical and analytical assessment of all of them. Therefore, as it aims to provide a global comparative overview of these organizations, we selected the most representative organizations in each continent: in Africa, the African Union (AU), the Economic Community of West African States (ECOWAS), the Intergovernmental Authority on Development (IGAD), and the Southern African Development Community (SADC); in the Americas, the Organization of American States (OAS); and in Asia, the Association of Southeast Asian Nations (ASEAN), the Commonwealth of Independent States (CIS), the League of Arab States (LAS), and the Pacific Islands Forum (PIF). Although the LAS is a cross-regional organization (situated both in Africa and in Asia) it was included in the Asia section since the majority of its 22 members are located in Western Asia (the Middle East). Finally, in Europe it includes the European Union (EU), and the North Atlantic Treaty Organization (NATO).

The book breaks down into three main areas. Chapter 1 provides an analytical background to the subject matter by tracing the relationship between the UN and regional organizations and ascertaining the comparative advantages and disadvantages of these organizations; coupled with this, it also highlights what are still the major challenges in regional security. Chapters 2–12 provide a critical analysis of the eleven organizations: Parts I–IV deal with, respectively, Africa, the Americas, Asia, and Europe. Chapter 13 assesses, from a comparative perspective, the major capacities of these institutions in conflict prevention, peacekeeping or peacebuilding.

1 International organizations in regional security

The realm of international relations comprises today not only states and global regimes such as the United Nations, but also many international organizations with a mandate in regional peace and security. Although these organizations, such as the AU, the OAS, the EU, or NATO have made significant headway over the last decade and are regarded as key actors in the prevention and resolution of conflicts, their role remains under-studied. How have they become prominent security actors? What are their comparative advantages and disadvantages? What are the implications for the United Nations as the prime actor responsible for peace and security? What are the challenges ahead?

The interest shown by policy-makers in regional organizations is fairly recent and it has been spurred by some changes in the global scene. The first is the realization that the majority of threats and security problems are primarily regional rather than local, national, or global.[1] Today it is difficult to envision a security problem that originates and is neutralized strictly within the confines of a single state. Be it inter-state or intra-state armed conflict, proliferation of deadly diseases, illegal immigration, or failed states, contemporary threats usually have a regional pattern that calls for regional mechanisms to confront them. Second, although the sovereignty axiom is still prominent, states— seduced by the potentially positive effects of economic integration and suffering the effects of globalization—are showing signs of being less orthodox and more malleable about external interventions. With increased frequency, humanitarian norms have been the source of calls for intervention to halt or prevent gross violations of human rights.

Third, regional institutions have been encouraged to take on a security mandate as a way to cope with the frailty of the United Nations. In the past, mostly in the context of the Cold War, regional institutions and regional conflicts were subordinated to the particular interest of the superpowers.[2] As former UN Secretary-General Boutros-Ghali stated in the 1992 *Agenda for Peace*, "the Cold War impaired the proper use of Chapter VIII and indeed, in that era, regional arrangements worked on occasion against resolving disputes in the manner foreseen in the Charter." This judgment seems justified as long as it was based on action by the OAS with regard to Cuba (1962) and the Dominican Republic (1965), the League of Arab States in Lebanon (1976–83), or the Organization of African Unity's (OAU) action in Chad (1981).[3] After the Cold War, however, a renewed interest in the global level and in the possibility of a new approach in terms of international peace was generated. Yet, the weak financial conditions of the United Nations, the poor record of its peacekeeping missions in the 1990s (e.g. UNPROFOR in the former Yugoslavia and UNOSOM in Somalia), and political pressure from Western powers for reform served as stumbling blocks on the UN's road toward complete self-sufficiency in peace and security.[4] This has been acknowledged even by the UN itself; on numerous occasions the secretary-general has recognized that the organization "lacks the capacity, resources and expertise" to address all the problems and therefore the support of regional organizations is "both necessary and desirable."[5] In 1994, the issuing of Presidential Decision Directive 25 (PDD-25) by President Bill Clinton was another blow to the universal aspirations of the UN. In the wake of the disastrous mission in Somalia, the directive prevented the United States from using peacekeeping operations as the centerpiece of its foreign policy. Interestingly, as a complement to America's unilateral actions, it foresaw supporting the improvement of regional organizations' peacekeeping capabilities. In 2000, this point was reinforced in PDD 71 of February 2000, which identified the strengthening of the capacity of regional organizations as a major objective.

It is clear today that the UN has neither enough resources nor political will to engage with all security problems. These impediments have, hence, paved the way for greater regional involvement. As Haas already pointed out during the Cold War, "regional security arrangements grow in direct proportion to disappointment with the UN collective security system."[6] The beginning of this renewed trend toward the regionalization of security mechanisms arrived with the Economic Community of West African Countries' (ECOWAS) armed intervention in Liberia in 1990 (see Chapter 3). Liberated from the suffocating forces of the Cold War, West African states seized the opportunity to take responsibility for their own interests.

As a result of the growth of regional action, this book presents a critical account of the role and capacities of international organizations in the realm of regional peace and security.

The United Nations and international organizations in regional security

During the early stages of planning for the post-war world, some of the leaders, such as Winston Churchill, aspired to a reliance upon regional agencies as the "massive pillars" of the world system. But the final result was a fine balance between global and regional dynamics, with the United Nations—the supreme authority—making permissive concessions to regionalism.[7] Regional bodies were not given exclusive jurisdiction over regional disputes, but they were given elbow room to deal with local disputes, and the Security Council was even urged to encourage and facilitate such efforts.

Until the end of the Cold War, however, regional agencies were far less active in the peaceful settlement of disputes than the framers of the Charter anticipated. The few active organizations (e.g. OAU, OAS, LAS) were not able to play any significant role in security issues. Today, however, the context is markedly different and there are approximately 38 international organizations that have a mandate and an interest in regional security (see Table 1.2), covering virtually the whole globe.[8] From a UN perspective, the combination of an increased demand for security management and limited resources has made the development of relationships with regional bodies a necessity. The cooperation was, however, not explicitly ordained not even universally desired; rather it "came about in an improvised way and in response to specific regional situations."[9]

Published at the end of the Cold War, when the new security environment was yearning for new actors and new approaches, the *Agenda for Peace* called for a greater involvement of regional organizations in UN activities. Both the *Agenda for Peace* and the *Supplement to an Agenda for Peace* highlighted the advantages and potential for the division of labor in using the regional arrangements for the mechanisms of peace (preventive diplomacy, peacekeeping, peacemaking and post-conflict peacebuilding).[10] This proved to be a shifting moment. Even if the UN and its member states were not capable of adopting clear guidelines on the role and division of labor between the global and the regional bodies,[11] the 1990s witnessed a proliferation of declarations where the role of regional organizations was clearly acknowledged and stimulated. As an illustration, in early 1994 the secretary-general signaled his intention to develop "a set of guidelines governing cooperation between the United Nations and regional organizations" and this was welcomed by the General Assembly.[12] Follow-up declarations have shied away, however, from clearly defining these practical guidelines.[13]

The escalating interest was complemented by several meetings between the UN and regional organizations. Since 1993, the UN Secretary-General has convened seven high-level meetings (HLMs) with regional organizations involved in security matters from all continents. The discussions have focused on challenges to international peace and security, the role of regional organizations in peacebuilding activities, and practical measures to promote greater coordination and coopera-tion in peacekeeping and peacebuilding. Symbolically, at the fifth HLM in July 2003 the secretary-general offered a "new vision of global secur-ity" that rested on a "network of effective and mutually-reinforcing multilateral mechanisms—regional and global."[14] At the sixth HLM in July 2005, the UN Secretary-General stated that strengthening the UN relationship with regional and other intergovernmental organizations was a critical part of the effort to reform the UN. This partnership, it was argued, should build on the "comparative strengths of each orga-nization."[15] Interest in these meetings has grown considerably, as testified, inter alia, by the increase in attendance (see Table 1.1). Nevertheless, with the inauguration of Secretary-General Ban Ki-moon and the new leadership at the Department of Political Affairs (DPA), the interest by the UN in multilateral regional cooperation has diminished. The high-level meetings have come to an end and will be replaced by a less formal and bureaucratic arrangement where the UN Secretary-General could recover his high profile and where the largest organizations will have more constraints in advancing their interests and agendas. At the time of writing, in early 2009, the arrangement that has been proposed in the UN secretariat is in the form of an annual retreat between the secretary-general and heads of regional organizations.

Next to these high-level meetings, the Security Council has also given more attention to regional organizations. From the first meeting in 2003 to 2008, the Security Council met seven times on the topic (including three times directly *with* regional organizations) even though the resolutions and presidential statements adopted have not proposed any substantial working plan nor led to any major breakthrough. For instance, the joint AU-UN panel set up to consider modalities for supporting AU peacekeeping operations (UNSC resolution 1809 of April 2008) submitted in December 2008 several recommendations.[16] Although they were discussed in a Security Council meeting in March the following year, they have not yet made any fundamental headway.

Even if enthusiasm does not necessarily lead to commitment, the interest mustered in the frame of the meetings convened by the secretary-general and the Security Council led to important declarations. In March 2005, Kofi Annan's Report *In Larger Freedom: Towards Development,*

Table 1.1 Meetings with regional organizations

High level meetings		Security Council meetings with regional organizations		
Date	Attendance	Date	Attendance	Outcome
August 1994	10	April 2003 (Mexican presidency)	6	No action
February 1996	13	July 2004 (Romanian presidency)	9	Presidential statement 27/2004
July 1998	14	October 2005 (Romanian presidency)	10	SC resolution 1631
February 2001	16	Security Council meetings on regional organizations		
July 2003	19[†]	Date	Outcome	
July 2005	20[†]	September 2006 (Greek presidency)	Presidential statement 39/2006	
September 2006	20[†]	March 2007 (South African presidency)	Presidential statement 7/2007	
		November 2007 (Indonesian presidency)	Presidential statement 42/2007	
		April 2008 (South African presidency)	SC resolution 1809	

Note:
[†] The EU counts as one organization although it was represented by the presidency of the Council of the EU, the Council Secretariat, and the European Commission.

Security and Human Rights for All proposed the introduction of memoranda of understanding between the UN and regional organizations in order to foster the exchange of information, expertise and resources, and reiterated the need to establish "effective regional and global intergovernmental institutions to mobilize and coordinate collective action."[17] Although this proposal had also been put forward the year before by the High-level Panel on Threats, Challenges and Change, it has never been properly adopted. In 2006, the secretary-general's report, *Regional-Global Security Partnership: Challenges and Opportunities*, which was meant to break new ground, emphasized that, "the opportunities before us lie in the establishment of a more effective partnership operating in close cooperation with the Security Council based on a clear division of labour that reflects the comparative advantage of each organization. As important is the development of a programme of action for capacity-building across the globe."[18] Despite the recurrent allusion to *partnership*, there is "a fundamental misconception, misunderstanding and misperception of what such partnership entail, and what should be the guiding principles of this relationship,"[19] says Kwesi Anning, the author of the UN Secretary General report on the *Relationship between the United Nations and Regional Organizations* (footnote 18). The key question is hence to what extent an increased interaction between regional organizations and the UN can lead to a more efficient UN and even to a rethinking of multilateralism as we know it today. On the ground, cooperation between the UN and regional bodies—even without guiding principles—is indeed likely to increase. It may either involve operational support, whereby a regional organization provides some form of technical cooperation according to the requirements on the ground (e.g. UNMIK, KFOR,[20] UNPROFOR); joint operation, where the staffing, direction, and financing are to be shared between the UN and a regional body (e.g. MICIVIH and UNAMID); or legitimization, where the UN only provides legal authorization for the deployment of the mission.

The UN Charter and international organizations

The UN has widely expressed the view that regional organizations complement—and not contest—the UN system. In part, this stance stems from a reading of Chapter VIII of the UN Charter which deals with "regional agencies and arrangements." Indeed, the Charter authorizes the regional bodies to engage in the peaceful settlement of local disputes (art. 52) before referring them to the Security Council, or with peace enforcement after Security Council authorization (art. 53). But the ambiguous content of Chapter VIII has sparked fundamental questions. First, what is the distinction between a "regional agency" and a "regional arrangement"? Second, do all international organizations that have a security mandate operate under Chapter VIII? If not, what chapters legitimize their actions? In 1992, the *Agenda for Peace* underlined that "the Charter deliberately provides no precise definition of regional arrangements and agencies, thus allowing useful flexibility for undertakings by a group of States to deal with a matter appropriate for regional action which also could contribute to the maintenance of international peace and security."[21] The "usefulness" of this ambiguity has, however, been put in question by empirical reality. Often organizations that are neither regional nor have a mandate to resolve "local disputes" have hijacked Chapter VIII in order to receive a band-aid of legitimacy. Others have renounced their own regional responsibility, causing conflicts to escalate and unaccountability to reign. There is, therefore, a need to inject some clarity into this political ambivalence.

The distinction between the concepts of "agency" and "arrangement" concerns the degree of formality of the entity in question. A regional agency is a recognized organization with legal personality and an organizational structure (i.e. secretariat) located in a member country. A regional arrangement, on the other hand, is a grouping of states under a treaty for a specified common purpose without any organization to personify that arrangement. In this second case, organizational functions are carried out by the member states themselves.[22] As the latter have no international legal personality they are not able, for instance, to enter into formal agreements. As mentioned, the report *In Larger Freedom* proposed to introduce memoranda of understanding with regional bodies in order to improve cooperation.[23] But what the report did not say is that some of the bodies that presently collaborate with the UN are, in fact, "arrangements" and thus not legally able to sign the memoranda of understanding (see Table 1.2).

Another important distinction seems to be between organizations that are considered to be regional organizations within the meaning of Chapter VIII and some that have not usually been so considered but which "have some similar characteristics."[24] The latter case includes (Table 1.2):

- Alliance organizations (collective defense), whose prime mandate is to contain and diffuse threats originated outside their jurisdictional area;
- Institutions that operate out-of-area, i.e. that have the legal and operational capacity to deploy security missions outside the geographical space formed by their member states;
- Agencies whose criteria for membership does not abide by any geographical proximity rule and therefore cannot be called "regional."

None of these organizations meets Chapter VIII requirements which explicitly evoke the "regional" component of these organizations and authorize their actions only intra-regionally, or in "local disputes." But although they are unsuited to use the Chapter VIII banner it does not mean that they are legally unsuitable. Alliance organizations may perform under article 51, whereas the other organizations operate in pacific settlement under Chapter VI and enforcement under Chapter VII. Do these distinctions matter? They do, because the clarification of

Table 1.2 Classification of actors with regional security mandate

	Agencies	Arrangements
Regional and sub-regional (Chapter VIII)	African Union (AU) Andean Community (CAN) Arab Maghreb Union (AMU) Association of Southeast Asian Nations (ASEAN) Black Sea Economic Cooperation Council (BSECC) Caribbean Community (CARICOM) Collective Security Treaty Organization (CSTO) Common Market for Eastern and Southern Africa (COMESA) Commonwealth of Independent States (CIS) Community of Sahelo-Saharan States (CEN-SAD) Conference on Interaction and Confidence-Building Measures in Asia (CICA)[1] Council of Europe (COE) East African Community (EAC) Economic and Monetary Community of Central African States (CEMAC) Economic Community of Central African States (ECCAS) Economic Community of West African States (ECOWAS) GUAM Organization for Democracy and Economic Development (GUAM) Gulf Cooperation Council (GCC) Intergovernmental Authority for Development (IGAD) League of Arab States (LAS) Mano River Union (MRU) Organization of American States (OAS) Organization of East Caribbean States (OECS) Shanghai Cooperation Organization (SCO) Southern Africa Development Community (SADC)	Community of Democratic Choice (CDC) International Conference on the Great Lakes Region (IC/GLR) Organization for Security and Cooperation in Europe (OSCE) Pacific Islands Forum (PIF)[2] Rio Group (GRIO) Union of South American Nations (UNASUR)[3]

Table 1.2 (continued)

	Agencies	Arrangements
Other Intergovernmental (Non-chapter VIII)	African-Caribbean-Pacific Group of States (ACP) Community of Portuguese-Speaking States (CPLP) European Union (EU) North Atlantic Treaty Organization (NATO) Organization of Islamic Conference (OIC) International Organization of Francophonie (IOF)	Commonwealth Secretariat (COMSEC)

Notes:
1 Although called "Conference," CICA is in fact an organization with legal personality. In 2006 it adopted the *Statute of the CICA Secretariat* laying down a legal basis for establishment and functioning of the secretariat (located in Almaty). The statute also defines the legal capacity of the conference.
2 PIF was established as an arrangement by the 1971 communiqué. At its 36th Leaders Meeting in October 2005, PIF adopted a formal agreement establishing the forum as an international organization. This will come into force when ratified by all 16 forum members and at that stage the PIF will become a "regional agency."
3 The UNASUR Constitutive Treaty was signed on May 23rd 2008 at the Third Summit of Heads of State held in Brasilia, but to come into force it needs to be ratified by at least 9 member states.

roles is the most basic prerequisite for an operational global–regional mechanism to work. We need to know who can be expected to do what if any division of labor is to be institutionalized between the UN and international organizations.

Since the first high-level meeting on cooperation with regional organizations in 1994, the United Nations has not made public any invitation criteria for participating organizations. Although the meetings are framed under a regional approach, some partaking organizations are clearly not regional, such as the Commonwealth (COMSEC), la Francophonie (IOF) or the Community of Portuguese Speaking-Countries (CPLP), whose area of membership encompasses several continents. More ironically, some participants do not regard themselves as a "regional agency" for the purposes of Chapter VIII of the UN Charter, such as NATO and the EU (even if some UN resolutions or US presidential decisions have described these organizations under that banner).[25] Only a few organizations, notably the Organization for Security and Cooperation in Europe (OSCE), Organization of Islamic Conference (OIF), CIS, ECOWAS, SADC, OAS, AU, and LAS have coined themselves as Chapter VIII organizations. Aware of this conundrum, the UN named the six and seventh high-level meetings as being on "cooperation with regional and *other intergovernmental organizations*" (italics added). But this distinction has never been adopted by the Security Council meetings neither by the latest Secretary-General reports mandated by the council. The same dubiety applies to the invitation criteria used for the Security Council meetings. Attendance is consequent upon selective invitations by whatever country is holding the presidency, and it is thereby "open to differing national perceptions and interests."[26]

What are the comparative advantages of regional organizations?

The empowerment of regional actors has taken place on the dual assumption that the UN retains primary responsibility for maintaining international peace and security and that regional organizations may offer some comparative advantages where the UN is either unable or unwilling to take action.[27] As reiterated by Kofi Annan in the second Security Council meeting (July 2004), "so while our cooperation is being enhanced, we have to consider more thoroughly the comparative strengths of different organizations, be they global, regional or sub-regional, and move towards the creation of strategic partnerships that meet today's and tomorrow's challenges."[28] But what are these comparative advantages?

First, as the members of an organization share the same cultural background, they are likely to be more in tune with a conflict at hand. Often conflict situations produce narratives and are caused by factors that fall off the radar of traditional or conventional wisdom and, hence, are difficult for foreigners to comprehend without judgment or misunderstandings. Ban Ki-moon has also recognized that these organizations are "well positioned to understand the root causes of many conflicts and other security challenges close to home and to influence their prevention or resolution, owing to their knowledge of the region."[29] In association to this, as often alerted by African military strategists, regional peacekeepers are also likely to have a similar immunological system to the parties in the conflict, which makes them less vulnerable to the virological specificities of some regions—an important factor in peacekeeping operations. Cultural affinity also includes the personal relationships that may exist between regional leaders, which results in greater understanding of the situation and may lead to fruitful dialogue based on personal trust. Sharing the same cultural background might have a downside, however. In some cases the cultural specificity might be at odds with the universal principles of the UN, as it was the case with the vehement repudiation by the AU of the arrest warrant issued in March 2009 by the International Criminal Court to President Bashir of Sudan.[30]

Second, as time is of the essence in a crisis situation, regional organizations could offer a more timely response, compared to bureaucratic global organizations such as the UN or foreign states. The Policy Framework for the Establishment of the African Standby Force (ASF) adopted in 2003 by the African Union, anticipates that the AU will be able by 2010 to deploy a robust military force in as early as 14 days, or a peacekeeping force within 30 days. In contrast, it takes on average three to six months from the time the UN Security Council decides to establish a peacekeeping mission until it is able to deploy such a mission.

Third, as the chief of staff of the ECOWAS Planning Element, Brigadier General Hassan M. Lai noted, regional conflict management is also likely to be less costly; it is logistically easier to sustain peacekeeping missions nearby than airlifting them from a more distant place.[31] Fourth, as the members of a regional organization are the ones who would suffer more directly the impacts of the conflict, they have a legitimate vital interest at stake in preserving regional stability.[32] States located thousands of kilometers away, "separated by vast differences in historical background, culture, language, and political and economic interests, may find it difficult to appreciate as fully as they should the mutual problem."[33] Although the UN and its member states have shied away from intervening in Somalia, the most dramatic failed state in the world, IGAD and AU's member states, who suffered directly the spillover effects of the critical political situation, have been engaged in the conflict with peacemaking (IGAD) and peacekeeping measures (AU) (see Chapters 2 and 4).

Fifth, in some situations regional organizations are better welcomed. For instance, cultural considerations were important in the decision to have Turkey take the rotational command of NATO's International Security Assistance Force (ISAF) in Afghanistan in 2005. In the case of Darfur, Sudanese president al-Bashir explicitly made the deployment of the hybrid UNAMID mission contingent on the recruitment of African peacekeepers only. He claimed that the presence of non-African peacekeepers, especially from the West, would threaten Sudan's sovereignty.

Finally, regional conflict management is also likely to give an opportunity to smaller and less influential countries to play a role in conflict resolution.[34] Uganda, a small land-locked country, is the largest troop contributor to the AU mission in Somalia, which has, to a large extent, paved the way for its international recognition.

But whereas the potentiality of regional organizations is salient, "there is no single formula for allocating security responsibilities either to global or regional forums."[35] Conflict-management incentives vary according to the issues at stake, the actors involved, and the regional context in which a problem originates.

The challenges ahead

Regional organizations vary widely in terms of structure, mandate, and capacity. Not surprisingly, in the policy and academic worlds we may also find a wide range of stances on the potentiality of regional action. Some authors have been emphatic in their criticism. Diehl, for instance, has pointed out that "regional organizations have some notable disadvantages vis-à-vis global efforts, especially the UN, at conflict management ... [and] are ill-designed to conduct enforcement and peacekeeping operations or facilitate judicial solutions to conflicts."[36] An undersecretary-general of the United Nations in charge of peacekeeping, Marrack Goulding, also warned that most regional organizations lacked the experience, bureaucratic structures, and resources necessary to conduct peacekeeping effectively.[37] Others have a more positive view. Lake and Morgan have observed that "efforts to cope with violent conflicts, as well to achieve order and security, will primarily involve arrangements and actions devised and implemented at the regional level."[38] Some other scholars have a cautious approach and claim that regional institutions are only particularly strong, for instance, in preventing the outbreak of armed conflicts among member states.[39] This multiplicity of visions is a reflection of how much we still do not know about the role of regional organizations. There are hence very pertinent challenges ahead.

First, and of primary importance, is the issue of capacity. Notwithstanding the eulogistic tone of the majority of political declarations, regional organizations can only exercise their security mandate if they have the capability to do so. Yet, only a handful of organizations have the administrative, logistical, and command structures needed to deploy and manage multinational military operations. The funding of peacekeeping missions of some organizations, such as the AU, has been ad hoc and unpredictable. Some of these funds tend to be provided by donors such as the EU, which normally attaches conditionalities to its disbursements. The Kofi Annan report on *Regional-Global Security Partnership* has also identified the promotion of regional capacity as a critical challenge that should be addressed. In fact we are currently living in a limbo where neither the UN nor the regional organizations are totally fit to do their business of providing security, leaving several conflict situations unattended.

Second, any consideration of regional organizations has to tackle the determining problem of partiality. Vicinity is not conducive for member states to remain impartial, and it is often the case that one or more states are party to a conflict, or simply determined to impose a solution.[40] Even if regional organizations were the first to intervene in Liberia, Sierra Leone, Tajikistan, Georgia, or Côte d'Ivoire, they were later supplemented (or replaced) by UN missions, partly to guarantee their impartiality.[41] Thus, if impartiality is part of the genetic code of the concept and practice of peacekeeping, it raises the issue of the genuine legal capacity for regional institutions to deploy peacekeeping operations.

Third, delegation of power to regional bodies has to account for the issue of hegemony. It is often the case—such as South Africa in SADC, France and Germany in the EU, Nigeria in ECOWAS, or the United States in OAS—that a member state has the political and functional capacity to hijack an organization to advance its national interests under a legitimate camouflage. Along the same lines, in 2000 the *Report of the Panel on United Nations Peace Operations* (the Brahimi Report) warned that a regional organization that is dominated by one of its members might serve as an impediment to short-term conflict prevention strategies.[42] During the Cold War, the United States' fears of communist encroachment into the Western hemisphere led to a distortion of OAS security concepts and, in many cases, to the installation of repressive regimes[43] (see Chapter 6). Also, Russia has notably projected its national security interests by hijacking the CIS and intervening under its flag in Georgia and Tajikistan (Chapter 8).

The fourth problem is the issue of priority. Once a conflict situation erupts in a particular country, who takes logical precedence and, in principle, is expected to come first? Even if the Security Council has the supremacy—the legal, political and moral authority and status— the UN Charter does not provide clear guidance over this important issue. In the past there have been numerous examples of jurisdictional struggle between the UN and regional organizations. For instance, in 1954 the government of Guatemala appealed to both the OAS and the UN, and the conflict was treated both as an "aggression" (calling for Security Council intervention) and a "local dispute" (appropriate for a regional organization). The Soviet Union favored the first definition, whereas the United States backed the latter.[44] What criteria should be identified thus to give priority to either of them? The reasons are not only legal but also practical, as greater reliance on regional organizations seems to be the result of an unwillingness to commit [by the Security Council] rather than because the idea has intrinsic merit.[45]

Fifth, another critical issue to bear in mind is regional overlapping and institutional proliferation. The clearest case is in Africa, where different countries are affiliated to various organizations, often with competitive agendas. Herbst describes the African situation as an "organizational junkyard of unsuccessful attempts to reduce the continent's balkanization."[46] But in other regions the division of labor is also an issue of heated debate; for instance in Europe the most pervasive example is the uneasy relationship between NATO and the EU. As pointed out by Keohane, "NATO and the EU could do so much more to help each other ... at a time when both are being called upon by the UN to provide troops, whether to Lebanon or Afghanistan, they should be talking to each other. Frankly, the dialogue in Brussels is truly dreadful."[47]

The sixth consideration deals with the discrepancy that exists between the praise given to regional action in general and the nonexistence of regional organizations in some areas of the world, or the nonexistence of legal mandates in some of them to engage in regional peace and security. Some organizations are, indeed, still largely attached to the sanctity of the principle of non-intervention. Malaysia's suggestion to establish an ASEAN peacekeeping force was shelved because it was seen as an attempt to turn ASEAN into a military alliance and a violation of the national sovereignty principles of the organization. Also the South Asian Association for Regional Cooperation (SAARC), the regional organization covering South Asia and one-sixth of the world's population, has resisted incorporating a security mandate. Pressured by India, SAARC's charter includes an article that states that bilateral and contentious issues shall be excluded from the deliberations (art. X-2). SAARC has never formally engaged with the Kashmir conflict, nor was the nuclearization of India and Pakistan debated under its auspices. When it was invited by the UN to take part in the fifth high-level meeting with regional organizations, it turned down the invitation.

Seventh, there is a need to foment inter-organizational information sharing. The diversity of capabilities and the expansion of mandates call for the development of forums where regional organizations may streamline their vocations. In this light, Security Council resolution 1809 (April 2008), adopted in the follow up of a meeting between the Council and regional organizations, also "encourages regional and subregional organizations to strengthen and increase cooperation among them."[48] This is gradually emerging and is reflected, for example, in the ongoing cooperation between the EU and almost all regional organizations in the world[49] or in the memorandum of understanding (MoU) signed between IGAD and ECOWAS in February 2009. However, such collaborations are generally carried out on a bilateral basis without a global sense of needs and demands.

The final issue to be taken into consideration by the policy community is the need to clarify the exact mandate of these regional bodies. The difference between a Chapter VIII organization and other organizations—more than semantic—carries legal implications. Presently, there is no clarity or consistency in the policy-making sphere on this issue. The task ahead is to determine, on the basis of their respective mandates and capacities, which institutions have the potential to cooperate most effectively with the United Nations in which areas, both geographically and functionally. None are excluded; each has a role to play. In 2006, Kofi Annan suggested that the Security Council could discuss the desirability of international organizations "identifying themselves either as regional organizations acting under Chapter VIII or as other intergovernmental organizations acting under other provisions of the Charter," but this has never materialized.[50]

This book will address these challenges, with the overall emphasis placed on the capacity of regional organizations. Capacity includes primarily organizational capacity, and operational experience. Organizational capacity indicates both the legal capacity (mandate) of an organization in security matters and its institutional capacity to make decisions, as well as the existence of organs, rules, and procedures necessary for their implementation. Operational experience encapsulates the procedural ability of an organization to undertake action in the field in the maintenance of peace and security. This depends on the mechanisms that the partner has developed to put into action the decisions it may have taken in conflict prevention,[51] peacemaking,[52] peacekeeping,[53] peace enforcement[54] or peacebuilding.[55] Even if significant, the book will not focus on constructivist or liberal measures—generally based on norm creation and information sharing—available to international organizations to bolster peace, consensus, and trust.[56] Neither it will concentrate on the impact of democracy and institutional design on conflict management effectiveness.[57]

Part I
Africa

2 African Union (AU)

The idea of a united Africa can be traced back to the "scramble for Africa" and the atomization of the continent by European powers. At the beginning of the twentieth century, the voices of Marcus Garvey, W. E. B. Du Bois, George Padmore and Léopold Senghor spearheaded political campaigns against the destructive legacies of the Berlin Conference (1884–85).[1] These pioneering ideas paved the way toward decolonization and triggered the belief that native and diaspora Africans should be unified as part of a global African community. The most notable herald of this message was Kwame Nkrumah, the first president of Ghana, who declared at independence:

> We are going to see that we create our own African personality and identity. We again rededicate ourselves in the struggle to emancipate other countries in Africa; for our independence is meaningless unless it is linked up with the total liberation of the African continent.[2]

The creation in 1963 of the Organization of African Unity warranted initial hopes that the continent was set for unification. However, pushed by countries such as Ethiopia, Nigeria, and Liberia (the so-called "Monrovia group"[3]), the OAU has from the beginning advocated an idea of unity that was intent on retaining the colonial demarcations of the new independent states and envisaged the formation of an "alliance" of African states rather than an "United States of Africa."[4] To reinforce the prevailing vision, the charter of the OAU specifically called for the respect of national borders and non-interference in the domestic affairs of its members.[5]

Regardless of how much praise African leaders have devoted to the OAU, it is unquestionable that the organization was marked more by failures than achievements. Its stated principles, such as to "promote the unity and solidarity of the African States" (article II-a), "achieve a better life for the peoples of Africa" (article II-b), or "respect the Universal Declaration of Human Rights" (article II-e) were not ful-filled and Africa reached the millennium with low levels of human development and high levels of human insecurity. According to most critics, the OAU protected the interests of African leaders without addressing the real problems that plagued the continent. The genocide in Rwanda and the atrocities committed in Sudan, the Democratic Republic of Congo (DRC), Somalia, Sierra Leone, and Angola were shamelessly neglected by the AU. At the same time it coddled dictators such as Uganda's Idi Amin, Mengistu Mariam of Ethiopia, Mobutu Sese Seko of Congo, or Ibrahim Babangida of Nigeria (all served terms as OAU chairman). The only interventions authorized by the OAU were in countries with white majority regimes such as Angola (before 1975), Zimbabwe (before 1980), Namibia (before 1989) and South Africa (before the early 1990s).

The limitations of the OAU were acknowledged even by some of its leaders. Issaias Afeworki, president of Eritrea, the last country to be accepted to the OAU, declared that "membership of the OAU was not spiritually gratifying or politically challenging [because] the OAU has become a nominal organization that has failed to deliver on its pro-nounced goals and objectives."[6] These failures paved the way for the creation of a new organization in 2000, the African Union.

The AU was first proposed in 1999 by Libyan leader Moammar Ghadafi, who in July that year extended an invitation for African lea-ders to attend an extraordinary summit in September in Sirte, Libya, with the objective of strengthening OAU capacity to enable it to meet the challenges of the new millennium. The meeting resulted in the adoption of the landmark Sirte Declaration, where African leaders pledged to establish an African Union in order to address the new social, political and economic realities in Africa and the world. Fol-lowing the Sirte Declaration, member states began working on a Con-stitutive Act, which was adopted at the 36th OAU summit in July 2000, in Togo, and in July 2002 the organization was formally laun-ched in Durban, South Africa. Similarly to the OAU, the new organi-zation reaffirmed the national sovereignty of states and the sacredness of national borders, which indicates the reluctance of African leaders to take ambitious steps to reformulate the political structure of the continent left behind by colonialism. Unlike the OAU Charter, how-ever, the AU allows interventions in grave circumstances, such as war crimes, genocide and crimes against humanity (AU Constitutive Act, art. 4-h; Protocol, art. 7-e)—one of the first organizations in the world to give itself such a clear mandate. Even though the AU is still far from being able to implement an efficient responsibility to protect regime, it is possible to make the case that the AU is committed to this principle, since it has taken an active and interventionist stance with regard to conflict situations in Burundi, Darfur, and Somalia.[7]

Despite these adjustments to the new post-colonial globalized order, the African Union still needs to show genuine commitment and seriousness to the pan-African ideal.[8] Several declarations have been issued by the Assembly of Heads of State committing states to an accelerated program of integration that would culminate in a United States of Africa. This seems to be the easier part of the task. As the 2007 audit of the AU points out, much more complicated is ensuring that member states remain committed to the development and implementation of the detailed roadmaps.[9]

Organizational capacity

The organizational capacity of an organization to undertake peace and security activities depends on the constitutional provisions according it the mandate to become active, and the institutional mechanisms through which it can function and exercise that mandate. Similarly to other African sub-regional organizations (e.g. SADC, IGAD, ECOWAS), the AU has adopted constitutional provisions to engage in peace and security. Its constitutive act clearly states that one of the objectives of the organization is "to promote peace, security, and stability on the continent (art. 3-f) and the 2002 Protocol Relating to the Establishment of the Peace and Security Council provides guidelines on how the organization should maneuver in the security field (Box 2.1). To reinforce its security profile, in 2004 the AU adopted the comprehensive Solemn Declaration on a Common African Defence and Security Policy to ensure collective responses to both internal and external threats to Africa. These two key legal instruments—the Protocol and the Solemn Declaration—are regarded by the AU to form the two legal pillars which underpin the continental peace and security architecture.

However, the organizational capacity of the AU refers not only to the legal mandate but also to its organic ability. In this regard, it is important to distinguish between structure and operationalization, or between façade and content. In terms of structure, the AU's pinnacle is centered on the Assembly, which lays out the general guidelines and provides strategic orientation. Under its strict dependency, the Executive Council, a ministerial organ composed of foreign ministers of all member states, is tasked to implement the decisions emanating from the summit and to elaborate work programs in its respective areas of intervention. The central executive organ of the AU is, however, the Authority (called Commission until July 2009), composed—since 2009—by a president, a vice-president, and the secretaries (former commissioners) holding individual portfolios, which manages day-to-day tasks and implements AU policies. Finally, the AU has established a Peace and Security Council (PSC) responsible for the formulation and implementation of key political decisions associated to conflict prevention, peacekeeping or enforcement. The AU has also set up a Panel of the Wise, a Continental Early Warning System, an African Standby Force, and a Peace Fund.

If the structure of the AU is fairly adequate to cope with security issues, its operationalization is more questionable. Operationalization is related to whether the organs, which are laid out in the legal documents, function in accordance to what is legally expected from them. The record of the AU is far from convincing in this regard.

The Peace and Security Council is a case in point. Article 2 of the Protocol Relating to the Establishment of the Peace and Security Council describes it as a collective security and early warning arrangement to facilitate timely and effective response to conflict and crisis situations in Africa. According to AU's former president, Joaquim Chissano, the PSC has been designed to be a strong signal to the African peoples and the international community of our determination to put an end to the conflicts and wars which have ravaged the continent for far too long.[10] Created in 2004, it has 15 member states representing all five sub-regions of the AU (Central, North, East, South, and West), elected for two- or three-year terms, with equal voting rights. The execution of its mandate has been hampered by some difficulties, nevertheless. First, the division of labor between the PSC and the commission is not very clear as it is the latter that has been setting the PSC timetable, proposing its agenda, preparing its draft reports, and drafting communiqués.[11] [12] Second, the secretariat of the council is under-staffed and many more personnel and operational tools are needed to handle the increasing volume, complexity of work, and frequency of PSC meetings. The members of the council themselves lack proper human resources. According to a senior AU official, "members come to the meetings without background preparation. They lack knowledge and sometimes true motivation. The embassies are poorly equipped with human resources and lack research capacity for PSC members to prepare themselves conveniently before the discussions."[13] Third, due to the conflicts in the continent, the PSC has been compelled to deal mainly with country-focused issues. But given the comprehensive nature of its mandate and the complexity of African security problems, the council should also cover transversal issues such as terrorism, illegal exploitation of natural resources, the phenomenon of child soldiers or the illegal trade in small arms. Finally, there is a need to add practical value to PSC decisions through the undertaking of fact-finding missions

---

Box 2.1   Protocol Relating to the Establishment of the Peace and Security Council of the African Union (excerpt)

Article 3

The objectives for which the Peace and Security Council is established shall be to:

(a) Promote peace, security and stability in Africa, in order to guarantee the protection and preservation of life and property, the well-being of the African people and their environment, as well as the creation of conditions conducive to sustainable development;

(b) Anticipate and prevent conflicts. In circumstances where conflicts have occurred, the Peace and Security Council shall have the responsibility to undertake peace making and peacebuilding functions for the resolution of these conflicts;

(c) Promote and implement peacebuilding and post-conflict reconstruction activities to consolidate peace and prevent the resurgence of violence;

(d) Co-ordinate and harmonize continental efforts in the prevention and combating of international terrorism in all its aspects;

(e) Develop a common defence policy for the Union, in accordance with article 4(d) of the Constitutive Act;

(f) Promote and encourage democratic practices, good governance and the rule of law, protect human rights and fundamental freedoms, respect for the sanctity of human life and international humanitarian law, as part of efforts for preventing conflicts.

Source: African Union website, www.africa-union.org

to conflict zones or post-conflict recovery areas. In the first five years of its existence, the PSC has only undertaken one field mission—to Darfur.

Despite these hindrances the AU, through the PSC, has brought visibility and credibility to Africa in the area of peace and security. It has led to a reversal of one of the key principles of the OAU, national sovereignty, by replacing the principle of non-interference with the principle of non-indifference. It has been able to bring parties to conflicts together through its mediation efforts as exemplified in Ivory Coast, Burundi, and the DRC. These first successful steps have certainly inspired the UN to accelerate the process of devolution and collaboration with the AU, symbolized in the Ten Year Capacity-Building Programme signed in 2006 and in numerous Security Council resolutions calling for more effective cooperation with relevant organs of regional organizations, "in particular the AU Peace and Security Council."[14]

Another potentially significant organ is the Panel of the Wise, which plays a conflict prevention and peacemaking role (e.g. to conduct shuttle diplomacy between parties in conflict, encourage parties to engage in political dialogue, adopt confidence building measures and carry out reconciliation processes). It is composed of five African personalities, each representing one of the AU sub-regions.[15] After the approval by the Peace and Security Council in November 2007 of the Modalities for the Function of the Panel, it was officially launched one month later and it became operational in 2008. The creation of the panel should be inserted in the overall capacity and experience of the AU in peacemaking and conflict prevention. For instance, the AU has been engaged in Sudan, where it helped negotiate an initial ceasefire and hosted peace talks from 2004 onward; or in Togo, where it reacted forcefully to the unlawful takeover of the Togolese presidency by Faure Gnassingbé following the death of his father, President Gnassingbé Eyadéma, in February 2005. In March 2009, it suspended Madagascar after an unconstitutional change of government. Nowadays it would be difficult to expect the AU not to be called upon whenever there is an outbreak of a new conflict. However, the AU has not yet made any systematic effort to study and capitalize on its accumulate knowledge in peacemaking. Most peacemaking efforts are ad hoc, based on personal initiatives, and do not have appropriate follow-up. The formation of the Panel of the Wise will supposedly give a more formal and concerted orientation to AU's peacemaking, but if so the deployment of members of the Panel would need to be followed by an agile administration in Addis Ababa responsible for providing technical support, supplying accurate data, and mobilizing political support. This seems, however, unlikely to materialize given the current lack of resources.

Another critical organ is the Continental Early Warning System, which consists of an observation and monitoring center (the Situation Room), and is responsible for data collection and analysis.[16] It is based on general structural indicators (the so-called Indicators Module) and is fed by dynamic open source information which is collected automatically through the Internet. Analysis is based on standard Strategic Conflict Assessments techniques.[17] At the time of writing in early 2009 the early warning system has already implemented an important part of the data and information gathering infrastructure but the continental coordination remains weak. Indeed, although it is expected to have a supervisory role over the early warning centers of the African sub-regional organizations (ECCAS, ECOWAS, SADC, IGAD, COMESA, CEN-SAD, EAC) it is still far from fulfilling its mandate. Partially, this may be explained by the political and financial emphasis that the AU tends to put on conflict management (peacemaking, peacekeeping and peace enforcement) rather than on early action, driving resources and political will away from the prevention of conflicts. But the continental system also suffers from weak communication between the AU and the sub-regional organizations, mostly because the regional mechanisms are at different states of development: while ECOWAS and IGAD have established their early warning systems (see Chapters 3 and 4) and ECCAS and SADC are in the process of doing so (see Chapter 5 for SADC), the EAC, CEN-SAD and COMESA have only reached a conceptual phase. According to the Situation Room coordinator, the memorandum of understanding between the AU and the African sub-regional organizations (signed in January 2008), and the creation of liaison offices at the AU by the sub-regional organizations were meant to remove some of these obstacles.[18] Charles Mwaura, the AU Early Warning Expert, notes that the harmonization of the different early warning mechanisms is not problematic. The only possible exception could be the integration of SADC's data—since it is based upon intelligence sources.[19] In any case Africa's early warning reflects the importance of promoting inter-organizational information sharing, and the adoption of the MoU, which was several years in the making, is an important milestone in this endeavor.

The AU's organizational capacity would not be complete without the enhancement of its peacekeeping and peace enforcement profile. At the third meeting of the African Chiefs of Defense Staff (ACDS), held in Addis Ababa in 2003, a Policy Framework for the Establishment of the African Standby Force and the Military Staff Committee (MSC)[20] was adopted, which commits the AU to set up an African Standby Force to serve as a rapid reaction force comprising 10,000 people (8,000 soldiers and 2,000 civilians) by 2010. The force will be drawn from the regional brigades. The current developments can be attributed to Kwame Nkrumah's original idea of a continental high command. The idea has gestated over the years and now there is a sentiment that integrated continental armed forces are necessary to conduct police action and peacekeeping operations across the continent. The ASF might be deployed in different scenarios. A scenario 1 approach would entail provision of military advice to a political mission, as was the case in Côte d'Ivoire. Under scenario 2, the AU or a regional observer mission is supposed to co-deploy with a UN mission, as was the case with the OAU/AU Liaison Mission in Ethiopia-Eritrea (OLMEE) or the Verification Monitoring Team (VMT) in the Sudan. A scenario 3 mission is a stand-alone AU or regional observer mission, such as the AU Mission in Burundi (AMIB) or the AU Mission in the Comoros (AMIC). Scenario 4 entails an AU or regional peacekeeping force for Chapter VI and preventive deployment missions (and peacebuilding), such as the AU Mission in Burundi (AMIB), while scenario 5 means an AU peacekeeping force for complex multidimensional peace-keeping missions, including those involving low-level spoilers. A scenario 6 mission would include intervention, for example, in genocide situations where the international community does not act promptly. In terms of the draft training policy the AU must define and fund a biennial training plan at continental and regional levels. The continental training plan provides for various workshops, an annual exercise for the AU PLANELM and one major exercise involving three regions in the lead-up to 2010.[21]

Although some progress has been made in doctrine, standard operating procedures, command, control, and communications and information policy, the establishment of ASF is lagging behind schedule.[22] Most sub-regional organizations are setting up their brigades with no clear supervision from the AU, whereas others—namely the central and the northern brigades—are at a standstill (see Chapters 3, 4, and 5). Other problems with the ASF include the lack of an integrated civilian, police, and military structure; the non-veto power decision-making structure; and the inclusion of conflict-prone countries as troop contributors. So far, the AU has limited planning capacity: there is no lessons learned unit attached to the Peace Support Operation Division (PSOD), no effective evaluation methodology to be employed on its military missions, no documentation center, nor are returning senior military personnel requested to debrief the PSOD. According to Cilliers, while Africa has seen good progress with regard to training, development of doctrine, SOPs [Standard Operating Procedures], command and control concepts and the like, the issue of ASF logistics remains hugely problematic.[23] The policy framework proposed a system of AU military logistic depots, consisting of the AU military logistic depot in Addis Ababa and regional logistic bases, aimed at rapid deployment and mission sustainability, but they have not yet been made operational.

Besides conflict prevention, peacemaking and peacekeeping, the AU also has organizational capacity in peacebuilding. In 2005 the AU Commission has developed a Policy Framework on Post-Conflict Reconstruction and Development (PCRD) and in 2007 the Conflict Management Division (CMD) produced a Handbook on Post-Conflict Reconstruction and Development, which serves as the Framework's guideline. According to former CMD's Expert in Post-Conflict Reconstruction and Peace Building, Naison Ngoma, the handbook was designed to be a flexible document—adjustable to the environment of the country (or sub-region) where it is employed.[24] AU officials acknowledge that AU's post-war reconstruction capacity is still not robust, but the handbook will aid the organization in being more pragmatic and more targeted.[25] The framework should be implemented as a tool to consolidate peace and prevent relapses of violence; help address the root causes of conflicts; encourage fast-track planning of reconstruction activities; and enhance complementarities, coordination, and coherence between the various actors engaged in post-war reconstruction and peacebuilding.

Operational experience

Even if the AU has some experience in peacebuilding and peacemaking, it tends to concentrate on military conflict management through peacekeeping and peace enforcement and has thus far deployed missions in Burundi, Sudan/Darfur, Somalia, and the Comoros. Military operations are conventionally deployed to supervise, observe, monitor, and verify the implementation of ceasefire agreements or to help broker ceasefires between government and rebel groups:[26]

- Burundi (April 2003–May 2004)—The mandate was to supervise, observe, monitor and verify the implementation of the ceasefire agreement (also known as the Arusha Agreement for Peace and Reconciliation for Burundi), signed in August 2000, in order to further consolidate the peace process in Burundi. In 2004, the UN took over the peacekeeping operations from the AU (ONUB). Overall, the mission helped to stabilize most of the country and it was successful in facilitating the delivery of humanitarian assistance.
- Sudan/Darfur (August 2004–December 2007)—It helped broker a ceasefire between the government of Sudan and rebel groups. It

initially had fewer than one hundred observers in Darfur to monitor the agreement, but gradually increased its presence to include soldiers and police. By 2005, the AU had nearly 7,000 troops in the region. A more sizable, better equipped UN peacekeeping force was originally proposed for September 2006, but due to Sudanese government opposition, it was not implemented. AMIS' mandate was extended repeatedly throughout 2006 and 2007, while the situation in Darfur continued to escalate. On 1 January 2008, AMIS was finally replaced by the United Nations African Union Mission in Darfur (UNAMID).

- Burundi (since January 2007)—The mandate of the AU Special Task Force in Burundi is to facilitate the implementation of the Dar es Salaam peace agreement of June 2006, between the government and the PALIPEHUTU-FNL (commonly known as FNL)—the most extreme Hutu group, which had not taken part in the Arusha Agreement. The force is composed of the South African battalion that served under the UN mission in Burundi. It was re-hatted under the AU mandate when the UN mandate came to an end on 31 December 2006.
- Somalia (since March 2007)—The objective is to carry out support for dialogue and reconciliation by assisting with the free movement, safe passage and protection of all those involved in a national reconciliation congress involving all stakeholders. It includes assistance with the implementation of the National Security and Stabilization Plan, and contribution to the creation of the necessary security conditions for the provision of humanitarian assistance. Although the AU is one of the best examples of a Chapter VIII organization, the Security Council decided to authorize the mission under Chapter VII, leading to further obscurity and legal confusion. AMISOM is expected to comprise 8,000 troops, but by March 2009 only a batch of approximately 4,000 AU peacekeepers (mostly from Uganda and Burundi) has been deployed. Given these difficulties, in January 2009 the UN Security Council expressed its intent to establish a UN peacekeeping operation in Somalia (resolution 1863).
- Comoros (March 2006–June 2006)—The AU Mission for Support to the Elections in the Comoros (AMISEC), comprising a team of election observers and monitors and 462 military and civilian police personnel, with South Africa as lead nation, was deployed with the objective to support the reconciliation process in the Comoros and to observe the electoral process. Although AMISEC arrested several individuals for fraud, the voting went smoothly.

- Comoros (March 2008–October 2008)—Shortly after AMISEC, the Comoros plunged again in instability after the renegade leader of the island of Anjouan, Mohamed Bacar, organized an illegal election. After nine months of negotiation led by South Africa, the AU deployed the African Union Electoral and Security Assistance Mission to the Comoros (MAES), which was composed of approximately 1,500 AU troops (from Sudan, Tanzania, and Senegal with logistical support from Libya) with the objective to re-establish peace and security to the archipelago. The mission was successful and Bacar sought political asylum in France. The AU's first engagement in Comoros, in order to prevent the fragmentation of the Comoros federation, dates back to 1997–1999 when it was still the OAU. To date it has deployed six missions to stop electoral processes from mutating into political turmoil.

These interventions have, however, been dogged by some controversy. First, the decision to deploy is not always preceded by a systematic evaluation of the technical and military resources available, causing severe political constraints and military limitations. In the Comoros (MAES), there was a disagreement between South Africa, who argued that diplomatic sanctions should have been given more time, and some of the troop contributing countries, such as Tanzania, who insisted that the AU had exhausted all available opportunities to end the political dispute.[27] In Sudan, Makinda and Okumu's description of the AU's intervention in Darfur is elucidatory:

> The deployment of the African Union Mission in Sudan faced enormous problems ... There were few countries with soldiers trained in peace operations of the Darfur nature, where there was no peace agreement to implement. ... The AU lacked equipment and had only a few vehicles and tents, and no aircraft. It took a while before the donors provided the promised equipment, some of which was incompatible. Once countries, such as Rwanda and Nigeria offered troops, there was a logistical problem of transporting them to Darfur. When Rwanda tried to send in 300 soldiers ... it was forced to postpone the deployment, as preparations to house them had not been made.[28]

Second, the interventions are often encouraged by member states' needs to project national and personal agendas. For instance, the underlying reason that prompted Mozambique and Ethiopia to deploy in Burundi was to accommodate the expectations of the national armies. Africa peacekeeping is often associated with an increase in salaries, exposure to new technologies and armament, and the learning of new military doctrines—all of which is likely to enhance the living conditions of the soldiers.[29] In addition, there were economic interests, mostly in the case of Ethiopia. The Great Lakes region was a focal point of instability in the whole continent and by contributing to its pacification Ethiopia would have better conditions to increase trade.[30] Moreover, the Mozambican political leadership was also led by a desire to reward African countries over their key contributions to the two-year long United Nations Operation in Mozambique (ONUMOZ), established to help implement the peace agreement that put an end to the civil war that had agonized the country.[31] Furthermore, encouraged by the end of the civil war (1975–92), Mozambique wanted to demonstrate to its African counterparts (and to the international community) that it was no longer a country that needed to be aided, but a country that could come to the rescue of other countries.[32] It was therefore, a struggle for international visibility.[33] According to AU officials, Ethiopia, as the host of the Union, also places great importance in being recognized as a herald of the African cause.[34] It should be recalled that according to article 5 of the protocol, a criteria to be qualified for election to the PSC is the capacity and commitment of a country to the promotion and maintenance of peace and security in Africa, including experience in peace support operations.

Third, these interventions should not camouflage the fact that the AU has shied away from intervening in other countries such as Zimbabwe, Libya, Equatorial Guinea, or Congo-Brazzaville, where atrocities are being committed and human rights are frequently violated. Regrettably the old culture of non-intervention and sacred respect for national borders is still present and will take time to eradicate. Obviously a young and under-resourced organization such as the AU should not be expected to intervene every single time an internal conflict erupts in a country, but in due time this mandate should indeed be improved and the AU should be prepared to advocate more creative approaches to complex problems.

Conclusion

For an organization that only became operational in 2002 the AU has demonstrated a strong political willingness to engage with the wider spectrum of conflict—from conflict prevention to peacebuilding. Its resource capacity is, however, limited. In total the AU has presently a staff of approximately 700, of which roughly 40 work in peace and security related issues (at headquarters).[35] The low number of staff and the level of qualifications is clearly inadequate to deal effectively with the new work being generated by the wider mandate of the AU compared to the OAU and the demands of member states. A thorough job evaluation has not yet been carried out as required by the 2003 Maputo summit, which has led to the retention of a number of former OAU staff without a clear responsibility, or being assigned to non-approved positions.[36]

The running budget of the AU for the year 2009 amounted to US $164.3 million. Although it clearly exceeds that of the OAU, it is seemingly insufficient to finance the running costs of 18-plus internal organs. In peace and security, the AU seems to be better equipped. Even if in 2007 the peace fund only amounted to US$12 million (generated primarily through a transference of 6 percent of the regular budget), the budget of the Peace and Security Department reached US$250.6 million as a result of contributions from Western (mainly European) donors. The main European contributors to the AU's security architecture are the European Union (African Peace Facility and Amani Africa/ Euro Recamp), Italy (Italian African Peace Facility), Spain (Spanish Peace Facility), and Denmark (Danish Africa Program for Peace).

Given the multiplication of international support, the AU should increase its auditing and oversight capacity in order to assure that the budget is managed rigorously. Often it is not. For instance, in 2007 the Pan-African Parliament was hit by a financial scandal. An audit commissioned by the permanent representatives has found that MPs have been granting to themselves undue benefits and denounced a "total and systematic non-respect of existing rules" regarding financial matters.[37] As pointed out by the director of the AU Peace and Security Department, "there is a notorious discrepancy between what is demanded from the AU and our capacity to deliver. The AU is still building its house, but the challenges on the ground are so outstanding that we are not able to finish our work."[38]

The AU's dependency on outside funds opens the door for external agents to shape the internal security agenda of the organization. Although this is acknowledged by some of its leaders,[39] the AU should be more unwavering at picking up the bill for its own problems before turning to Western donors. And even if it is unquestionable that African states have poor financial conditions, this alone does not explain the poor resources of the organization. It would be possible for the AU to overcome its over-dependency if its members showed an unbending determination to advance the Pan-African cause and if they articulated, in a more effective way, national and regional strategies to increase AU's reliance on its own resources. For instance, as pointed out by Murithi, a substantial amount of funds can be re-directed from the draining military budgets in all African countries.[40] Other alternatives include the creation of an AU trust fund to be financed by diasporan Africans, and a one-dollar levy on all international airline flights to and from Africa.

3 Economic Community of West African States (ECOWAS)

In the African context, the sub-regional organization which arguably has the most robust security mechanism is ECOWAS. Founded by the Lagos Treaty in May 1975, ECOWAS was conceived as a means toward economic integration and development intended to lead to the eventual establishment of an economic union in West Africa, fostering economic stability and enhancing relations between its member states.[1] Since it was launched as a traditional customs union regime, ECOWAS has grown to become a robust organization designed to meet challenges beyond those presented by a tariff-harmonization scheme. In reality, ECOWAS was an attempt to overcome the isolation of most West African countries following the colonial period and the period of post-independence nationalism. In the decade after independence, West Africa was jolted by a series of bloody military coups against constitutional governments, a three-year civil war in Nigeria, inter-state wars, extra-regional interventions and a spate of foreign-backed mercenary activities in Guinea, Benin, and Cape Verde, which compelled Western African leaders to consider regional integration schemes.[2] In practice, however, ECOWAS was meant to provide an institutional framework for Nigeria's leadership and the erosion of France's political and economical influence.[3] In 1973 France provided political capital for the creation of the all-Francophone West African Economic Community (CEAO), which according to French president Georges Pompidou would serve to counter-balance the heavy weight of Nigeria,[4] a country that after the discovery of oil and the 1973 crisis converted itself into a major power. The creation of ECOWAS, spearheaded by Nigerian president General Yakubu Gowon and President Eyadema of Togo (with observer status in CEAO), was thus an upshot of Nigeria's regional leadership.

ECOWAS has developed in a very volatile context. The diversity of West Africa is reflected in its history with a Francophone, Anglophone and Lusophone colonial divide, and socio-cultural, ethnic, and linguistic differences. Moreover, as McGowan and Johnson noted, West Africa is the region *par excellence* of the military coup d'etat. According to them the sub-region accounted for 55 percent of all coups d'état in Africa in the period 1960–1984.[5] Francis adds that West Africa is therefore a regional conflict complex because armed conflicts are not just confined and localized within state borders, but the regional dimensions and dynamics often fuel and sustain these wars through the activities of the shadow economy and peace spoilers.[6] Even so, ECOWAS has successfully managed to become the most dominant sub-regional organization in sub-Saharan Africa.[7]

Organizational capacity

When ECOWAS was established in 1975 the Lagos Treaty did not accord the organization any juridical mandate in the areas of peace and security. The gradual incorporation of a security dimension only arrived slowly in 1976, when Nigeria and Togo proposed a formal defense treaty that resulted the following year in the Accord on Non-Aggression and Defence (ANAD). The Protocol compelled member states to refrain from "committing an act of aggression against the territorial integrity of a member state" (art. 2), but it not foresee any response mechanism in case that occurred. This void was filled in 1981 when ECOWAS adopted the Protocol on Mutual Assistance and Defense (PMAD), which envisioned among other things the bold creation of the Allied Armed Forces of the Community (arts. 5–18) and permitted the legitimate intervention in the internal affairs of member states when a situation is "likely to endanger the security and peace in the entire Community" (art. 4). Thus, in the 1980s ECOWAS set the stage for the responsibility to protect, at least at the declaratory level, since in practice the principles of national sovereignty have always prevailed and the Protocol was to a large extent a dead letter, since none of its procedural or integral decision-making aspects had been implemented.[8]

From a legal perspective, ECOWAS has only integrated indisputable security provisions into its juridical architecture with the revised Treaty of ECOWAS (adopted in 1993), which enshrines the need to establish and strengthen appropriate mechanisms for the timely prevention and resolution of intra-State and inter-State conflicts (art. 58). This security profile of the organization was reinforced with a series of declarations and treaties adopted in the early 1990s, which included the 1991 Declaration of Political Principles, committing member states to uphold democracy and the rule of law; the 1998 Moratorium on Import,

Export and Manufacturing of Light Weapons; and the 1999 Protocol for Conflict Prevention, Management, Resolution, Peacekeeping and Security, signed at the ECOWAS Summit in Lomé. This protocol was an attempt to rectify the poor planning, coordination, command, and control that characterized ECOWAS' operations in Liberia and Sierra Leone.[9] The interventions in these countries, along with the one in Guinea-Bissau, have also put into evidence the fragile status of democracy in the region and led the organization to expound in 2001 the Protocol on Democracy and Good Governance Supplementary to the Protocol for Conflict Prevention, Management, Resolution, Peacekeeping and Security. An interesting aspect of the Protocol for Conflict Prevention is that it revitalizes the possibility to intervene in internal disputes that "threaten to trigger a humanitarian disaster" or that pose "a serious threat to peace and security in the sub-region." Intervention is also authorized in situations of "serious and massive violations of human rights and the rule of law," or "in the event of an overthrow or attempted overthrow of a democratically elected government" (art. 25).

In 2007 ECOWAS adopted a comprehensive new plan for the future, coined as ECOWAS Vision 2020, which envisioned the consolidation of a peaceful environment and the strengthening of an effective conflict prevention, peace and security system. Although this plan was set in motion primarily due to regional economic interests, it brought to light the specificities of post-conflict states and alerted its readers to the importance of investing in development as a vehicle for conflict prevention. The adoption of these various legal documents endowed ECOWAS with a strong juridical capacity to operate in the full cycle of conflict: from prevention to post-war reconstruction. But despite all these provisions aimed at finding solutions to the causes of conflicts in West Africa, the region is still unstable. This raises the need to look beyond the legal mandate and focus on the institutional capacity of the organization to prevent and resolve conflicts.

ECOWAS central decision-making organs in the sphere of peace and security are the Commission (which in January 2007 replaced the Executive Secretariat), the Defense and Security Commission, and the Mediation and Security Council. Although some executive secretaries have proved to be more competent than others, over the years the Commission (or the previous Executive Secretariat) has emerged as the soul of the organization, which may be explained by the stability and predictability of its leadership—regular mandates of four years—and by the extension of its powers assigned by the 1999 protocol which recognized it as "the legal representative of the institutions of the Community in their totality" (art. 19-2) (Table 3.1). It is the Commission, namely

Table 3.1 Executive secretaries of ECOWAS

Mandate	Name	Country of Origin
1977–1985	Aboubakar Ouattara	Côte D'Ivoire
1985–1989	Alhaji Momodu Munu	Sierra Leone
1989–1993	Abass Bundu	Sierra Leone
1993–1997	Édouard Benjamin	Guinea
1997–2002	Lansana Kouyaté	Guinea
2002–2006	Mohamed Ibn Chambas	Ghana
Presidents of ECOWAS Commission		
2007–present	Mohamed Ibn Chambas	Ghana

the Commissioner for Political Affairs, Peace and Security, that supervises the Observation and Monitoring Center[10] (the headquarters body of the early warning system—ECOWARN) and the peacekeeping activities of the organization.

Another key body is the Defense and Security Commission, comprising the chiefs of defense staff, mandated to examine all technical and administrative issues and evaluate the prerequisites for peacekeeping operations. Finally, the Mediation and Security Council, composed of 10 members,[11] oversees the activities of ECOWAS devoted to conflict prevention, peacemaking, peacekeeping, and peace enforcement. The members to the council are selected on the basis of elections, which is a way to curtail accusations of Anglophone decision-making dominance. Besides these transversal decision-making bodies, ECOWAS has created specific bodies tailored to execute its mandate in conflict prevention and peacemaking, and peacekeeping and peace enforcement.

Conflict prevention and peacemaking

In 2008, ECOWAS adopted the ECOWAS Conflict Prevention Framework (ECPF), a very ambitious and well-crafted document that attempts to address both structural and operational prevention by providing guidelines and entry points for actors to engage in prevention initiatives. Conflict prevention is defined as:

> Activities designed to reduce tensions and prevent the outbreak, escalation, spread or recurrence of violence. Conflict prevention strategies may distinguish between operational prevention (measures applicable in the face of imminent crisis) and structural prevention (measures to ensure that crises do not arise in the first

place or, if they do, that they do not reoccur). The emphasis is not on preventing conflict per se (conflict being a natural consequence of change) but in halting its descent into violence.

(para. 18)

Conflict prevention is to be achieved through a variety of mechanisms that include for example preventive diplomacy, democracy and political governance, cross-border initiatives, youth empowerment or early warning. The latter is absolutely central in any conflict prevention strategy and ECOWAS takes pride for having a substantial capacity in this regard. The organization's early warning mechanism—ECOWARN—comprises a situation room at headquarters, field stations in all member states and four zonal bureaus of early warning (in Banjul, Ouagadougou, Monrovia, and Cotonou) mandated to assess political (human rights, democracy), economic (food shortages), social (unemployment), security (arms flows, civil–military relations), and environment (drought, flooding) indicators on a daily basis. ECOWAS work in the area of early warning is carried out in close partnership with civil society, and is being coordinated mainly through two West African civil society networks: the West Africa Network for Peacebuilding (WANEP) and the West African Civil Society Forum (WACSOF). The zonal bureaus are, however, not yet functional. There is still a lack of technical and qualified staff to operate and maintain the equipment, and also to collect, collate, and analyze data. The second problem with the early warning mechanism is its end-use. In most cases, there is no insufficiency of information on the root causes of violent conflicts in West Africa. The perpetrators of some of the recent conflicts, Doe, Vieira, and Momoh, were aware that their mismanagement could pave the way for social turmoil. One of the goals of ECOWAS' early warning system should be, therefore, to gather compelling data to demonstrate that conflict prevention is about the efficient promotion of a democratic culture, institutions, and governance. Associated with this, some field monitors may have difficulties collecting data. As Souaré warns, "it is unlikely that civil servants loyal to an undemocratic, if not dictatorial, regime will be able to effectively monitor and report human rights situations, press freedom and civil-military relations in their country or another country friendly with theirs."[12] To overcome this shortcoming WANEP and WACSOF have been given room for maneuver in data collection.

ECOWAS' organizational capacity in conflict prevention and peacemaking is also centered on the Council of Elders, a group of 15 persons (one from each member state) mandated to use their good offices in the prevention of violent conflict.[13] Some years after the setting up of the council the UN cooperated with ECOWAS in the identification of "eminent" people in order to inject much needed credibility in the selection process. Indeed, when the council was inaugurated in 2001 its chairman was General Yakubu Gowon, who came to power in Nigeria in 1966 through a coup d'état and was accused of corruption and mismanagement on a grand scale.[14] This is not the background expected from someone who is expected to act as a reference point and peacemaker. ECOWAS counter-argues by spotlighting Gowon's role as chairman of the Committee of Eminent Persons that drafted the revised 1993 treaty.

The adoption of the Conflict Prevention Framework is also a step forward in terms of coordination among ECOWAS institutions and agencies on conflict prevention, which to date has been weak, incoherent or non-existent. Initiatives such as ECOWARN that promote good governance, democracy, gender equality, and youth empowerment, have operated in isolation, causing overlap and inefficient use of resources. This would be a very difficult endeavor, as old habits die hard and "implementing the ECPF will have to involve various departments in ECOWAS ceding their turfs and consciously including other related departments in programmes' design and implementation to yield better results."[15] Collaboration between member states, civil society, and external agents has also been limited and therefore the Framework is an important vehicle to promote cooperation and harmonization. The challenges ahead are manifold and include the need to generate political will to implement the Framework and not allow it to become a cosmetic document. Conflict prevention is also an expensive program which is likely to stretch even further ECOWAS finances.

Peacekeeping and enforcement

The peacekeeping capacity of ECOWAS has been centered on its monitoring group (ECOMOG), established in 1990 to intervene in the civil war in Liberia (see below). ECOMOG represented the first attempt at a regional security initiative since the OAU tried to establish an Inter-African Force to intervene in Chad in 1981. This standby force became a de jure organ of ECOWAS in the 1999 Protocol and it is currently being overhauled into the ECOWAS Standby Force (ESF), under the African Standby Force. The force, composed of 6,500 soldiers, police and gendarmes, is sub-divided between an ECOWAS task force composed of 2,773 personnel that could be deployed within 30 days, and an ECOWAS main brigade of 3,727 personnel that could be deployed within 90 days.[16] The established a task force headquarters (in Abuja) and has an operational PLANELM. All countries have pledged their support and the Commission has undertaken a verification mission to confirm the levels of readiness among member states and has also conducted a number of command post exercises.[17] Additionally, three training centers have been designated, however, to offer ECOWAS troops training in peacekeeping operations: the National Defense College in Nigeria is aimed at the strategic level, the Ecole du Maintien de la Paix in Mali operates at the tactical level, and the Kofi Annan International Peacekeeping Training Center in Ghana is focused on the operational level. Despite the interesting set-up these institutions have poor administrative capacity, which hinders their capacity to provide effective technical support. Nevertheless, the ESF has attained the highest level of readiness to deploy when compared to the other sub-regional brigades. In this process, the military exercises so far conducted to assess the status of the troops, their operational readiness, equipment and training level, has been noteworthy. In 2004 an exercise under the Renforcement des Capacités Africaines de Maintien de la Paix (RECAMP) framework was organized for ECOWAS member states in Benin. In December 2007, some 1,600 troops from West Africa and France participated in Exercise DEGGO XXVII, a command post and field training exercise starting at Thies, Senegal. In June 2008, experts from the military, police, gendarmerie, and their civilian counterparts and troops from all 15 member states, participated in an exercise in Bamako, which evaluated the capacity of the ESF Task Force Headquarters to plan and conduct peacekeeping operations as well as the capacity of the dedicated transmission company to establish reliable communications. It was the first drill organized solely by ECOWAS. The second took place in June 2009 in Ouagadougou, Burkina Faso and its main objective was to evaluate the logistic component of the ESF.

The organic and operational record of ECOWAS is, however, not faultless. The organization has only demonstrated a modest interest from the military/security side in drawing out the linkages between their work and development programs for conflict prevention. Indeed, despite the adoption of the Conflict Prevention Framework, the defense and security staff still regards peace and security as a mainly military responsibility involving the ECOWAS Standby Force and other techniques involving military forces supported by formal structures. ECOWAS should therefore enhance the conceptual basis for peace and security in general, and conflict prevention in particular, so that a distinction between operational prevention and structural prevention becomes visible, and is able to increase understanding of conflict prevention related opportunities, tools and resources at technical and political levels. Strangely, the Conflict Prevention Framework includes the ECOWAS Standby Force as one of the components of its conflict prevention strategy, reinforcing the paradoxical idea that the use of force is an apposite strategy to prevent violence breaking out.

Operational experience

ECOWAS is the African sub-regional organization with the largest operational experience in peace and security, whose work in pacific settlement and peacekeeping has been encouraged by numerous UN policy declarations. Its experience lies primarily at the intersection between peacekeeping and enforcement, although the organization is also active in conflict prevention and peacemaking.

Peacekeeping and enforcement

The peacekeeping experience of ECOWAS is well documented as the negative record of the operations in terms lack of unified command and control; major differences in capabilities of national contingents; absence of a central logistics system or lack of capacity to effect the transition from peacekeeping to peacebuilding (see below).[18] In total ECOWAS has deployed five military missions in the following countries:

- Liberia I (1990–97). Following the outbreak of the civil war that pitted Charles Taylor (NPFL) against government forces (led by President Samuel Doe), ECOWAS deployed a mission with the mandate to conduct military operations for the purpose of monitoring the cease-fire and restore law and order to create the necessary conditions for free and fair elections. ECOMOG, however, soon found its mandate complicated by the violence of the warring factions. Not long after its deployment, ECOMOG shifted from being a peacekeeper to performing peace enforcement tasks.
- Liberia II (2003). After President Taylor resigned office and departed into exile in Nigeria, conditions were created for the deployment of what became a 3,600-strong ECOWAS peacekeeping mission in Liberia (ECOMIL). The UN took over security in Liberia in October 2003, subsuming ECOMIL into the United Nations Mission in Liberia (UNMIL), a force that grew to its present size of nearly 15,000.
- Sierra Leone (1997–99). It was established after the Nigerian leader, General Sani Abacha, diverted peacekeepers from the successful

Liberia mission to Sierra Leone in an attempt to crush a military coup by the Sierra Leonean army in May 1997. Nigerian troops reversed the coup in February 1998 and restored President Ahmed Tejan Kabbah to power.

- Guinea-Bissau (1998–99). The goal was to end civil conflict between President João Vieira (backed by Senegalese and Guinean military forces), and his former army chief, Ansumane Mané. Given the continuous degradation of the conflict and its poor capacity to cope with it, ECOWAS withdrew its forces before the conflict was resolved.
- Côte d'Ivoire (2003–4). Deployed in order to facilitate the implementation of the Linas-Marcoussis Agreement that put an end to the civil war that had broken out in September 2002. In February 2004, the UN Security Council passed a resolution authorizing a full peacekeeping operation for Côte d'Ivoire and mandating nearly 7,000 UN troops to monitor and help implement the peace agreement. The ECOWAS forces have been, as a result, subsumed within the UN-mandated operation.

ECOWAS military interventions have been marred by controversy. The first flaw was the absence of community-wide logistical arrangements prior to the deployment of ECOMOG forces, which led to panicky responses to underestimated threats from rebel forces; and lop-sided national reinforcements that served to further complicate regional diplomacy.[19] ECOMOG in all its operations relied on an inadequate and very poor military capability, logistics, and structure. The improvisatory nature of its deployments also catalyzed the lack of clarity of its mandate, especially relating to peacekeeping and enforcement.[20] ECOWAS interventions illustrate the need to address the critical issues of capacity and of the suitability of delegating responsibilities to malfunctioning institutions.

Second, the military interventions in Western Africa also embody the opportunism of dominant countries. Nigeria, for instance, has widely used military interventions to project its political and economic interests, to cement its hegemonic role, or to market its international image abroad.[21] During the Liberian war, timber and minerals were transported across the frontlines between rival forces, earning ECOMOG the anecdotal acronym of "Every Car Or Moving Object Gone."[22] In fact, some authors argue that Nigerian generals personally benefited from revenues written off as ECOMOG expenses.[23] But if Nigeria's interests have been discussed extensively in the literature, other ECOWAS interventions have also been sparked by national agendas. For example, in Guinea-Bissau, Senegal's president Abdou Diouf's interest in saving the Vieira government stemmed primarily from a desire to prevent a government friendly to the Casamance rebels from ruling Bissau. Indeed, Dakar believed that Ansumane Mané was sending weapons to his Mandingo kin in the secessionist Casamance region.[24]

Conflict prevention and peacemaking

As a joint EU-UN assessment mission to ECOWAS observed, the West African organization has been more effective in crisis management through the deployment of peacekeepers than in conflict prevention.[25] Nonetheless, ECOWAS has some field experience in conflict prevention and peacemaking. For instance, in Guinea-Bissau (1998) mediation efforts (in collaboration with CPLP) led to a ceasefire agreement between President Vieira and dissident General Mané, whereas in Sierra Leone (2000) it was directly involved in securing the Abuja ceasefire agreement. In Côte d'Ivoire (2002) ECOWAS dispatched a high-level ministerial delegation to Abidjan to begin efforts to restore peace between the government of President Laurent Gbagbo and rebel soldiers, and it became a member of the follow-up committee established to monitor the implementation of the agreement. In Liberia (2003), ECOWAS facilitated peace talks between the government of Liberia, civil society, and the LURD and MODEL rebel groups. In 2005, ECOWAS was instrumental in lowering tensions between Senegal and The Gambia that were sparked by the conflict in Casamance. In 2009, it also played an important role in stabilizing Guinea-Bissau after the assassination of its president, Nino Vieira. A report supervised by the United Nations Office for West Africa (UNOWA) has clarified that "ECOWAS mediation has led to the signing of nearly two dozen peace agreements to end destructive wars in West Africa."[26] Despite this, ECOWAS has not yet fully capitalized on the potential of its Council of Elders, as many of the council members lack training and knowledge in conflict prevention, resolution, and management. Nor are these missions properly registered and monitored in order to create a bank of empirical knowledge and to extract lessons learnt.

Conclusion

Several assessments carried out by independent consultants have indicated that the ECOWAS secretariat is in need of training and equipment to operationalize the framework set up by the Protocol. A UN assessment mission to ECOWAS has concluded that ECOWAS still lacks the "resource capacity (both human and financial) to complete the organization's institutional capability to maintain regional stability over the long-term."[27] ECOWAS staff dealing with peace and security need to enhance their capacity in program/project identification, formulation, practical and financial management. Moreover, financial administration remains weak and needs to be strengthened. Although ECOWAS approved, in 2008, a budget of US$210 million for the operations of the secretariat and institutions of the community,[28] dependence on external funding is growing as an increased number of donors show interest in fostering the capacity of the secretariat. Such funding is either channeled through the ECOWAS internal budget or allocated directly to the department concerned. The assistance is more based on the availability of funds and budgetary deadlines from donors rather than on systematically assessed needs.

Another characteristic of the secretariat is its poor human resource capacity, in inverted proportion to the growth of its mandate and areas of operation. Although there is no reliable source, ECOWAS staff is estimated to be approximately 300 people. Recruitment is still often driven by political appointments and promotions, hindering a progressive professionalization.

Yet, West Africa's future looks auspicious. After years of virtual stagnation largely occasioned by unstable markets for primary products (the mainstay of most countries in the region), and the distraction of more than a decade of conflicts, the prognosis looks better. Regional economic growth manifests itself in improvements in the regional GDP—from US$141.9 billion in 2005 to US$199.1 billion in 2007. To sustain this growth it is important that ECOWAS be able to coordinate its regional programs and projects with other bodies located in the region, such as the Mano River Union and the Co-Prosperity Zone (COPAZ). Indeed, when regional overlapping is a problem (see Table 13.1) it is essential that sub-regional bodies coordinate their actions and adopt a clear task-sharing program. ECOWAS is nevertheless the dominant organization in Western Africa and it seems to be keen on strengthening and overhauling its institutions to adapt to regional challenges. Indeed, at the 2008 ECOWAS summit, Sierra Leone's President Ernest Koroma affirmed that "the organizational transformation we are looking for is therefore one that will develop institutions that could work with national and international bodies to address global problems as well as the felt needs of our people." ECOWAS is on the right track, but still has a long way to go.

4 Intergovernmental Authority on Development (IGAD)

IGAD is the successor organization to the Intergovernmental Authority on Drought and Development (IGADD), created in 1986 by six drought-stricken East African countries (Djibouti, Ethiopia, Kenya, Somalia, Sudan, and Uganda)[1] with a narrow mandate around the issues of drought and desertification. With the active encouragement of the United Nations Environmental Program (UNEP), IGADD was created in order to improve the regional response to natural disasters.[2] In the mid-1990s the founding members of IGADD decided to revitalize and transform the organization into a fully fledged regional political, economic, development, trade, and security entity similar to ECOWAS and SADC (founded in 1975 and 1992 respectively). One of the principal motivations for the revitalization of IGADD was the existence of many organizational and structural problems that made the implementation of its goals and principles ineffective. To tackle these problems IGADD leaders met in April 1995 and resolved to revitalize the authority and expand its areas of regional cooperation. In March 1996 at the Second Extraordinary Summit in Nairobi they approved and adopted an Agreement Establishing the Intergovernmental Authority on Development. In April 1996 on the recommendation of the Summit of the Heads of State and Government, the IGAD Council of Ministers identified three priority areas of cooperation: conflict prevention, management and resolution, and humanitarian affairs; infrastructure development (transport and communications); and food security and environment protection.

The initial enthusiasm soon encountered various obstacles and the leaders quickly realized that the efficiency of IGAD is hampered by several factors. This was even acknowledged by IGAD's former executive secretary, Attalla Hamad Bashir (2000–8), who has noted that the region is idiosyncratic as first, it often suffers from natural calamities (floods, famine, water shortages, droughts), second, IGAD countries are devastated by civil wars and political instability, third, they are the poorest countries in the world, finally, the illiteracy rate reaches 80 percent.[3] Indeed, the prevalence of identity politics and processes or state formation and disintegration are identified as common structural features of conflict in the region.[4] In addition to this problematic scenario, two of its key member states, Ethiopia and Eritrea, have been involved in a deadly conflict from 1998 to 2000, and have been engaged in a process of mutual accusations ever since that has unquestionably affected the work of the organization.

However, it seems more pertinent to evaluate IGAD not by juxtaposing its initial objectives with its accomplishments, but rather by recognizing that the organization has already accomplished a great deal in a context that is adverse and detrimental. Some authors have nonetheless contended that "IGAD has not been successful in ending current conflicts and bringing stability to the region. IGAD's inability to foster peace and security cooperation among the countries in the Horn stems fundamentally from the persisting suspicions, geographical rivalries, and ideological differences among its members."[5] It could be argued however that the name change from IGADD to IGAD was not merely cosmetic and has had a bearing on the ability of the Djibouti-based secretariat to promote peace and security more directly. And in this light, IGAD has performed well in the areas of peace and security, namely in Sudan and Somalia—where it has been involved with mediation efforts since the early 1990s.

Given the socio-economic disparities, societal heterogeneities, and geographical boundaries, it has always been difficult to create a stable regional security identity in the IGAD region. Culturally and historically speaking, various fault lines, which have successfully been politicized in the course of the last century, criss-cross the arena. One is the line between Arabic and Black Africa linked with lines between Muslim and Christian culture, or the line between peasant culture and nomadic pastoralism.[6] There are other factors that curtail regional integration, namely the absence of a leading power (like South Africa in SADC or Nigeria in ECOWAS), heavily differing forms of national government and types of state constitution, diverging domestic policies, and self-centered nationalist leaders who may minimize efforts toward integration and cooperation.[7] But violent conflict constitutes perhaps the single greatest barrier to economic and social development in the IGAD region. The Horn of Africa has been embroiled in endless wars for more than 40 years and represents one of the most complex regional peace and security clusters[8] in the world. Interactions *between* the states of the region support and sustain the conflicts *within* the state of the region in a systematic way.[9] Despite this background, and with very low resources, IGAD has been able to set up an effective security agenda, most notably in conflict prevention and peacemaking.

Organizational capacity

The constitutional provisions of IGAD have accorded it a mandate to operate in peace and security. In the Agreement Establishing IGAD of 1996, article 18a determines that "Member States shall act collectively to preserve peace, security and stability, which are essential pre-requisites for economic development and social progress." To reach this goal, IGAD members shall take effective collective measures to eliminate threats to regional cooperation, peace and stability; establish an effective mechanism of consultation and cooperation for the pacific settlement of disputes; and be prepared to deal with disputes between member states within this sub-regional mechanism before they are referred to other regional or international organizations.

In the late 1990s IGAD took a turn to focus on conflict prevention. In 1998, IGAD heads of state mandated the secretariat in Djibouti to establish a Conflict Early Warning and Response Mechanism, and a team of international consultants was brought into to develop the pilot project.[10] Four years later, at the 9th summit in Khartoum, IGAD heads of state and government signed the Protocol on the Establishment of a Conflict Early Warning and Response Mechanism (CEWARN), reinforcing the legal mandate of the organization in peace and security.[11] Although article 6A-b of the Agreement Establishing IGAD states that one of the principles of the organization is the "non-interference in the internal affairs of Member-states," IGAD has in place functioning sub-regional mechanisms for collective intervention, through early warning and conflict prevention (CEWARN) and peacekeeping (EASBRIG).

The organizational capacity of an organization is also associated with its institutions and the way they are operationalized. The internal structure of IGAD includes the Assembly of Heads of State and Government, a secretariat, the Council of Ministers, and the Committee of Ambassadors. The assembly is the supreme policy-making organ of the authority, and determines the objectives, guidelines and programs for IGAD. The secretariat assists member states in formulating regional projects in the priority areas, facilitates the coordination and harmonization of development policies, mobilizes resources to implement regional projects and programs approved by the Council, and reinforces national infrastructures necessary for implementing regional projects and policies. Within the secretariat the small Peace and Security Division is mandated to deal with issues related to political affairs, conflict prevention/resolution and humanitarian affairs. The Council of Ministers is composed of the ministers of foreign affairs and one other minister designated by each member state, and its primary task is to formulate policies and to approve the work program and annual budget of the secretariat. Finally, the Committee of Ambassadors is composed of IGAD member states' ambassadors or plenipotentiaries accredited to the country of IGAD headquarters, and is mandated to advise and guide the executive secretary. This decision-making architecture has some limitations, nevertheless, primarily in terms of operational capacity derived from the internal disputes between some member states, which cause decision-making blockades and result in operational slowness. As an illustration, in April 2007, Eritrea decided to suspend its membership of IGAD due to the fact that "a number of repeated and irresponsible resolutions that undermine regional peace and security have been adopted in the guise of IGAD."[12] In an organization that has a strong intergovernmental nature the absence of a member state restrains to a worrisome level the regional decision-making process. As observed by Fanta, "even when they are not engaged in an open war, the countries in the region [Horn of Africa] remain very suspicious towards one another obliging them to take into account each other's moves and political decisions."[13] This reiterates the idea that vicinity and national interests condition the capacity of a regional organization to take transparent decisions on behalf of the common regional interest.

Despite the recurrent tension that punctuates the decision-making process, IGAD has still been able to gain the status of a sub-regional organization with strong expertise and experience in security issues which translated into the creation of decision-making mechanisms strictly devoted to early warning/conflict prevention, peacekeeping, and counter-terrorism.

Early warning and conflict prevention

Following the signature of the protocol on early warning, IGAD set up the early warning mechanism in Addis Ababa with support from donors. The mechanism developed at a quick pace and over time it became the hub and clearing-house for early warning in East Africa. Its tasks are manifold and includes the managing of databases and the recommendation of regional responses to cross-border and trans-border conflicts. To collect the data it counts on an extensive network of field monitors, country coordinators, national research institutes, and Conflict Early Warning and Response Units (CEWERUs). CEWARN is primarily tailored to monitor the pastoral conflicts that affect the region. Eastern Africa is the sub-region in the world with the highest concentration of pastoralists, and as grazing land is shrinking as a result of many internal and external factors, including the expansion of cultivation, human and animal population growth, and climate change, competition over pasture and water results in frequent armed conflicts. The molding of IGAD's early warning mechanism according to the nature of local conflicts is a good example of the capacity of regional organizations to be more in tune with the specificity of the local dynamic and to provide local solutions to local problems. IGAD is also conscious of the political problems affecting the organization and therefore CEWARN creates room for NGOs to collect data (similarly to ECOWAS). This is a major step, as practice has shown that NGOs may act as whistle blowers and they are closer to the grassroots where the most effective early warning of conflict can be discerned.[14]

But although the focus on "livestock rustling; conflicts over grazing and water points; smuggling and illegal trade; nomadic movements; refugees; landmines; banditry" (Protocol, part II) is a reflection of the nature of the region, Eastern Africa is mostly tormented by inter-state and intra-state conflicts, issues that the mechanism does not yet address. As pointed out by Daniel Yifru, director of IGAD's Peace and Security Division, "monitoring pastoral conflicts was the easiest entry point into the field of conflict prevention in East Africa. As most countries in the region are in tension with one another, embracing hardcore inter-state or intra-state armed conflicts was considered a premature and impudent step."[15] This shortcoming is amply acknowledged by IGAD officials and the organization is currently considering the possibility of monitoring hardcore security issues from 2012 onwards (from the end of pilot phase).

Another shortcoming of CEWARN, and generally of early warning mechanisms in Africa, is that it lacks an effective response component. Indeed, early warning presupposes early action and IGAD is not logistically fully prepared to respond to pastoral conflicts. The decision to intervene (or not) in conflicts is taken by the Assembly—which generally takes a long time to reach a decision due to divergent state interests—and it meets only once a year. The most significant challenge for CEWARN is hence the translation of a hypothetical member state commitment to conflict prevention to a meaningful and action-oriented one.[16] The IGAD protocol does not have enforcement mechanisms, nor is there an obligation for the governments to act upon the conflict early warning information that CEWARN will avail to them. Despite all the warnings, IGAD could not force the Sudanese government to prevent the humanitarian emergency in the Darfur region. To address some of these issues, CEWARN has developed a five-year strategy (2007–11). According to Raymond M. Kitevu of CEWARN, the areas of focus of the five-year strategy include expansion of the reporting to cover all member states; strengthening the early response side of the mechanism; and strengthening the institutional and functional capacity of the mechanism.[17] A step in this direction was taken in August 2008 when IGAD organized a forum aimed at discussing the creation of a Response Framework and the establishment and operationalization of a Rapid Response Fund (RRF) for CEWARN.

Another shortcoming of early warning practices in East Africa is that although CEWARN is a complex and authoritative system it still requires the establishment of a single, integrated and comprehensive conflict prevention, management and reconstruction framework. Even if IGAD launched the IGAD Strategy on Peace and Security in October 2005, its formulation and proper implementation is lagging behind in time. IGAD officials recognize that the organization's involvements in Somalia and Sudan were spontaneous and did not follow any doctrine.

Peacekeeping

The organizational capacity of IGAD is not solely concentrated on early warning but also on peacekeeping. In 2003, IGAD was requested by the AU to spearhead the conceptualization and formation of the Eastern Brigade of the African Standby Force. In February 2004, IGAD convened a meeting of experts on the establishment of the Eastern Africa Standby Brigade (EASBRIG) and in the same month the Eastern African Chiefs of Defense Staff drafted a policy framework and a legal framework to operationalize EASBRIG, which were adopted in April 2005. The operational structure of EASBRIG is not very complex and includes only the brigade headquarters located in Addis Ababa, the planning element based in Nairobi, and the logistics base located with the brigade headquarters in Addis Ababa. It also uses the Karen Centre in Nairobi to train the troops for peace support operation. In May 2007, as previously determined, IGAD handed over the responsibility of operationalizing EASBRIG to an independent organ, the Eastern African Standby Brigade Coordination Mechanism (EASBRICOM), which is administratively attached to the planning cell in Nairobi and has been formed in full consensus with AU and IGAD's decision-making bodies. The reason why IGAD is not holding on to its mandate until the end is centered on the fact that some members of the Eastern Africa sub-region are not part of IGAD, such as Burundi, Rwanda, Seychelles, Madagascar, Tanzania, Comoros, and Mauritius. EASBRICOM is hence responsible for overviewing the training of the EASBRIG and it has coordinated the first Command Post exercise (CPX) in 2008. But to be able to fulfill the parameters laid out by the AU, the EASBRIG still needs to rectify some inconsistencies. As it was discussed in a workshop of the expert Working Group of the Eastern Africa Region held in September 2007, these shortcomings are related to the fact that the EASBRIG structures do not provide for the non-military components of the brigade as required by the ASF and, furthermore, it does not incorporate peacebuilding, conflict resolution and post-war reconstruction responsibilities, as also required by the African Standby Force.[18]

East Africa requires a comprehensive and integrated system that includes military, police and civilian components to undertake peace-keeping and peacebuilding missions when assigned and mandated to do so by the AU. Member states supporting EASBRIG have contributed sufficient troops to make up the brigade as required by the ASF frame-work. However, the brigade is not prepared to undertake modern peace-keeping operations. As noted in Chapter 1, peacekeeping has changed greatly since the end of the Cold War. In the process, it has become a more complex, comprehensive, and dangerous activity. Today, the classical task of serving as a neutral buffer between consenting parties has evolved into operations geared toward managing political, economic, and social change, often under difficult circumstances—a trend fueled by the fact that most modern peacekeeping operations are responses to intra-state, rather than inter-state, conflicts. And in this light EASBRIG still lacks a robust civilian-police component.

Counter-terrorism

Finally, IGAD is also involved in counter-terrorism through the IGAD Capacity-Building Program Against Terrorism (ICPAT, launched in 2006). The program revolves around five components: enhancement of judicial measures (adoption by member states of an adequate legislative network to prevent terrorism), interdepartmental cooperation (enhancement of national cooperation between the ministries of defense, justice and external relations, central banks, tourism agencies and chambers of commerce), border control (governance enhancement, electronic surveillance, and training of border police), institutional linkages with other agencies to avoid duplication (namely extra-regional agents such as the UN), training, and sharing of information and best practices. The Institute of Security Studies (Pretoria-based) is the implementation agency of the Program and it thus provides technical administration.

According to Hiruy Amanuel, head of ICPAT, the objective is to provide a genuinely idiosyncratic approach to regional counter-terrorism.[19] In the light of the ongoing war on terrorism, ICPAT provides an interesting approach to counter-terrorism based on preventive and legal measures rather than on ad hoc military action. And in a region so sensitive to external interventions, ICPAT leaders make a point in side-lining their counter-terrorism approach from the major world dynamics. Some of the components of the program, namely border control or interdepartmental cooperation, reflect the peculiar context of the Horn of Africa, marked by problems of border demarcations and governmental fragmentation. The counter-terrorism program of IGAD is thus another case study of the comparative advantages of regional organizations, that is the capacity to provide a more accurate reading of the problems and the solution of the region.

Operational experience

As stated in the Agreement Establishing IGAD, one of the objectives is to promote peace and stability and create mechanisms within the sub-region for the prevention, management, and resolution of inter and intra-state conflicts through dialogue (art. 7-g). In the field of peace-making IGAD has a good record. Since 1993, it has been involved in negotiating a peace settlement in Sudan. If initially the mediators relied mainly on improvisation and were singularly unable to structure the talks to avoid sliding into the usual deadlock,[20] in 1999 a secretariat was created in Nairobi to ensure continued engagement with the parties to the conflict. In 2002, the Machakos Protocol agreed by the government of Sudan and the Sudan People's Liberation Movement/Army (SPLM/A) under the auspices of IGAD opened the way for the signing of Sudan's Comprehensive Peace Agreement in 2005. While the agreement ended one of Africa's longest and bloodiest civil wars, it was an agreement between only two parties, the (SPLM/A) and the ruling National Congress Party (NCP). In any case, Uganda's President Museveni claimed that the achievement was an illustration of IGAD's conflict resolution capacity: "We in IGAD region and Africa as a whole have created a viable partnership, which reduces chances for outsiders to jump into solving regional conflicts yet they have very little knowledge of them."[21]

Besides Sudan, IGAD is also involved in Somalia. In 1998, in cooperation with the IGAD Forum Partners Liaison Group, IGAD members created a standing committee on the Somali peace process, chaired by Ethiopia. This committee was mandated to organize a peace process in

Somalia by providing a consultative forum for negotiations aimed at reconciliation and restoration of a government in Somalia. The current Transitional Federal Government is a result of Ethiopia's effort in finding a solution for Somalia, and it received the approval of IGAD. In March 2005, IGAD proposed a Chapter VIII Peace Support Mission to Somalia involving 10,000 troops, at a cost of US$500 million for the first year. However, the mission never materialized due to lack of international support and funding. But in 2006, Islamists took power in Somalia, prompting the United States to put the country back on the map of the global war on terrorism and to withdraw its reservations over an intervention. The mission was assigned nevertheless to the African Union and not to IGAD, an organization whose members (for example Ethiopia) were deeply entrenched in the conflict. In 2006, Ethiopian troops had entered Somalia to protect their allies in the country's virtually powerless government from Islamic militants. This is also an illustration of the lack of coherence in the global–regional mechanism regarding priority. When a conflict erupts, who should be given the priority to intervene? The UN, regional organizations, or the sub-regional? As Chapter 1 highlighted, the criteria seem to be more related to power struggles and national opportunities rather than to clear legal principles of the use of power. Despite the flawed military operation, IGAD's involvement in the Somali peace process is recurrent. In October 2008 it issued an important declaration instructing the Transitional Federal Institutions of Somalia (TFIs) to disband the government and to draft a new constitution.

Conclusion

IGAD represents the African sub-region with the lowest resource capacity if measured by the number of staff or the volume of its budget. The secretariat, based in Djibouti City, has a staff of approximately only 50 and its budget runs at approximately US$3 million a year. If IGAD could only count on these meager financial resources its institutional and operational experience in conflict resolution would be much lower. But its early warning mechanism, the counter-terrorism program, and the peace initiatives for Somalia and Sudan were supported by external donors (primarily GTZ, USAid and the EU). Although this could render the organization vulnerable to external agendas, the secretariat has been able to decline support from Western countries whose security agenda may be regarded as too embroiled with the Horn of Africa. In fact, even though the physical and administrative conditions of the secretariat are poor and the organization is under-resourced financially,

IGAD staff have been able to capitalize on the scarce resources available. Despite all limitations, the relation between IGAD and donors seems to be based more on pragmatic partnerships than on hierarchical financial directives. With a degree of legitimacy, IGAD is often praised for its accomplishments. Keller notes that both the Sudanese peace process and the reconciliation conferences in Somalia highlight the viability of subregional mediation to address intractable domestic conflicts where dialogue offers the only way out from stalemates.[22]

At the 12th Ordinary Summit of IGAD, in June 2008, heads of state directed the secretariat to undertake an inventory of what has been achieved so far in terms of harmonization and regional integration, and make recommendations on the way forward. Despite the difficult terrain on which IGAD has been built, and its scarce resources, the inventory is likely to flag up how much the organization has already achieved. That would be a legitimate appraisal.

5   Southern African Development Community (SADC)

The attempt to create a regional security structure in Southern Africa began in earnest in 1974 with the formation of the Frontline States (FLS) Alliance.[1] With the independence of Zimbabwe in 1980, the expanded FLS and its military component, the Inter-State Defense and Security Committee (ISDSC), continued to support liberation movements and provide some resistance to South Africa's forces, which were clearly superior, both quantitatively and qualitatively.[2] In Lusaka in 1980, the FLS adopted the declaration Southern Africa: Towards Economic Liberation, which committed the signatory governments to pursue policies aimed at economic liberation (i.e. to reduce economic dependence on South Africa) and the integrated and equitable development of the economies of the region. The Southern African Development Coordinating Conference (SADCC) was subsequently established in July 1981 by the governments of the nine Southern African countries of Angola, Botswana, Lesotho, Malawi, Mozambique, Swaziland, Tanzania, Zambia, and Zimbabwe[3] through the signature of a memorandum of understanding. SADCC stemmed from a frank acknowledgment that Southern Africa was economically dependent on South Africa, the hub of the regional transport and communications network, an important destination for exports and source of imports, and an important destination for many workers from across the region.[4]

In 1989 the Summit of Heads of State or Government, meeting in Harare, decided that SADCC should be formalized to give it an appropriate legal status by replacing the MoU with an agreement, charter or treaty. Hence, in 1992 the SADCC transformed itself into the Southern African Development Community. The SADC Treaty was signed in Windhoek in August 1992 and on the same day member states adopted the SADC Windhoek Declaration, the framework for SADC cooperation which included the purpose to strengthen regional solidarity, peace, and security. With the adoption of this document and with the end of apartheid in 1994, the FLS dissolved.

Organizational capacity

SADC's legal capacity in the area of peace and security was laid out in its foundational treaty of 1992, which lists as one of the objectives of the organization to "consolidate, defend and maintain democracy, peace, security and stability" (art. 5). In order to streamline its mandate, the SADC secretariat coordinated the formulation of a regional policy on peace and security which paved the way for the adoption of SADC's Framework and Strategy, which called for the forging of common political values based on democratic norms, the creation of a non-militaristic security order, and the establishment of mechanisms for conflict prevention, management, and resolution. This process culminated in the SADC Workshop on Democracy, Peace and Security, held in Windhoek in July 1994, which paved the way for the formal involvement of the SADC in the field of security, conflict mediation, and military cooperation. Two years later, SADC foreign ministers recommended the establishment of an SADC Organ for Politics, Defense and Security, which would allow for more flexibility and timely response, at the highest level, to sensitive and potentially explosive situations. The organ was formalized in the Gaborone Communiqué of June 1996. In 2001, once tension abated amongst SADC members (see below), Southern African leaders signed the Protocol on Politics, Defense and Security Cooperation at a summit in Blantyre, Malawi, which clarified the goals and determined the structure of the organ. According to the preamble of the protocol, the SADC operates in peace and security under Chapter VIII of the UN Charter (similarly to OSCE and OAS) and in this light it reaffirms the primary responsibility of the UN Security Council in maintaining international peace and security. This was a way to shed some light upon the problem of priority and authority in the follow-up of the 1998 SADC interventions which were epitomized by total disarticulation between the UN and the sub-regional organization.

Also in 2001, SADC leaders adopted at the Windhoek Summit a Report on the Review of Operation of SADC Institutions, which marked the beginning of the SADC's restructuring process. The report argued that article 5 of the SADC Treaty—which enumerates the objectives of the organization—was not clearly articulated and effectively operationalized. Hence, in order to give some strategic direction and fulfill the organ's capacity, the 2003 SADC Summit adopted a Strategic

Indicative Plan, divided into four sectors: political, defense, state security, and public security, which pinpoints the challenges, determines the objectives, and suggests strategies/activities to address them. In what concerns the prevention and resolution of conflicts, the plan encourages the contribution of civil society, suggests the development of appropriate policies for the social reintegration of ex-combatants, and recommends the definition of common standards to identify conflicts. In the field of democratization and human rights protection, the plan suggests establishing an SADC electoral commission, and indicates the need to create a regional commission for the promotion of, and the respect for, human rights. Finally, the plan establishes a new sub-structure within the SADC secretariat: the Department for Politics, Defense and Security, comprised of a Directorate for Politics and Diplomacy, a Directorate for Defense and Security, and a Strategic Analysis Unit, also responsible for the early warning situation room.

In the same year, the SADC adopted a Mutual Defense Pact, in Dar es Salaam, Tanzania, whereby "an armed attack against a state party shall be considered a threat to regional peace and security and such an attack shall be met with immediate collective action" (art. 6-1). By taking this step, the SADC became constitutionally equipped to operate not only as a Chapter VIII organization, but also as an alliance organization, with latitude of action under article 51 of the UN Charter. We should note, however, that should the Summit fail to agree on whether to order collective self-defense action, the attacked state party and other states (including non-SADC states) could already take defensive action as provided for under international law (including the UN Charter). Nevertheless, the importance of the comprehensive defense pact was flagged up by South Africa's minister of defense, Mosiua Lekota, when he stated that the pact was aimed at "stabilizing the region ... cultivating an atmosphere conducive to investment and long-term stability ... providing a mechanism to prevent conflicts between SADC countries, as well as with other countries, and for SADC countries to act together against aggression by outsiders."[5]

Despite the wide mandate, SADC has remained a hollow security organization, which has led some authors, already in the mid-1990s, to argue that "in the foreseeable future" it will not "move beyond the level of rhetoric."[6] Vale adds that, "the region lacks an appropriate regional institution to handle security issues."[7] Ngoma, on the other hand, refutes this idea by arguing that the legal documents of SADC often allude to "common cultural and social affinities," a "vision of shared future," or "common problems and aspirations" signaling that SADC holds, accurately, the idea of a security community.[8] This might be an over-statement, and an analysis of the operational capacity of some of SADC's internal organs is elucidative.

The institutional apparatus of the organization is composed of the Summit of Heads of State and Government, the Council of Ministers (usually foreign or finance ministers), the Integrated Committee of Ministers which bears responsibility for the implementation of the Regional Indicative Strategic Development Plan, the secretariat, and the Organ on Defense, Politics and Security Cooperation—modeled on the OAU's Central Organ of the Mechanism for Conflict Prevention, Management and Resolution—is the main peace and security hub of the organization.

The coordination of the organ has been assigned to a Ministerial Committee comprised of the ministers responsible for foreign affairs, defense, public security, and state security from each of the member states. Ministers of foreign affairs of each member state perform the functions of the Organ relating to politics and diplomacy within the Inter-state Politics and Diplomacy Committee (ISPDC). Ministers for Defense, Public Security and State Security work through the Inter-state Defense and Security Committee (ISDSC). The responsibilities of the latter two are not clearly defined and delineated. Oosthuizen argues that this may put a strain on their relationship, and affect the efficacy of their work and that of the Organ. Compounding this danger is the relative strength of the ISDSC and the traditional preference of many member states for military and security solutions to issues that could be solved by diplomatic and political means.[9]

According to some authors the organ has developed into a critical structure whose function has become a major determinant of the direction that peace and security in the sub-region will take.[10] Its creation was first conceived in 1994. As the genocide in Rwanda ended, the SADC secretariat convened a workshop in Windhoek for ministers responsible for democracy, human rights, and peace and security to discuss how the region could cooperate in these areas. According to Oosthuizen, the workshop seemingly galvanized efforts to place political and security cooperation among SADC member states on a new, or new-looking, footing.[11]

Since its formation, however, the organ has been marked by internal political disputes, lack of resources and overall lassitude.[12] Various reasons have been advanced for the factors underlying the disputes about the organ. Among them is the absence of common political values and practices among its members, despite the official declarations saying otherwise. The members, previously mythically united in their struggles for political liberation, had developed divergent geostrategic and national interests which became evident only after the end of apartheid. One camp preferred the peaceful resolution of disputes, while another, composed of governments that placed a high premium on national sovereignty and the centrality of the states in the ordering of national and regional affairs, preferred military means to settle conflicts.[13] As pointed out by Oosthuizen, Nelson Mandela—the democrat—stole the limelight that Robert Mugabe—an autocratic hero of the liberation struggles in the region and FLS chairman from 1980 to 1994—had enjoyed in regional political and security affairs, and the two disliked each other.[14] Khadiagala adds that,

> whereas Zimbabwe preferred a more autonomous security mechanism on the line of the previous FLS, South Africa and most of the SADC members insisted that the Organ must operate fully within the overall institutional framework of the SADC. ... To reconcile these positions, SADC agreed on rotating the chairmanship of the Organ among the heads of state on an annual basis and placed the oversight responsibilities in the ministerial Interstate Defense and Security Committee.[15]

This slugging match between two combatants had the potential to engulf the entire region in a political conflict that adversely affected the operations of the Organ.[16] Over the last years however, the Organ has been properly integrated in the internal organic structure of SADC and the competition between South Africa and Zimbabwe no longer leads to a standstill. Its structure, functions, powers, and procedures are clearly set out in the Organ's protocol, the defense pact, the indicative strategic plan, and the SADC election guidelines.

Associated with these institutions, the Regional Peacekeeping Training Center, located in Harare, became a fully fledged SADC structure in August 2005. The SADC's goal is to transform it into a center of excellence for training in peace support operations, thus enhancing its capacity to respond to conflict and to maintain stability within the region. So far, however, the Center is at a standstill due to fund cutting by international donors who fear that the funds could be diverted by the Zimbabwean government. It is not clear how many civilian, police, and military personnel the Center has trained and how many of them were deployed to participate in UN and AU peace support operations.

Unlike the AU and ECOWAS, the SADC does not, therefore, have a peace and security council, or a committee with reduced membership that acts on behalf of member states. Instead, all countries are involved within its peace and security framework below the heads of state level. The function of the SADC and Organ troikas is to serve as a steering committee so that decisions ultimately depend upon agreement at summit level. These security institutions are important steps toward the operationalization of peace and security in the sub-region, but they remain mostly empty structures waiting to be filled through the implementation of policies and actions.

Although the organization recognizes the strict respect for sovereignty and the territorial integrity of each member state (preamble of Protocol), it has a mandate to prevent, contain and resolve not only inter-state, but also intra-state conflicts (Protocol, art. 2-e; art. 11-1c). This enforcement capacity derives from article 53 of the UN Charter and it presupposes authorization from the UN Security Council (Protocol, art. 11-13d). Besides peacekeeping, SADC is also in the process of setting up an early warning mechanism, which will further challenge the conventional principle of non-interference.

Peacekeeping

The most visible organizational capacity of the SADC in the peace and security dominion has been in peacekeeping. In 2004, the Interstate Defense and Security Committee met in Maseru, Lesotho, and mandated the Ministerial Defense Sub-Committee to assemble a technical team to plan the setting up of an SADC Standby Brigade (SADCBRIG). According to the Colonel P. S. Manyemba of the SADCBRIG Planning Element, SADC operations are conducted under the framework of the African Standby Force for preventive diplomacy, peacemaking, humanitarian intervention, peacekeeping, peace enforcement, and peace-building.[17] There is, however, a distinction between the high ambitions at the political level and the shortcomings of the brigade at the operational. Although it was launched officially in August 2007 and pledged forces and elements are in place, as is the brigade headquarters, it still faces numerous shortcomings: (i) largely dysfunctional national armies with different military doctrines; (ii) lack of a civilian dimension (e.g. police, rule of law); (iii) lack of effective coordination and communication; and (iv) lack of a clear-cut strategy and doctrine (the size and type of national contributions abide more by national constraints than by any SADCBRIG program).[18] Even though some states in the southern region have engaged in common regional military exercises,[19] only two, the SADC Dolphin Phase-I and II, have been conducted under the frame of the SADCBRIG. They took place in Angola and Mozambique in February and April 2009, respectively.

Currently, the only physical structure of SADCBRIG is the planning element with a staff of about a dozen people. The planning element is subdivided into different sections: operations, logistics, and communications. Although it is difficult to forecast the shape of SADCBRIG, it is likely to become a loose force that will only be mustered when there is a compelling need to do so. If so, it might fall prey to the national interests of the major players in the region.[20] How realistic is it to expect the development of effective and properly harmonized training modules and mission doctrine given the interests of the various national and regional actors?

Early warning

In the late 1980s, the SADC (SADCC) created a regional early warning system (REWS) to advance information on food security through analysis and monitoring of food crop production prospects, food supplies, and requirements in order to alert member states and the humanitarian community of impending food shortages in sufficient time for appropriate interventions to be made. This was a response to a severe drought that affected Southern Africa and nearly 100 million people. Later in 2001, the SADC Organ adopted a new agenda and provided for the establishment of an early warning system in order to facilitate timeous action to prevent the outbreak and escalation of conflict (Protocol, art. 11-3b). The Early Warning System is comprised of national early warning centers and a regional early warning center/situation room located at SADC headquarters in Gaborone. SADC's early warning has the peculiarity of being more focused on traditional security concerns, superseding the earlier focus on food security,[21] and is based to a very large extent on classified intelligence information. Although the center was eventually inaugurated in 2007, at the time of writing (June 2009) it is not functioning properly, mostly due to lack of human and financial resources. Moreover, the involvement of civil society organizations is not foreseen, raising concerns about the real capacity of the mechanism to collect information in an apolitical and transparent way. Indeed, several questions arise: Will the SADC early warning mechanism only consider information passed on to it by national units? Will mechanisms be created to prevent national and regional interference in the collection and processing of information? How will SADC and member states react when a conflict warning is issued?

Operational experience

Although the SADC has adopted a comprehensive and fairly agile organizational structure to handle issues of peace and security, it still has a limited record in the field. In the area of peacekeeping and enforcement, SADC's interventions have been as follows:

- Lesotho (1998): South African troops entered Lesotho to prevent mutinous soldiers of the Royal Lesotho Defense Force (RLDF) from staging a military coup. The South African contingent was part of a SADC Combined Task Force. Its objectives were to prevent a military coup, to disarm the mutineers, and to create a safe and stable environment for the diplomatic initiative to find a peaceful solution to the political crisis in Lesotho. However, because of the way in which the intervention was authorized, structured, and deployed, it has been marred by overall criticism. Critics point out that the intervention was a South African intervention aimed at entrenching the rule of the governing Lesotho Congress for Democracy (LCD) party. The intervention in Lesotho did not have the approval of the UN Security Council.
- Democratic Republic of Congo (1998): The military intervention in DRC by Angola, Namibia and Zimbabwe has also been widely discussed, and views differ as to the appropriateness of the action. The participating countries argued that they were acting on the basis of collective self-defense, but the fact that only some members of SADC participated has sparked controversy. There were claims of an intense internal rivalry in SADC. The intervention by only three member states was facilitated by the fact that until its 2002 restructuring, the organ had more independence from the rest of SADC's institutions. The military intervention was only retroactively recognized by SADC and it did not have the approval of the UN Security Council.

Indeed, SADC's military interventions have been marred by controversy. In Lesotho, critics point out that the intervention was a South African intervention aimed at entrenching the rule of the governing Lesotho Congress for Democracy (LCD) party and at protecting the Lesotho Highlands Water Project (LHWP).[22] The official discourse is different, however. According to General Louis Fisher, then Botswana's chief of defense forces, "the disobliging role of the defense forces and the way they led Lesotho to political paralysis was the major trigger for the intervention. Ultimately SADC intervention was aimed at neutralizing the defense forces."[23]

In the DRC the military intervention by Angola, Namibia, and Zimbabwe has also been widely criticized. The participating countries argued that they were acting on the basis of collective self-defense. In fact, however, Zimbabwe, Angola, and Namibia intervened to protect their national (geostrategic, political, economic) interests.[24] Although the military intervention received SADC approval retroactively, Berman and Sams argue that it did not signify a true consensus or transform the coalition into a "SADC Force."[25] The problematic handling of these crises has hence jeopardized SADC's reputation as an effective conflict resolution actor. There is thus a notable discrepancy between the policy speech where regional organizations are praised for developing regionally accepted norms and standards and for using the right mechanisms for monitoring and enforcement, and events on the ground.[26]

Besides peacekeeping and enforcement, the SADC has also been active in peacemaking. For instance, in October 1994, SADC members strongly pressured Mozambican RENAMO leader Afonso Dlakhama not to withdraw from the elections in Mozambique.[27] Also in the late 1990s, the presidents of South Africa, Botswana, and Zimbabwe paid "fatherly visits" to King Mswati III of Swaziland to advise him not to curb popular democratic demands. As pointed out by Khadiagala, "democracy and pluralism have been on the regional agenda, but SADC has enforced them selectively: Its military intervention in Lesotho put subtle pressure on Swaziland to democratize, but it has been conspicuously silent when Zambia and Zimbabwe have infringed on human rights and civil liberties."[28] In 2007 and 2008, SADC—through South Africa's then president Thabo Mbeki—was involved in Zimbabwe. The talks constituted the most comprehensive and sustained attempt to reduce tensions between Zanu-PF and opposition parties and resolve the issue of free and fair elections.

Conclusions

In 1997, a report entitled Review and Rationalization of the SADC Program of Action contained some pointed conclusions about the work of the organization. It argued that cooperation in SADC was constrained by an inadequate management framework which could clearly articulate goals, policies, strategies, and time-frames, and it added that national policies and plans lacked a regional dimension. There was no prioritization of areas of cooperation, and in general, no prioritization of policies and strategies. SADC has naturally progressed and rectified some of its past shortcomings. But it remains a politically weak organization in the peace and security sector, serving mostly as an umbrella for member states to advance their interests or legitimize their actions. From a human and financial perspective the 2007/8 budget amounted to only US$18.9 million[29] and the staff numbers only about 200, of whom only about 30–40 are assigned to issues of peace and security. With this low capacity, SADC is unlikely to fine-tune and develop its conflict prevention, management, and resolution framework in the near future.

Part II
Americas

6   Organization of American States (OAS)

The first statement about the Americas as a whole came in 1823 from US president James Monroe, who declared unilaterally that the Americas were not to be considered as subjects for future colonization by any European powers. This incipient idea of hemispheric community was reinforced later by Simón Bolívar who, at the 1826 Congress of Panama, proposed creating a league of American republics with a common military, a mutual defense pact, and a supranational parliamentary assembly. Bolívar's dream soon floundered with the withdrawal of Ecuador and Venezuela from "Gran Colombia" and with the disintegration of Central America.[1]

The pursuit of regional cooperation came to the forefront again in the context of the International Conferences of American States (1889–1954).[2] It was under their auspices that the first permanent inter-American organization was created: the Commercial Bureau of American Republics (at the first conference in 1889–90), which at the fourth conference in 1910 became the Pan American Union.[3]

In 1947 regional cooperation reached another landmark. The experience of the Second World War convinced hemispheric governments that unilateral action could not ensure the territorial integrity of the American nations in the event of extra-continental aggression. This inspired 20 Latin American states to sign the Inter-American Treaty of Reciprocal Assistance (Rio Treaty), which provides for collective defense, not only from foreign attacks but also from any action or threat posed by one member against another. In this light acts of aggression are subject to sanctions that may include the recall of diplomatic missions, the breaking of diplomatic relations, the partial or complete interruption of economic relations, and the use of armed force (article 6). The treaty was invoked numerous times. For instance, in the 1950s economic sanctions were levied against the Dominican dictator Rafael Trujillo following an assassination attempt on Venezuelan president Romulo

Betancourt. According to Pastor, despite the Rio Treaty "few would call the region a 'security community', a region in which there were no expectations of conflict."[4] The emergence of democracy had dampened the likelihood of war but, in part because many of the democracies were fragile, there were still conflicts.

In parallel, the International Conferences of American States produced myriad conventions and treaties. These ranged from the establishment of unions and confederations to promotion of hemispheric solidarity and defense alliances to peaceful settlement procedures.[5] These meetings culminated in the birth of the OAS as it stands today, with the signature by 21 American countries of the Charter of the Organization of American States on 30 April 1948 (in effect since December 1951) at the ninth international conference. The meeting also adopted the American Declaration of the Rights and Duties of Man, the world's first regional human rights instrument, and the American Treaty on Pacific Settlement (also known as the Pact of Bogotá) whose purpose was to impose a general obligation on the signatories to settle their disputes through peaceful means. The treaty was adopted in fulfillment of some of the principles of the OAS Charter.

Following the League of Arab States, OAS is the oldest regional organization in the world, covering the totality of the American continent's 35 member states.[6] The OAS has a wide mandate (e.g. cooperation in the fields of culture, education, science and technology, human rights, international law, foreign trade, drug trafficking), including an explicit mandate to act in the arena of peace and security. But despite its bold objectives, OAS was paralyzed in the 1970s and 1980s by the deep divisions that existed between the USA and Latin America over the crisis in Central America, the unilateral decisions by the United States to intervene both in Grenada in 1983 and in Panama in 1989, and the marginal role OAS played in the Falklands/Malvinas War.[7] Yet the salience of OAS has increased dramatically in the 1990s, prompted by a wide sense of failure, the admission of Canada in 1990, different interests of regional actors, and the wider debate on the redefinition of the concept of security. Although its role in the traditional field of peace and security remains somewhat limited, it has adopted a much more forceful position with the regard to the support of democracy. The first sign of a significant move toward a pro-democracy doctrine came in 1979 with the passage of a resolution condemning the human rights record of the US-backed Somoza regime in Nicaragua.[8]

Even if the Americas constitute a region in which the bonds connecting the various sub-regions are more symbolic than substantial,[9] many now see the effective collective defense of democracy as forming the heart of a renewed and strengthened inter-American political and military system.[10] The Summit of the Americas, a sequence of summits led largely by the United States bringing together the countries of the Americas for discussion of a variety of issues (first in 1994), has also provided OAS with a renewed agenda.

Organizational capacity

The OAS' explicit mandate in security matters is enshrined in its founding document, where it coins itself as a regional agency for UN purposes (Chapter VIII of the UN Charter), one of the few regional actors to do it so clearly. Furthermore, member states also proclaim in the charter that the purposes of OAS include "to strengthen the peace and security of the continent" (art. 2-a), "to promote and consolidate representative democracy, with due respect for the principle of non-intervention" (art. 2-b), "to prevent possible causes of difficulties and to ensure the pacific settlement of disputes that may arise among the Member States" (art. 2-c), and "to provide for common action on the part of those States in the event of aggression" (art. 2-d). The mandate for peaceful settlement of disputes is further elaborated in article 3-i where it is stated that "controversies of an international character arising between two or more American States shall be settled by peaceful procedures." This mandate is encapsulated in Chapter V ("Peaceful Settlement of Disputes," arts. 24–27), which enumerates the peaceful procedures for the settlement of disputes available to the organization: "direct negotiation, good offices, mediation, investigation and conciliation, judicial settlement, arbitration, and those which the parties to the dispute may especially agree upon at any time" (art. 25). The dispute settlement capacity of the organization is reiterated in the 1948 American Treaty on Pacific Settlement (Pact of Bogotá).

The OAS Charter also envisages a collective defense mechanism, set out in article 3-h), which states that "an act of aggression against one American state is an act of aggression against all the American states" and is further elaborated in Chapter VI ("Collective Security," arts. 28–29). This regional mechanism established during the Cold War to address Soviet threats is still in place and could presumably be invoked should an extra-hemispheric threat arise that needed to be addressed collectively. States in the region are, however, much more concerned about threats to democracy.[11] This concept of "multidimensional security" established itself in a number of agreements, but especially those arising out of the 32nd regular session of the OAS General Assembly held in Bridgetown, Barbados, in 2002, the Special Conference on Security held in Mexico City in 2003—which adopted the key Declaration on Security—and the Special Summit of the Americas in Monterrey, Mexico, in 2004. In the Declaration member states unequivocally contended that their "new concept of security" in the hemisphere includes "traditional and new threats," and is based on "democratic values." Also significant in the Declaration is the shift from state security—so characteristic of Latin American states—to human security (Box 6.1). This landmark declaration identifies a comprehensive program for addressing ever-changing security threats in the Americas through action in a number of areas. These include strengthening democracy, combating terrorism, fostering the peaceful resolution of conflict, furthering

---

Box 6.1   Declaration on Security in the Americas (Excerpt)

II. Shared values and common approaches

2   Our new concept of security in the Hemisphere is multidimensional in scope, includes traditional and new threats, concerns, and other challenges to the security of the states of the Hemisphere, incorporates the priorities of each state, contributes to the consolidation of peace, integral development, and social justice, and is based on democratic values, respect for and promotion and defense of human rights, solidarity, cooperation, and respect for national sovereignty.

[...]

4e In our Hemisphere, as democratic states committed to the principles of the Charter of the United Nations and the OAS, we reaffirm that the basis and purpose of security is the protection of human beings. Security is strengthened when we deepen its human dimension. Conditions for human security are improved through full respect for people's dignity, human rights, and fundamental freedoms, as well as the promotion of social and economic development, social inclusion, and education and the fight against poverty, disease, and hunger.

Source: OAS website, www.oas.org/documents/eng/DeclaracionSecurity_ 102803.asp

---

confidence and security building measures between states, curbing the proliferation of weapons of mass destruction, combating transnational organized crime and illicit trafficking in firearms, preventing and mitigating the effect of natural disasters, and addressing issues of health and poverty. In 2007 a "Special Meeting" on Implementation of the Declaration on Security in the Americas was held where OAS' bodies and member states made detailed presentations about their individual contributions. They concluded that while there is a long way yet to go and much work remains, cooperation is increasing and a number of important joint initiatives have begun and are bearing fruit.

The organizational capacity of OAS not only includes its legal mandate but also the institutional capacity to execute it. The principal decision-making body, convening annually to establish the work plan and the political agenda of the OAS is the General Assembly, composed of heads of state and government. The implementation of the General Assembly decisions is carried out by the Permanent Council consisting of the permanent ambassadors to the OAS. The Council keeps vigilance over the maintenance of friendly relations among the member states and, for that purpose, effectively assists them in the peaceful settlement of their disputes. It includes a committee on hemispheric security with a mandate that includes handling of actions against anti-personnel mines, arms trafficking, cooperation for hemispheric security, or natural disaster reduction. The main coordination and implementation body of the OAS is, however, the General Secretariat, managed by the secretary-general, who might bring to the attention of the General Assembly or the Permanent Council matters that might threaten the peace, security, or development of member states.[12] In the 1990s the secretary-general has been involved in facilitating negotiations between Belize and Guatemala, Costa Rica and Nicaragua, and Ecuador and Peru.[13] Within the secretariat, the major secretariats handling security issues are the Secretariat for Multidimensional Security, which coordinates OAS actions against organized crime, illegal drugs, border control, and other threats to public security, and the Secretariat for Political Affairs, responsible for political dialogue, international security, and democracy.[14] Within the latter, the Department of Sustainable Democracy and Special Missions provides technical expertise in matters pertaining to conflict resolution, threats to democracy, good governance, and democratic dialogue. The Department also manages the Fund for Peace (established in 2000) and the Inter-American Peace Forum (created in 2008). The first provides a pool of immediately available funds to enable the OAS to react swiftly to an unforeseen political dispute. But it aims to be more than just a material fund. It offers the parties to a dispute a series of negotiation and mediation mechanisms and affords them access to OAS technical expertise in conflict resolution, including its experience with diplomacy and international and inter-American law. Complementarily, the Inter-American Peace Forum operates within the framework of the Fund for Peace and it seeks to create an opportunity for the development of programs aimed at creating a culture of regional peace. It also maintains an exhaustive database of institutions and NGOs involved in promoting peace and peace research, in order to facilitate the exchange of information, experiences, and best practice.

Finally, the OAS has established several specialized organizations such as the Inter-American Human Rights system (commission and court) and the Inter-American Defense Board, all of these bodies being accountable to the General Assembly. The Inter-American Commission was established in 1959 and began its work in 1960, long before it had the legal foundation of the American Convention on Human Rights, which entered into force in 1978. The commission represents all member states of the OAS, and its principal function is to promote the observance and protection of human rights and to serve as a consultative organ for the organization.[15]

The OAS security structure was originally designed for collective security operations and diplomatic consultations. Regarding conflict between states in the hemisphere, the emphasis lay on peaceful means for the settlement of disputes. Nevertheless, in recent years the range of activities in which the organization is involved has grown considerably and new capabilities have been generated.[16] We will turn our attention to OAS organizational capacity in conflict prevention and early warning.

Conflict prevention and early warning

One of the principal contributions that the OAS makes toward structural conflict prevention is through democratic institution-building in member states. In 1991, the Unit for the Promotion of Democracy (UPD) was created within the General Secretariat to support the consolidation of democracy in the region (in the meantime it was dismantled in 2006 and its functions were distributed between the Department of Sustainable Democracy and the Department of State Modernization and Good Governance). Also in 1991, OAS foreign ministers approved the Declaration on the Collective Defense of Democracy (Santiago Commitment), which promised firm support for democracy and resolved that any "sudden or irregular interruption of the democratic political institutional process" of any of them would result in the calling of an emergency meeting of foreign ministers.[17] Resolution 1080,[18] which accompanied the declaration, creates automatic procedures for convening the OAS Permanent Council in the event of a coup or other disruption of constitutional order. It states that, "representative democracy is an indispensable condition for the stability, peace, and development of the region" and includes an automatic procedure to respond to democratic breakdown—allowing the OAS to undertake a wide range of collective activity so long as these actions are approved by the foreign ministers of its member states and/or the General Assembly. Resolution 1080 was applied when a condemnation of the 1991 coup in Haiti led to sanctions, and again over Peru (1992), Guatemala (1993), and Paraguay (1996). In addition, in 1992 the General Assembly approved the Protocol of Washington, allowing it to suspend a member state whose democratically elected government is overthrown by force. Peck has pointed out that "these developments mark a real turning point in the organization's history, in which domestic political circumstances (the interruption of a democratic government) can become the grounds for collective action."[19] In 1997 a reform of the OAS Charter took place incorporating the postulates of the Protocol of Washington (current art. 9). The adoption in 2001 of the Inter-American Democratic Charter further institutionalized the democratic paradigm. In the same year, the UPD established the Special Program for the Promotion of Dialogue and Conflict Resolution to assist member states in developing national and sub-regional capacities in dialogue, consensus building and conflict resolution. The mission of the Special Program was to contribute to the development of responses to deep-rooted socio-political conflicts and critical challenges facing member states and their societies. Next to the Council of Europe, the OAS has thus the most well-developed and active human rights machinery of any regional organization.

Also associated with conflict prevention is early warning. The General Secretariat of OAS does not have an indicator-based conflict early warning center at the time of writing. However, the Department of Sustainable Democracy and Special Missions through its Political Analysis and Multiple Scenarios System (SAPEM), is working to enhance OAS' capacity for early warning and response.[20] The new system aims at designing and implementing a comprehensive early warning mechanism, including the use of political analyses, to monitor, assess, and address nascent threats to democratic stability.

Operational experience

Even if the OAS Charter envisaged a collective defense mandate for the organization, in reality OAS experience is largely focused on peacekeeping, peacebuilding and to a smaller extent also on peacemaking. In 1997 it promoted political reconciliation and mediated in the territorial dispute between Venezuela and Guyana along with CARICOM. It also established in 2004 a mission to support the peace process in Colombia (MAPP/OEA), and has sponsored discussions between Honduras and Nicaragua (2001), Belize and Guatemala (2003),[21] and Colombia and Ecuador (2008)[22] to help them resolve their territorial and political differences. In Bolivia, the OAS had an active role in fomenting institutional strengthening and governability in the country (2008).[23] In addition to peacemaking, OAS has also been involved in significant military operations.

Military actions

In 1955, the OAS stationed military observers on the borders between Costa Rica and Nicaragua and created a frontier buffer zone. The deployment was sparked by a rebel incursion from Nicaragua into Costa Rica that seized the northern border town of Villa Quesada, near the Pacific coast. Later a commission created by the OAS discovered that the rebels' supplies and war material were coming from Nicaragua. In 1957, the OAS also sent a military observers' group to address the inter-state conflict between Honduras and Nicaragua. After Honduras created a new state (Gracias a Dios) in the border region, Nicaragua claimed that some Nicaraguan territory had been included and occupied Mocoron in the area claimed by both sides. In 1960 the boundary was demarcated also through OAS support.

In 1965, the OAS supported the United States' unilateral military intervention in the Dominican Republic to prevent a left-wing government from coming to power. In the wake of the US invasion, the OAS created an Inter-American Military Force (IAPF), with troops from the United States, Brazil, Honduras, Paraguay, Nicaragua, Costa Rica, and El Salvador, which kept the peace in the Dominican Republic until new elections were held there in 1966. This intervention serves as a good example of US manipulation of the organization. After the US Marines were deployed ostensibly to protect American citizens and in order to stop the escalation of international criticism, the United States pushed for the intervention to be brought under OAS auspices.[24] Ironically, in 2003 at the first Security Council meeting with regional organizations, the United States pointed out that although a troop-contributing country may share language and cultural elements "it may also have its own agenda independent of the peacekeeping agenda. We need to watch carefully for that possibility, given the goal of long-term peace and stability."[25]

In 1969, the OAS was also involved in the so-called "Soccer War" between Honduras and El Salvador. The day after the fighting began, the OAS met in an urgent session and called for an immediate ceasefire and a withdrawal of El Salvador's forces from Honduras. Although a ceasefire was eventually arranged, El Salvador continued for several days to resist pressure to withdraw its troops. OAS deployed a peace commission (military observers) seeking to end the conflict. A new group of military observers was sent once again between 1976 and 1981 to supervise disarmament efforts. More recently, the OAS has also facilitated the ceasefire in Suriname through the OAS Special Mission to Suriname (1992–2000).

Peacebuilding

The OAS has been heavily involved in peacebuilding activities, namely in the fields of disarmament, demobilization, and reintegration (DDR); truth, justice, and reconciliation; rule of law, human rights, good governance, and electoral assistance. The OAS's involvement in DDR activities includes past experiences in Suriname, Nicaragua, and Guatemala. Furthermore, the OAS Mission to support the Peace Process in Colombia is currently undertaking DDR activities in that country (since 2004). In Nicaragua, the OAS International Support and Verification Mission (CIAV-OAS, 1990–97) demobilized 22,000 ex-combatants and developed programs to help combatants and others affected by the conflict to reintegrate into the economic and political life of the country. Some authors argue that CIAV-OAS played a fundamental role in favor of former Contras and ex-combatants in general. Tacsan contends that, "the Contras in particular have benefited from CIAV-OAS because they were disarmed without having negotiated their demobilization and the OAS helped them ... If not for CIAV-OAS, who provided them with land and human support at the time they were badly needed, war would have probably regained intensity and the peace process may have been reversed."[26]

In Suriname, the OAS Special Mission (1992–2000) facilitated a ceasefire, promoted the demobilization of former combatants, provided electoral and legislative assistance, mediated disputes between ethnic groups and the government over economic rights, and developed job-training programs for young people. Through the Department for the Promotion of Democracy (now Department of Sustainable Democracy and Special Missions), the OAS has been furthering the peace process in Guatemala since 1995 (via the program "Culture and Dialogue: Development of Resources for Peacebuilding in Guatemala—OAS/PROPAZ").[27] In Haiti, the International Civilian Mission for Haiti

(MICIVIH, 1992–99), in cooperation with the UN, monitored the human rights situation, provided technical assistance in judicial reform, facilitated human rights training for police officers, and organized civic education programs on citizen's rights to local NGOs.

The OAS has also managed several de-mining operations in Central America in the last 15 years, through its Mine Action Program (AICMA). AICMA's first mandate was given in 1995 and since then the program has operated in Ecuador (completion by 2004), Guatemala (concluded in 2005), Honduras (concluded in 2004), Nicaragua (2003–5), Peru (completion by 2003), and Colombia (ongoing since 2003).

The major shortcomings of the OAS, in its organizational and operational capacity, are to a large extent a consequence of the specific context where the organization is located. The first is related to the adherence to consensus decision-making and the sanctity of sovereignty. In the Latin American context, "given the history of state formation among the different nations, the struggle for independence during the first decades of the nineteenth century, and the difficulty in realizing the Westphalian model in the face of great power influence and lack of central government authority over parts of the territory in several cases"[28] compelled states to be sensitive about sovereignty and separation. Even if the OAS has extended its mandate to allow it to take bold measures when the democratic credentials of a member states are in jeopardy, the phantom of intervention still prevails. National sovereignty comes hand-in-hand with consensus decision-making, as the search for consensus serves as a mechanism for guaranteeing the protection of state sovereignty. On higher-profile issues where there are profound differences of opinion, the process is prone to some considerable stalling if not immobilization.[29] This was most obvious in the case of Haiti in 1994, over the issue of coercive intervention after the overthrow of President Aristide and the invocation of resolution 1080. The OAS was only able to send a small grouping (18 members) of a civilian mission known as OAS-DEMOC.

Second, there is a lack of a coherent policy regarding the extent and role that the organization should have in intra-state conflict prevention and resolution at various levels. Coupled with this, there is also a need to increase public awareness (among its member states as well as the international community) of the organization's acquired expertise and successes in the peacebuilding and post-conflict reconciliation arenas. A striking example of this is the popular idea that the OAS has a camouflaged US agenda. In fact, research has demonstrated, on the basis of a thorough study of 30 cases of conflict resolution in the OAS over a 50-year period, that relations among member states are more nuanced than many observers might anticipate. Not every case involved tensions between US and Latin American preferences. And if there are cases when the USA dominated the organization, there are also cases when Latin American members resist US pressure and reject US proposals.[30]

Third, although the Summit of the Americas held in Miami in 1994 has tagged the OAS as the main organization for the defense and consolidation of democracy within the Americas, other overlapping initiatives have also came about. As noted by Cooper and Legler, there has been a proliferation of agencies sharing this agenda, including the Rio Group, the Esquipulas Group, the Andean Group, CARICOM, and the Mercado Común del Sur (MERCOSUR).[31] The division of labor is far from being clear. Institutional proliferation is not only expensive but leads to political competition, deviation of resources, and unaccountability. It is true, however, that at certain instances, like the 2008 dispute between Colombia and Ecuador, the OAS is the only organization with a specific mandate to contribute to the prevention of potential squabbles in the fragile border area between the two countries. But the OAS suffers from lack of funding for this kind of mediation activity.

Conclusion

For an organization founded approximately six decades ago the OAS has shown over the last decade a substantial capacity to adjust to new political situations and to find a new raison d'être. The core of its activities is presently centered on the nexus between democracy and security. The latter is defined by the organization in a modern and comprehensive way; the Declaration on Security states that, "the traditional concept and approach [of security] must be expanded to encompass new and nontraditional threats, which include political, economic, social, health, and environmental aspects" (II-4i). But OAS still has a long path ahead in order to fulfill its potential. Particularly when enforcement becomes a requirement for success, the OAS is not prepared for robust operations and does not even present a formal mechanism for compulsory cost sharing for peace missions. The regional culture does not support this option. In countries where a violent conflict is protracted, such as today's Colombia, the organization does not have the political clout or the necessary resources to make an impact.[32]

Moreover, to deliver on its ambitious mandate the OAS needs better human and financial resources. This has been suggested even by the Declaration on Security which underscores the need to "revitalize and strengthen the organs, institutions, and mechanisms" of the organization in order to achieve "greater coordination and cooperation among them" (IV-42). Yet, although the OAS is one of the largest intergovernmental organizations in the world—if measured in terms of membership—it remains in a relatively weak financial position.[33] For the year 2008, OAS's total budget stood at only US$157.3 million, of which US$25.6 million was allocated to democracy and governance (including prevention and resolution of conflicts) and US$23.4 million was allocated to multidimensional security (terrorism, drugs, and other threats to public security). The weak financial position has also led to a reduction in human resources. From close to 700 in 1996, the organization went down to approximately 500 employees in 2006. Ultimately the governments of the region will need to take the necessary steps to make resources available for the OAS, to expedite the decision-making process, modernize the organization's internal procedures, and generate a more robust institution.

Part III

Asia

7   Association of Southeast Asian Nations (ASEAN)

The idea of Southeast Asia is a recent political invention. The lexicon derives from the South East Asia Command (SEAC), the military body set up during the Second World War to be in overall charge of Allied operations in the area between China and Australia. The most striking characteristic of the region is its sheer diversity—geographic, religious, linguistic, political, ethno-social—which has led some authors to argue that what makes Southeast Asia a *region* is indeed its heterogeneity.[1] In the past, the region was typified by the relative lack of contacts between the various countries, centuries-old inter-group strife, and authoritarian and controlled political systems.[2] The political fragmentation of Southeast Asia is further reflected in the numerous conflicts that erupted after the Second World War. In the early 1960s, the decision to unite Singapore and the Borneo territories of Brunei, Sabah, and Sarawak with the Federation of Malaya triggered a series of regional conflicts: the Philippines broke off diplomatic relations with Malaysia,[3] rebels in Brunei launched an armed rebellion, and Indonesia launched a low-level war against Malaysia known as *konfrontasi*. Thailand also had latent conflicts with Myanmar, Cambodia, Laos, and Malaysia of a historical nature and as a result of colonization, the Second World War, and the subsequent decolonization. Vietnam and Myanmar were born into civil wars and Indonesia had a record of expansionist policies.

The hostility in this regional peace and security cluster fell prey to the Cold War dynamic.[4] As early as in 1955, the United States instigated the creation of the Southeast Asian Treaty Organization (SEATO) conceived as a bulwark against communism in the region. In practice it was part of the worldwide US-led system of anti-communist military alliances rather than a true Southeast Asian regional arrangement. All countries in the region, except Singapore, had a local communist insurgency to deal with and for this reason China's Cultural Revolution rhetoric was regarded as a threat to the whole region. The Association of Southeast Asia (ASA) and MAPHILINDO followed in 1961 and 1963 respectively, but lasted only until tensions in the region forced them to be abandoned. Even more ill-fated was the Asian and Pacific Council (ASPAC), established in 1966, which brought together most of the leading non-communist nations of the Western Pacific to deal with external threats and to provide a framework for more widespread cooperation. As argued by Öjendal, these projects were not initiated from within and they neither solved regional problems nor addressed regional needs as defined from within.[5]

The Cold War context and primarily the internal conflicts that marred the region were pivotal events in Southeast Asian history because the intense diplomacy required to resolve them created a new communications network among Southeast Asian leaders who had previously been isolated from one another.[6] The desire to institutionalize that communications network and promulgate a regional code of conduct to prevent future conflicts led to the creation of the Association of Southeast Asian Nations (ASEAN) in 1967. ASEAN was therefore created not *despite* the propensity to become the Balkans of Asia[7] but *because* it was so conflict-prone.

ASEAN exceeded the early expectations. If at first it was typically regarded as just the latest in a series of failed organizations in Southeast Asia, it revealed surprising progress in overcoming these barriers and striving for the possible gains from regional cooperation. Palmer calls it a miracle.[8] The original five states who signed the 1967 Bangkok Declaration—Indonesia, Malaysia, the Philippines, Singapore, and Thailand—had the following objectives: (i) to establish good relations in the neighborhood; (ii) to create a bulwark again the perceived expansion of communism and counter the internal communist insurgencies; and (iii) to foster economic cooperation, social progress, and cultural development. The framers of ASEAN insisted that the new organization would not deal directly with security matters and would also avoid controversial political issues, leaving these problems to national action and multilateral cooperation through other channels. Narine explains with lucidity why some ASEAN states are still vehemently opposed to any substantial redefinition of these established practices:

> The reasons for this are clear: most ASEAN members are weak states that are in the process of state-building. They joined the organization to enhance their sovereignty and, in the case of the newer members, enjoy greater international standing ... opening themselves to criticism from their fellow members evokes tensions

that the organization cannot resolve and creates disunity that undermines ASEAN's influence.[9]

In the 1980s and 1990s ASEAN grew both in mandate and membership, including presently all 10 Southeast Asian states.[10] In 1997, ASEAN leaders adopted the *Vision 2020* where they declared that "ASEAN shall have, by the year 2020, established a peaceful and stable Southeast Asia where each nation is at peace with itself and where the causes for conflict have been eliminated, through abiding respect for justice and the rule of law and through the strengthening of national and regional resilience".[11] To estimate whether ASEAN will be able to attain this objective, one should reflect upon its organizational capacity and operational experience.

Organizational capacity

The mandate of ASEAN in peace and security derives from the Bangkok Declaration of 1967 where the maintenance of peace and security is enumerated as one of the objectives of the organization. Furthermore, the Association has specified a set of norms to govern the conduct of relations among its members and has established procedures for conflict management in five major documents: the Zone of Peace, Freedom and Neutrality—ZOPFAN (1971), the Treaty of Amity and Cooperation in Southeast Asia (TAC) (1976), the Declaration of ASEAN Concord (1976), the Declaration of ASEAN Concord II (2003), and the ASEAN Charter (2008).

ZOPFAN, created in 1971 in the wake of the Kuala Lumpur Declaration, represents one of ASEAN's first political actions. It commits all ASEAN members to "exert efforts to secure the recognition of and respect for Southeast Asia as a Zone of Peace, Freedom and Neutrality, free from any manner of interference by outside powers," and to "make concerted efforts to broaden the areas of cooperation." Despite the signature it was understood that some ASEAN members would maintain foreign bases on their soil.[12] In 1976 ASEAN was given a greater momentum when the heads of government held their first summit, in Bali. At this meeting, not only was an agreement reached for the first time to establish an ASEAN secretariat, but also two other important documents were adopted. The first was the Treaty of Amity, which provides guiding principles for cooperation and states that ASEAN should "promote regional peace and stability by enhancing regional resilience" (articles 2. d and 13–17). The treaty also envisioned the establishment of a High Council tasked to resolve intra-regional disputes. The Council is to recommend to the parties in dispute appropriate means of settlement such as good offices, mediation, inquiry or conciliation. Yet, it has never been invoked not even after its Rules of Procedure were approved in 2001. Saravanamuttu points out that "the formal mechanisms of the Amity Treaty are window-dressing rather than true instrumentalities for conflict resolution."[13] While this is indeed a sign of institutional weakness, ASEAN leaders found in it a vindication of the "ASEAN Way" (see below).[14] If so, it would be difficult to understand why, for instance, Malaysia and Indonesia settled their maritime border conflict through formal adjudication by the International Court of Justice rather than by any informal and consensus-building mechanism. In 2003, Malaysia and Singapore similarly submitted their cases to the Court in relation to Pedra Branca/Pulau Batu Putih.

A more specific program of action was outlined in a second agreement, the Declaration of ASEAN Concord I (1976). It envisioned concrete programs of cooperation in the political, economic, social, and security fields. It also adopted principles for regional stability which included settling regional disputes "by peaceful means as soon as possible" and strengthening political solidarity by promoting the harmonization of views, coordination of positions and, where possible and desirable, taking common action.

But it was not until the Ninth ASEAN Summit in Bali (2003) that the region set itself on more ambitious path. The summit adopted the Declaration of ASEAN Concord II (Bali Concord II), which stipulated the establishment of an ASEAN Community resting on three pillars: an ASEAN Security Community, an ASEAN Economic Community and an ASEAN Socio-Cultural Community. This was reiterated in early 2009 with the adoption of the Cha Am-Hua Hin Declaration on the roadmap for an ASEAN Community. To give shape to the Security Community, ASEAN adopted a Security Community Plan of Action (2004) and a Political-Security Blueprint (2009). The documents reaffirm ASEAN's well known principles of peaceful settlement of disputes, renunciation of the use or threat of force, respect for sovereignty, and non-interference in internal affairs. Yet, they also envisage the strengthening of regional cooperation in the fields of conflict prevention, conflict resolution and post-conflict peacebuilding, and embrace new proposals such as organizing and conducting regional military exchanges among high-ranking officials; the creation of an Experts Advisory Committee (EAC) or an Eminent Persons Group (EPG) attached to the High Council to provide advice on the settlement of disputes; establishment of an ASEAN Institute for Peace and Reconciliation; and to create a mechanism to mobilize necessary resources to facilitate post-conflict peacebuilding (e.g. a stability fund).

The lengthy period for implementing the ASEAN Community (2015) indicates a realistic assessment of the challenges involved. The ASEAN agenda remains loose and highly voluntaristic, with very limited supranational and institutional aspects. Hence, deep integration, coercive rules, and any serious erosion of the non-interference principle—necessary for the effective implementation of Concord II—are potentially divisive.[15] Moreover, Concord II does not take proper account of new security threats. In Southeast Asia most traditional security threats have waned and large-scale foreign military interventions are unlikely. However, new transnational threats have emerged including refugees, illegal labor flows, and transboundary environmental destruction.

The most recent document re-affirming ASEAN's legal capacity in security issues is the new ASEAN Charter formally adopted in 2008. Article 1 emphasizes that one of the purposes of the Association is "to maintain and enhance peace, security and stability and further strengthen peace-oriented values in the region." Even more significant is Chapter VIII (Settlement of Disputes) which legally equips ASEAN with a dispute settlement mechanism "in all fields of ASEAN cooperation" and permits conflicts to be resolved through good offices, conciliation, and mediation. Chapter VIII will substitute the High Council created by the Treaty of Amity. Moreover, it can also be deduced from the ASEAN Charter that the Association does not recognize itself as conforming to Chapter VIII of the UN Charter. In fact, article 28 of the ASEAN Charter postulates that "member states have the right of recourse to the modes of peaceful settlement contained in Article 33(1) of the Charter of the United Nations." Nowhere in the ASEAN Charter is it suggested that the Association should engage in peaceful settlement under article 52(2) of the UN Charter (Chapter VIII).

Decision-making and institutional capacity

As it has been amply discussed elsewhere,[16] ASEAN often adopts a collegial style of decision-making: one based on friendship rather than power and on stability rather than adventurism. Davidson describes this so-called ASEAN Way as follows:

> it involves processes including intensive informal and discreet discussions behind the scenes to work out a general consensus which then acts as the starting point around which the unanimous decision is finally accepted in more formal meetings, rather than

across-the-table negotiations involving bargaining and give-and-take that result in deals enforceable in a court of law.[17]

Even if the ASEAN Way has been regarded as a mere catchword, simplistic, and an overvaluation of culture[18] it is still fair to underline that ASEAN does have an idiosyncratic decision-making procedure—if compared to Western organizations. In ASEAN's decision-making process the idea of "regional resilience" is also often employed, meaning that the country with the most vested interests has the greatest say in any particular conflict. Some ASEAN members, such as Indonesia, Thailand, and the Philippines, also advocate the idea of "flexible engagement" and "enhanced interaction" which presupposes that ASEAN states should be able to freely discuss fellow members' domestic policies, especially those that have regional externalities. Emmers argues that such debates within ASEAN "may result in a multi-layered or two-speed arrangement including members opting for the current level of institutionalization and other moving forward in specific areas."[19] Aware of some of the obstacles inherent to the practice of consensus, the Eminent Persons' Group (EPG), which was assigned to produce a draft of the ASEAN Charter, proposed that decision-making should be based upon majority vote and not consensus. The proposal was discarded.

The informal decision-making process matches ASEAN's weak institutional capacity. The main decision-making body governing the organization is the Meeting of Heads of State and Government—or ASEAN Summit, preceded by a Joint Ministerial Meeting (JMM) composed of foreign and economic ministers. The ASEAN Standing Committee, under the chairmanship of the foreign minister of the country-in-chair, is mandated to coordinate the work of the Association in between the annual ASEAN Ministerial Meeting (AMM).

Numerous other ministerial groups also meet regularly. ASEAN has developed over the years a high number of sectoral ministerial meetings (28 in total at present) focused on coordinating regional cooperation and more recently, the implementation of the Vientiane Action Program 2004–2010[20] and the Blueprints that will serve as bedrock for the ASEAN community. The institutional architecture of ASEAN also includes the ASEAN Secretariat in Jakarta which provides advice, initiates actions, and implements cooperation activities. For the moment, it does not have any unit or department on peace and security.

In the Kuala Lumpur Declaration on the Establishment of the ASEAN Charter (12 December 2005), ASEAN leaders recognized the importance of having "an appropriate institutional framework"—to confer legal personality, determine the functions, and develop areas of competence of ASEAN's key bodies. Following the ratification of the Charter in 2008, the ASEAN structures were transformed and enlarged to include:

(i)   a *Coordination Council*, composed of ASEAN foreign ministers;
(ii)   *Community Councils* with relevant sectoral ministerial bodies, which will include the ASEAN Political and Security Council (APSC), the ASEAN Economic Community Council (AEC) and the ASEAN Socio-Cultural Community Council (ASCC);
(iii)   the Ministerial Meeting (AMM of foreign ministers) will be renamed the *ASEAN Foreign Ministers Meeting* and will be one of the four sectoral ministerial bodies of the APSC Council;
(iv)   a *Committee of Permanent Representatives* to ASEAN will be established in Jakarta—comprised of one permanent representative from each ASEAN member state. This new committee will take over many of the regional functions of the ASEAN Standing Committee (ASC), including external relations and supervising the ASEAN Secretariat; and
(v)   an ASEAN *Human Rights Body.*

In addition to its own institutional architecture, ASEAN relies on dialogue processes with non-ASEAN partners. Some of these linkages have security implications. For instance, through the ASEAN Plus Three (China, South Korea, Japan) regular meetings are held to strengthen security cooperation. In addition, the bi-annual Asia-Europe Meeting (ASEM), which includes all ASEAN countries, is another forum that may play an important role in addressing issues of transnational security in both regions, mainly in the field of "soft" and non-traditional security affairs.[21]

Some authors argue convincingly that ASEAN's institutional changes in the post-Cold War era have occurred with respect to geographical focus and issue scope rather than institutional strength. Emmers underlines that "the institutional changes have primarily derived from a need to move beyond a subregional approach to security, as well as from a widening of the security agenda."[22] The extension of the geographical focus of the Association was consummated with the establishment of the ASEAN Regional Forum, the central decision-making forum on regional security issues.

ASEAN Regional Forum (ARF)

Despite the treaties and declarations signed in the 1970s, security only started to be discussed openly at the fourth ASEAN summit in Singapore in 1992, setting the stage for the creation of the ARF in 1994.[23] Presently it comprises the 10 ASEAN states, plus the 10 ASEAN dialogue partners (Australia, Canada, China, EU, India, Japan, New Zealand, South Korea, Russia, and the United States), one ASEAN observer (Papua New Guinea), as well as North Korea, Mongolia, Pakistan, East Timor, Bangladesh, and Sri Lanka. The ARF was created with a mandate to discuss political and security issues, and is presently the principal forum for security dialogue in Asia. The ARF is characterized by consensus decision-making and minimal institutionalization. Interestingly, Khong and Nesadurai argue that "intrusive rules and mechanisms may not be necessary for meaningful cooperation. In fact, the 'ASEAN Way' slow and cumbersome as it is, as served the ARF well."[24] Proponents of more institutionalization are Singapore, the Philippines, and Thailand. These states are more willing to engage in peacekeeping than Malaysia, or Vietnam.[25] Even if ARF abides by minimal institutionalism, in 1995 it adopted a concept paper setting out a three-stage, evolutionary approach to the ARF's development, moving from confidence-building to preventive diplomacy and, in the long term, toward a conflict resolution capability. A definition of preventive diplomacy was also accorded.[26]

Some authors correctly underline that ARF "was an extraordinary achievement."[27] Unlike NATO and many other security arrangements, it has not been established in response to a threat or crisis. In fact it has been established at a time when the Asia-Pacific region was enjoying an economic boom and had a stable level of peace. The ARF is also seen by many as a tool for socializing China to accept the legitimacy of multilateralism, transparency, and reassurance as a basis for security.[28] Other authors, however, point out that given the sheer expanse of the ARF's geographic footprint, not to mention the political, economic, and cultural diversity that comes with it, the ARF has been hampered in its attempts to move at a more desired pace to push its three-stage agenda.[29]

The ambitious objectives of ARP are not mirrored in its institutional capacity. Its only permanent body is the ARF Unit, which was established inside the ASEAN Secretariat in June 2004 with the objective to provide secretarial support to the ARF chair; to function as depository of documents; and to manage a database/registry. Another body associated with ARF is the Register of Experts and Eminent Persons, created in 2001, which provides a pool of expertise on regional security issues that may be drawn upon by the ARF chair or individual ARF members. The Experts met for the first time in a plenary session in 2006 and have in the course of its mandate provided recommendations on ARF's future course.

Operational experience

Despite ASEAN's traditional reluctance to express its views on security, the ideal of regional peace and stability has always ranked high on the list of priorities of the Association. Adam Malik, Indonesia's third vice-president and one of the founders of ASEAN, has acknowledged that "whether consciously or unconsciously, considerations of national and regional security also figured largely in the minds of the founders of the ASEAN."[30] Over the years ASEAN's activities in the field of peace and security have been limited to conflict prevention and peacemaking and they generally involved little publicity. And even if ASEAN is gradually adopting a more assertive profile, the traditional "behind-the-scenes" strategy is still very salient.

One of the most important chapters in the history of ASEAN's diplomacy took place in the 1980s and 1990s during the Cambodian conflict. ASEAN sponsored resolutions at the UN General Assembly with constant support from the international community, and maintained a dialogue with all parties to the conflict. This eventually led to the Jakarta Informal Meetings, at which the four Cambodian factions discussed peace and national reconciliation. The process extended to the early 1990s, culminating in the 19-nation Paris Conference on Cambodia (chaired by France and Indonesia), which produced the Comprehensive Political Settlement of the Cambodian Conflict, leading to the holding of elections supervised by the UN, to which the ASEAN sent an observer mission.

ASEAN has consistently pursued a policy of cooperation in seeking the peaceful settlement of conflicts in the common territorial disputes faced by Southeast Asian member states. With reference to the South China Sea dispute, ASEAN recognized that an escalation of the conflict could directly affect peace and stability in the region, and therefore in 1992 issued a declaration on this matter urging all parties to solve all disputes peacefully, without resort to force (the Manila Declaration). Ten years later ASEAN has made an additional Declaration on the Conduct of Parties in the South China Sea at the eighth ASEAN summit, reaffirming member states' commitment to resolve their territorial and jurisdictional disputes by peaceful means.[31]

In the case of the self-determination of East Timor, ASEAN made several official declarations and political statements supporting implementation of the agreements between the UN and the Indonesian and Portuguese governments on modalities for the popular consultations of the East Timorese (held in August 1999). As violence shook the territory following the referendum, ASEAN leaders gathered to address the problem, and some of them agreed to contribute to an international force for East Timor. Other ASEAN members extended humanitarian and other forms of assistance. ASEAN's role in East Timor should, however, not be overemphasized. In reality, ASEAN was divided. Myanmar, not surprisingly, opposed any external intervention in East Timor, and Vietnam was unenthusiastic about the UN's regional role.[32]

ASEAN has also shown interest in its membership's neighborhood, whose stability naturally influences its own. The participation of North Korea in the ARF for the first time in 2000 was an important step in this direction. ASEAN expressed support for the historic summit between North and South Korean leaders, held in Pyongyang on 13–15 June 2000. It also commended the North–South Joint Declaration, the first agreement signed at the highest level since the division of the Korean Peninsula in 1945. Although ASEAN does not intervene directly in the conflict it supports the 6 Party Talks mediation process, and it has encouraged the six countries (China, South Korea, North Korea, the United States, Russia, and Japan) to take advantage of their presence at the ASEAN Regional Forum "to fully utilize this opportunity for dialogue as a means to move forward in achieving a peaceful resolution of the issue."[33]

But the most difficult test case for the "enhanced interaction" policy has been on Myanmar (ASEAN's full member since 1997). Despite the rhetoric by member states that Myanmar has to deliver on its commitments to political reform, and the discussions over the Myanmar's possible expulsion from ASEAN (recurrent since the junta's detention of democracy activist Aung San Suu Kyi at the end of May 2003 and after the large anti-government demonstrations in September 2007), at a formal level the Association has allowed for a considerable let-down. During the 13th ASEAN summit (2007), the ASEAN chairman produced a statement on Myanmar[34] wherein member states accepted that this was an internal affair of Myanmar not to be dealt with by ASEAN but directly between Myanmar and the UN. The year before, an ASEAN ministerial meeting joint communiqué acknowledged that "Myanmar needs both time and political space to deal with its many and complex challenges."[35] If at its June 2003 ministerial meeting ASEAN leaders demanded Suu Kyi's release, more recently the Association has hence adopted a more compliant position. For the Human Rights Watch, ASEAN's continuing failure to hold the Burmese military government accountable for abuses and ASEAN's unwillingness to provide refuge for those fleeing oppression in Burma are two sides of the same coin.[36]

Despite these significant achievements, it should be noted that the Southeast Asia still has various latent conflicts of low and medium intensity. The boundaries of the region—mostly imposed by the European colonial powers—were often ill-demarcated, leading to periodic border disputes. The dispute over Sabah for example, continues to be an irritation between Malaysia and the Philippines after more than 30 years. And there have been occasional border skirmishes (notably between Thailand and Myanmar in 2001). ASEAN's successes should not be exaggerated. In East Timor in the late 1990s, ASEAN was deemed to have been totally ineffective in responding to a major regional security crisis.[37]

Conclusion

The financial and economic crisis of 1997–98 caused a widespread perception that ASEAN was no longer relevant in an increasingly globalized world. However, ASEAN's accelerated pace of regional cooperation has transformed it into an indispensable tool to preserve peace and security in the region. In 2000 Kofi Annan affirmed in Jakarta that "today, ASEAN is not only a well-functioning, indispensable reality in the region. It is a real force to be reckoned with far beyond the region. It is also a trusted partner of the United Nations in the field of development. I hope that in the field of peace and security, too, we will see the beginnings of closer cooperation between ASEAN and the United Nations."[38]

Despite its political ambitions, ASEAN remains a week organization from a financial and human resource perspective. The secretariat in Jakarta has only 60 openly recruited staff from 9 member states (none from Brunei Darussalam), and about 200 support staff (almost all Indonesians).[39] There is no specific staff allocated to conflict prevention, peacebuilding or peace and security in general. And the only permanent organ devoted to these issues is the ARF Unit, placed under the Office of the Secretary-General. For the financial year of 2007, the organizational core budget was only US$9 million. There is a need, therefore, for the pace of ASEAN institutionalization to be in tandem with that of the ASEAN external relations process.[40]

The sacrosanct principles of sovereignty and non-intervention in domestic affairs have also hampered ASEAN's agility in peace and security.[41] With globalization and the rise of the post-Cold War era, the traditional practices of conflict resolution—coercive power, military deterrence, and sovereignty protection—cannot guarantee permanent, durable, and stable peace in the region.[42] ASEAN institutional architecture and decision-making procedures are out of tune with the current pattern of global threats which are inconsistent and transnational.

ASEAN was incapable of responding to the Asian financial crisis of 1990s, and it has not been able to respond to the phenomenon of air pollution (often originated by forest fires) that periodically affects the region.

In summary, the capacity of ASEAN to handle conflicts can be regarded in two different ways. If conflict resolution implies physical intervention in a member state—as could be the case with Myanmar—ASEAN is more of an impediment than a help as its baseline norms are at odds with the idea of violating the sovereignty of a member country.[43] Yet, insofar as conflict resolution is concentrated on preventing the outbreak and escalation of violence, ASEAN has played a meaningful rule. No territorial dispute has led to a militarized inter-state conflict since the establishment of the Association in 1967. In this light Australian prime minister Kevin Rudd affirmed assertively in 2008 that "Before ASEAN, [the post-Second World War situation in Asia] was very bad: Chinese civil war, Vietnam War, Cambodian war, confrontation in Indonesia, internal insurgency in Malaysia, security messes, not much economic growth. Forty years later, these security problems have disappeared and economic growth has been good; it is evidence that a good institution can encourage co-operation on security and the economy."[44] This is showcased by ASEAN itself. Speaking on behalf of ASEAN at a Security Council meeting on cooperation with regional organizations held in November 2007, Singapore's representative offered ASEAN as a model of a regional structure that had "succeeded during a 40-year period to not only keep the peace, but also to expand to economic, socio-cultural and cross-regional cooperation, through working methods that relied heavily on consensus."[45] In any case, its success must not be exaggerated. Even if the potential for the ASEAN identity to shape its members' behavior does exist, in practice ASEAN members will adhere to its collective norms insofar as these are in tune with their national interests.[46] ASEAN states have not rejected violence as a matter of cultural affiliation, but as a matter of pragmatic political and economic calculation.

8 Commonwealth of Independent States (CIS)

In the early 1990s the disintegration of the Soviet Union led to the transformation of Central Asia from a coherent region into a patchwork of independent sovereign states. This disintegration is something of an illusion, however, as most parts have subsequently engaged in a process of reintegration.[1] In fact, Caucasia and Central Asia have many common denominators and patterns of regional interaction. The Soviet Union gave the two areas a common infrastructure and political culture, and its legacy permeates economic, social, and cultural life. They also have a common history, being part of the Silk Road in historic times. The route was central to cultural transmission by linking merchants, pilgrims, and soldiers from China to the Mediterranean for thousands of years. Nevertheless, it would be a mistake to lump all eight of these "Asian" states together. In fact, the three Caucasian states are in Europe, whereas the Central Asian states are firmly part of the Asian political dynamic. In any case, connecting points are still obvious. The most salient one is the hegemonic role of Russia.

Developments in the post-Soviet space over the last 20 years have brought to evidence the existence of a state—Russia—that dominates the political and economic interactions through the formation and reshaping of various institutional patterns. There are two groups of factors that support Russian domination and hegemony. The first one flows from the previous status of the Russian Federation in the former USSR as the nucleus of a vast political space. With the lowering of the Soviet flag over the Kremlin, Russia's position as a catalyst of the disintegration processes in the former Soviet region has been reversed.[2] The second, Fedunyak argues, is connected to the current agenda of international relations post September 11. Over the years Moscow has efficiently played out the terrorist agenda to promote its own interests and to foment the reintegration processes in the post-Soviet space (2004). MacFarlane adds that "it is clear that Russian policy-makers are uncomfortable with the idea of a prominent role being granted to external actors in dealing with conflict in the former Soviet space."[3]

Another important characteristic of post-Soviet states is that even though all communist leaders and parties in Central Asia have made cosmetic and rhetorical changes, the political systems and structures of the Soviet period basically remain intact. Few leaders are ready to leave power voluntarily, and this complicates the challenges of political and economic reform.[4]

The region is also integrated by the pattern of its conflicts. In fact, the conflicts experienced in the CIS area—intra-state, inter-state and conflicts with states on the periphery or outside the region—all have left a mark in the region. Internal conflicts have broken out in Russia (Chechnya), Tajikistan, Georgia (South Ossetia and Abkhazia), and Moldova (Transnistria); Armenia and Azerbaijan are engaged in a protracted dispute over Nagorno-Karabach; and, finally, Turkey, Iran, China, and to some extent also the Western countries, are involved in a new "Great Game" over control of the region's energy resources.

This is the context in which the Commonwealth of Independent States (CIS) (Sodruzhestvo Nizavislmykh Gosudarsty—SNG) was created. It has its origins in early December 1991, when the leaders of Russia, Ukraine, and Belarus signed the Agreement Establishing the CIS (aka the Minsk Agreement), which laid down two fundamental decisions: first it declared that the USSR as a subject of international law and a geopolitical reality no longer existed; and second it proclaimed the establishment of the CIS, which comprised the above three states, but was open for accession to all member states of the USSR, as well as by other states sharing the purposes and principles of the founding agreement. The declaration of the end of the USSR without formal ratification by all members was juridically controversial, and former Soviet states met again in the same month to form a broader-based Commonwealth. At the Alma-Ata summit in 1991 the leaders of 11 states of the Soviet Union, apart from Georgia, hence confirmed the Minsk postulates by signing the Protocol to the Agreement Establishing the CIS, which was to enter into force for each of the parties from the moment of its ratification.[5]

The somewhat unskillful way in which the CIS was established provides ground to believe that its founders shared no long-term plan and were therefore obliged to choose a cautious step-by-step approach. This was clearly seen in their attitude to the CIS institutional structure, which was initially loose and lacked a clear statutory basis. Some states, especially Azerbaijan, Moldova, Turkmenistan, and Ukraine were mindful of their previous experience of the Soviet Union's central authorities, and were quite reluctant to create any powerful institutions which could threaten their newfound sovereignty.[6] Instead, they put the emphasis on the economic issues that urgently needed to be resolved. Accordingly, during the first year of the CIS members states adopted more than 200 arrangements on economic, military, ecological, social, and other matters. However, the quantity did not turn into the expected quality.[7] Consequently, although the political leadership clearly understood the benefits of cooperation and appreciated the costs of failure to cooperate, in practice cooperative relationships among all of the CIS members were limited.

Organizational capacity

The Council of Heads of State adopted the CIS Charter in January 1993. The document ascribes a wide range of objectives to the CIS, including in security matters. Article 2 states that one of the objectives of the CIS is "cooperation between member states to ensure international peace and security, the realization of effective measures for the reduction of arms and military expenditures, the elimination of nuclear and other types of weapons of mass destruction, and the achievement of universal and full disarmament." The same article ties member states to the principle of "peaceful resolution of disputes and conflicts between states of the Commonwealth," which in article 3 is linked to the "rejection of force or the threat of force against the political independence of a member state."

CIS' mandate in the peace and security sector is reinforced by sections III and IV of the Charter. Section III (Collective Security and Military-Political Cooperation) stipulates that "in the event that a threat arises to the sovereignty, security or territorial integrity of one or several member states or to international peace and security" the organization shall immediately initiate a mechanism of joint consultation to coordinate positions and further action (art. 12). Threats here are both intra-regional and extra-regional. The first is to be handled through peacemaking and peacekeeping. The latter is to be dealt with "in accordance with the procedure for exercising the right to individual or collective defense according to Article 51 of the UN Charter."

Section IV (Prevention and Resolution of Conflicts) calls on member states to "undertake all possible measures for the prevention of conflicts, and to try to achieve a fair and peaceful resolution to disputes through negotiations, or reach agreement on an appropriate alternative solution" (arts. 16–17). If they do not successfully resolve a dispute they shall call upon the Council of Heads of States.

In January 1996 the CIS strengthened its legal capacity by adopting the Concept of Prevention and Resolution of Conflicts in the Territory of Member States of the CIS. The Concept delineates the conflict prevention and peacemaking instruments available to the CIS, which encompasses good offices, mediation, negotiation, and confidence-building measures (e.g. agreement on the non-use of force, exchange of information, observer envoys). In certain cases the Concept envisages the possibility of preventive deployment of police, civilian, and military personnel in the region of possible confrontation. It also foresees the possibility of carrying out enforcement actions under article 53 of the UN Charter after requesting Security Council authorization. The concept clearly places the organization within the frame of Chapter VIII of the UN Charter, in the same line as other organizations such as the OSCE, OAS, or SADC.[8]

Over the years CIS has adopted some declarations that provide guiding principles for Russian/CIS peacekeeping. The first is the Agreement on Groups of Military Observers and Collective Peacekeeping Forces of the CIS Member States (also known as the Kyiv Agreement), signed in March 1992. The agreement defines peacekeeping forces as "created for the purpose of providing each other with assistance, on the basis of mutual agreement, in settling and preventing conflicts on the territory of any member" of the CIS[9] and postulates that the deployment should be done only in the event of a request made by all the conflicting parties. Interestingly, article 6 of the Kyiv Agreement provides for the participation of CIS peacekeepers in missions outside the CIS—as is presently the case with NATO and the EU—although this provision has never been invoked.

The next major step in defining and delimiting CIS peacekeeping was the Protocol on the Temporary Procedure for the Formation and Use of Collective Peacekeeping Forces in Zones of Conflict Between or Within Member-States of the CIS, signed in July 1992. The protocol enumerates the responsibilities which CIS peacekeepers could be expected to carry out, which includes, for instance, monitoring the implementation of the conditions of armistice or separation of conflicting parties. As of summer 1992, when the peacekeeping missions in South Ossetia and Moldova were established, these were the only two guiding principles with which Russian peacekeepers had to work. It was only in 1993 that Russia adopted its military doctrine.

In the legal documents that confer on Russia/CIS a mandate to deploy military operations, the UN's standard distinction between peacekeeping and peace enforcement is generally not adopted and the term "peacecreating operations" (*mirotvorcheckie operatsii*) is preferred. On top of this problematic ambiguity, no substantial progress has been made in transforming legal documents and memoranda into a working and reliable mechanism for conflict prevention and management. Yermolaev argues that "part of the reason for this is that Russia and some leading CIS states (including Ukraine, Georgia and Azerbaijan) have sometimes held clearly opposing views not only on the methods and means of conflict management, but on the very essence of collective peacekeeping and international security."[10]

Another sign of the obscurity of the CIS mandate is the adoption in May 1992 of the Collective Security Treaty (CST) by Armenia, Kazakhstan, Kyrgyzstan, Russia, Tajikistan, and Uzbekistan. The treaty reaffirmed the desire of all participating states to abstain from the use or threat of force and stressed that an aggression against one signatory would be perceived as an aggression against all. This would give an article 51 (UN Charter) mandate to act in self-defense, similarly to the mandate of other organizations such as NATO and OAS. However, in October 2002, the six members of the CST, signed a charter in Chişinău, expanding and institutionalizing it into the Collective Security Treaty Organization. What remains to be clearly delineated is the division of labor between both organizations.

In order to execute its mandate, the CIS has created a dense institutional architecture. At the top of the pyramid there are the two councils: the Council of Heads of State (the supreme organ) which holds its regular meetings twice a year and decides the general action and policy of the organization, whereas the Council of Heads of Government holds meetings four times a year and coordinates the cooperation of the member states' executive organs in economic, social, and other spheres of common interests. The two councils may have joint sessions, and create working and auxiliary bodies of both permanent and temporary operation. The CIS Charter also provides for the establishment of the Council of Ministers of Foreign Affairs, an executive body mandated to ensure cooperation in the foreign policy field. In between meetings of the highest bodies (Council of Heads of State and Council of Heads of Government) it is the highest decision-making body. There is also the Council of Ministers of Defense tasked with coordinating military cooperation (including legal harmonization in the field of development of armed forces and conflict prevention) and the Council of Commanders of Border Troops. All of them are subordinate to the Council of Heads of State, but the Charter does not reveal their decision-making competence, which is expected to be specified in the relevant regulations on these organs. The other institutional bodies include the Coordinating-Consultative Committee (executive organ), the High Command of the United Armed Forces, the Economic Court, the Commission on Human Rights, and the Inter Parliamentary Assembly. The organs of sectoral cooperation (councils, committees) may also be set up for cooperation in particular economic, social, and other matters.

Operational experience

Within one year of the fall of the USSR, five serious wars had broken out on the territory of the former Soviet space. The roots of each of these conflicts lay in Soviet nationality and linguistic policies, and most of them had been brewing since the late 1980s.[11] To address most of these cases, peacekeeping operations were deployed, which Russia has sought to present as being in some way or another CIS-led rather than Russian-led. This reflects a belief that the CIS umbrella could offer greater legitimacy, or at least respectability, and add efficiency to Russia's peacekeeping.[12] Nevertheless, the CIS states, other than Russia, have been very hesitant in their actual commitment to peacekeeping, despite the adoption of fine-sounding resolutions at CIS meetings. Some have been able to dispute Russia's ambitions, as did Azerbaijan, which in 1994 did not agree to Russia's plan for Nagorno-Karabach and therefore, as a conflict party, did not consent to the deployment of a Russian/CIS operation.[13]

Peacekeeping operations

- Moldova (since 1992): The deployment of this peacekeeping operation was preceded by the signing of the ceasefire in the Yeltsin-Snegur Agreement (21 July 1992) between the Moldavian national armed forces and the Transdniesteria separatist group. The joint Russian, Moldavian, and Dniesterian peacekeeping force was deployed under a Joint Control Commission command in August 1992.
- Georgia, Abkhazia (since 1994): The CIS peacekeeping forces in Georgia were deployed under the provisions of the Agreement on a Ceasefire and Separation of Forces between Georgia and Abkhazia (the Moscow Agreement) signed in May 1994. The main tasks for CIS peacekeepers were to maintain the ceasefire, implement the conditions of the agreement, supervise the withdrawal of heavy weapons, and promote safe conditions for the returning of displaced persons. Under the agreement, a coordinating commission has been established in order to discuss requirements from both sides. The CIS peacekeeping forces are still present on Georgian territory, and

some clashes between peacekeepers and Georgian authorities have erupted. The main problem is linked to the fact that the peacekeeping forces are composed solely of Russian troops, presently 2,000 soldiers.

- Tajikistan (1993–2000) is the largest operation carried out by CIS in the former Soviet space.[14] The peacekeeping forces were deployed according to a decision of the Council of Heads of State adopted in September 1993, which regarded the civil war between political factions of Tajikistan (the fighting began in May 1992) as a serious threat to the stability of the entire CIS. The peacekeeping forces included the Russian 201st Motorized Rifle Division (MRD) and Uzbek, Kazakh, and Kyrgyz battalions, which were operationally subordinated to the Collective Peacekeeping Force (CPF). In February 1994 the CIS' role was formally extended when nine CIS defense ministers (excluding Ukraine, Belarus, and Moldova) signed a document committing each to send peacekeeping troops to Tajikistan. In March 1994 a Standing Consultative Commission on Peacekeeping Activity was established under the CIS Council of Ministers of Foreign Affairs. After the end of the Tajik civil war and the disbanding of peacekeeping forces, Russia and Tajikistan agreed on transforming the 201st Motorized Rifle Division, stationed in the country, into a military base. Although the agreement was not implemented, the division is still stationed in Tajik territory and has become part of the Collective Forces of Rapid Deployment, which operates within the framework of the Collective Security Treaty Organization.

Russia has also undertaken a peacekeeping operation in Georgia, South Ossetia, which is often mistaken for a CIS operation. It started in July 1992, after the Sochi Agreement was signed between the Georgian and Russian presidents, settling the Georgian–Ossetian conflict. A Joint Peacekeeping Force (JPKF) was created, in order to guarantee the ceasefire, withdraw armed forces, disband self-defense units, ensure the security regime, and supervise peacekeeping forces. However, the initiative was Russian; no approval from international organizations (including the CIS) was sought.[15] When war erupted again in South Ossetia in the summer of 2008, the CIS remained paralyzed as Russia's military agenda did not permit the CIS to play any role in dispute settlement or peacekeeping.

Overall, CIS/Russian peacekeeping was marred by several limitations. First, if the peacekeeping activities are assessed from the point of view of classical UN peacekeeping theory and practice, several mistakes have been made. For instance, most of the missions were deployed on the basis of bilateral (sometimes oral) agreements between the Russian president and the leaders of warring factions, rather than under multilateral mandates. Often Russia deployed unilaterally its military contingents with the mandate approved only later by the CIS Council of Heads of State, as in Tajikistan and Abkhazia.[16] Russia dismisses the issue of impartiality by pointing to the consent of the warring parties to the interventions. However, the problem of consent must be considered in the larger context of Russian involvement in these countries. As argued by Jonson and Archer, "proclaimed consent can be forced and be the result of political blackmail by the peacekeeper."[17]

Also in friction with UN practices, CIS missions offer egregious examples of partiality on the part of the Russian troops. For instance, in Moldova/Transdniestria commanders of the Russian 14th Army accepted cabinet-level posts within the administration of the breakaway republic of Transdniestria, and were allowed to briefly keep both those posts and their command within the Russian army.[18] Russian forces were also accused of equipping both the separatist elements in South Ossetia and the pro-communist forces in Tajikistan. Mackinlay is right when he argues that "Russian peacekeeping ... is not a transferable operational technique and has only been used to deal with emergencies arising in the former Soviet space. Russian peacekeeping operations are regulated in each case by locally formulated procedures and are not based on recognized international doctrine."[19]

Second, the Russian military has never been trained for such peacekeeping activities and there is no military doctrine, no peacekeeping concept, not even manuals for peacekeeping training.[20] In the chaotic post-Soviet Union situation, political declarations about Moscow's strategic intentions did not always translate literally into the way Russian forces were deployed on the ground.[21] In this light, there was often a misunderstanding among military commanders on the essence of peacekeeping and its difference from enforcement operations. Yermolaev argues that "this meant that Russia's peacekeeping terminology, or *mirotvorchestvo*, was often applied to a range of very different military activities."[22] Even before the UN had begun its own move toward robust peacekeeping, the Russians were intervening in conflicts where there was no peace to keep—where the ceasefire agreements between warring factions had not been reached or were clearly being violated. This implied imposing a peace on warring factions and violating the Kyiv Agreement, which stressed the importance of peacekeeping as a measure for the promotion of a political solution.[23]

Fourth, peacekeeping contingents included military representatives from warring factions—apparently to create confidence-building—violating basic UN standards. This was the case, for instance, with the operation in Moldova, which included forces from Moldova and Transdniester, and the operation in South Ossetia which included contingents from Georgia, North and South Ossetia. A peacekeeper's mission is to maintain peace between two or more warring factions of the same country and therefore it would be paradoxical to use the disrupters of peace also as peacekeepers. It obviously negates the most fundamental aspect of peacekeeping: neutrality.

Finally, the CIS' operations made it clear that Russia has clear hegemonic aspirations in the former Soviet space. As explained by Mac-Farlane, this is evident "in their efforts to restore Russian control over the external borders of the former Soviet Union, to reassume control over the Soviet air defense network, to obtain agreements on the basing of Russian forces in the non-Russian republics and by their obvious sensitivity to external military presences (including multilateral ones) on the soil of the former Soviet Union."[24]

The capacity of a dominant power to manipulate a regional organization depends partly on the latter's institutional capacity. The more substantial and embedded the organization, the less likely it is to become a creature of particular dominant states within the region.[25] In this light, the CIS is an instrument of Russian foreign policy in the former Soviet space. The Abkhazia operation is illustrative. Russian peacekeepers were deployed in 1993 by a decision of the Russian government and without the imprimatur of the CIS, which caught up in June 1994 by authorizing the deployment of a regional peacekeeping force. However, the contingent was exclusively Russian and no other states in the CIS contributed financially to the force.

Conclusion

In 1991 many feared that the collapse of the Soviet Union would lead to unrestrained competition and conflict in Central Asia. Many observers believed that the region would return to communism or undergo violent revolution. But in fact, no major efforts were made to alter borders, nor has any state sought to subordinate its neighbors or create a unified new entity. The challenges that arose were primarily not from state-to-state conflict but from insurgent movements fueled by revolutionary doctrines emanating from Afghanistan or by the drug trade or by a combination of both.[26] Russia and the CIS should be credited for keeping a sense of stability in the region, even if that implied smoothing autonomy claims and projecting Russia's foreign policy agenda. Indeed, reliance on a regional agency in conflict resolution reduces pressure on the UN and increases the likelihood that a substantial effort will be made in the area of conflict management. As argued by MacFarlane, "it is fair to say that, in the Georgian case, had it not been Russia that intervened to stabilize the region, no one else would have."[27]

It is legitimate the claim that the CIS provides Russia with a perfect opportunity to control domestic processes in the former Soviet region.[28] For that purpose it was crucial to promote the regional agenda in the UN and to stress the legitimacy of regional agencies and arrangements to operate under Chapter VIII of the UN Charter. This was the central intention of Russia when in 1994 it presented the Draft Declaration on the Improvement of Cooperation Between the United Nations and Regional Organizations. As we saw in Chapter 1, the proposal suggested that regional organizations should set up peacemaking and peacekeeping forces to be at the disposal of the Security Council.

Nevertheless, as acknowledged even by Russian authorities, the CIS is still "experiencing certain difficulties in its development."[29] This derives not only from the political fragmentation and manipulation of the CIS' decision-making process, but is also due to its poor financial and human resources. The latest available information on the CIS's budget is from 2001, according to which the budget was only about US $8.54 million.[30] The Coordinating Committee has a staff of about 220, which includes approximately 120 attached to the Executive Committee in Minsk, and roughly 100 working at an affiliated branch of the Executive Committee, located in Moscow.

Some authors have forecast the disbanding of the CIS in a new context where the leaders of Georgia, Ukraine, and Moldova fiercely challenge Russia's political patronage.[31] But while Russia is able to channel its national interests through the CIS the organization is not likely to dissolve. In any case Russia is aware of its neighbors' reluctance to engage in political integration and excercises its power also through bilateralism. Many states in the region (most notably Armenia, Kazakstan, Kyrgyzstan, Tajikistan, and Turkmenistan) have bilateral security treaties with Russia that go far beyond the CIS treaties.

9   League of Arab States (LAS)[1]

The League of Arab States (or Arab League) was the first regional organization to be formed after the Second World War. In fact the official establishment of the League on 22 March 1945 even predates the setting up of the United Nations. The origin of the League can be traced back to the adoption of the Alexandria Protocol in 1944 by the representatives of Syria, (then) Transjordan, Iraq, Lebanon, and Egypt.[2] It was driven by an attempt to unite Arab states (especially for Syria and Transjordan), to resist colonial forces (especially for Lebanon), and to react to the Jewish presence. This protocol eventually opened the way for the establishment of the League of Arab States a year later. During the discussion at the Alexandria Conference there had been heated debate about what form would better represent Arab unity. Syrian and Transjordanian representatives were particularly eager to form a very advanced union that would resemble a confederate structure. However, representatives of Saudi Arabia were less enthusiastic about such a prospect.[3] In the end, with the help of the Egyptian delegates, a compromise was found between the two sides and the protocol stated that the future organization's decisions would only be binding for those that accepted them.[4] The protocol also made way for the setting up of a special sub-committee to reflect on the future organization that was to be established among the Arab states. The composition of this sub-committee was very different from the preparatory committee that had participated to the Alexandria Conference. Changes of governments in Egypt and in Lebanon led these two states to adopt a stronger stance against any form of organization that would threaten their national sovereignty. The Lebanese foreign minister thus openly admitted that they "did not want the Arab League to become a state above the states or a federation."[5] The participation in the talks of states that had only been observers in Alexandria also favored a scaling-down of the ambitions regarding Arab unity. As a result, the outcome of the sub-committee and the document that was drafted to serve as the Pact of the League of Arab States greatly undermined the prospects for an empowered supranational body. The pact did in fact represent a step back from what was proposed in the Alexandria Protocol. The Council of the new organization no longer had the ability to take any kind of binding policies and could only act as a mediator between conflicting parties if they asked the League to do so (article 5).[6] The pact also made out a special provision to enable the Council to work with what was to be the United Nations (article 3).

Egypt clearly came out as the victorious side following the signing of the pact.[7] Not only had it succeeded in getting the scaling-down of the powers of the organization, but it also managed to ensure that the seat of the League would be in Cairo and that an Egyptian, Abdul Rahman Hassan Azzam, would be elected to the post of secretary-general.[8] In fact, Egypt would retain the post of secretary-general except when it was expelled from the League between 1979 and 1989 for having signed an agreement with Israel. During this period the seat of the organization was moved from Cairo to Tunis. Egypt and Saudi Arabia would remain at the forefront of the organization, and would manage to temper down the far going integrative efforts supported by Syria, Iraq, and later on Libya.

One good example of how Egypt has been able to maneuver the League so as to have it more in line with the aspirations of Egyptian heads of state is provided by the adoption of the Treaty of Joint Defense and Economic Cooperation.[9] In 1949, a joint Iraqi–Syrian plan to unify in order to thwart the Israeli menace and with the aim of clearing the ground for a greater Arab unification was being negotiated (the plan is also known as the Fertile Crescent). Alarmed by this prospect, Egypt soon proposed a new framework that would allow member states to increase their military cooperation. This new plan was to eventually provide for an Arab Collective Security Pact (ACSP) while possible Iraqi–Syrian unification was officially considered as an internal affair that was beyond the League's competency.[10] The Treaty of Joint Defense and Economic Cooperation Between the States of the Arab League was eventually signed on 17 June 1950. The treaty provides a framework for collective security between the member states and calls for increased cooperation in the security and military fields. It also makes provisions for the establishment of a Permanent Military Commission tasked with the drawing up of plans for joint defense and their implementation in order to encourage the cooperation and coordination of the contracting states' armed forces. The treaty also introduced a Joint Defense Council which is under the supervision of the Arab

League Council and is composed of the foreign ministers and the defense ministers of the contracting states. It is in charge of ensuring the collective security of the contracting states and facilitating the cooperation and coordination of the armed forces, and it supervises the work of the Permanent Military Commission. Nevertheless, most of the conditions of the treaty were never implemented by the member states, on the one hand because the treaty itself was established to prevent a "too" integrative Iraqi–Syrian plan, and on the other hand because the signing of the Baghdad Pact in 1955.[11]

In regard to the history and evolution of the League of Arab States, two predominating factors need to be mentioned as they have continuously played a role in the relationship between the member states and the organization, as well as in the capacity of the regional organization itself.

The first major factor is Arab nationalism. Even before the setting up of the League, there had been many calls for a unification of all the Arab states within one entity. This political ideal also received a very strong support among the citizens of the region attracted by the prospects of a pan-Arab state.[12] This support for Arabism allowed some leaders among the member states to push forward their own agenda:

> The concept (albeit not the reality) of Arab unity provided an invaluable tool to mask what was at heart an inward-looking, state-building political strategy of regime survival. Arabism became a powerful tool of domination in the hands of regimes that relied on the military as an instrument of control by ethnic minorities or tribes, as with Syria's Alawi, Jordan's Hashemite officer corps, and Iraq's predominantly Takriti Sunni military command.[13]

The pressure coming from other Arab states and also from pan-Arab calls from among their populations eventually enabled the League to somehow punish defection and enforce compliance. The expulsion of Egypt between 1979 and 1989 was the very result of its non-compliance with the Arabist norm and more specifically with the League's call for the non-recognition of the state of Israel. Since the 1990s, however, the appeal of Arabism has cooled and has been under challenge from the resurgence of Islamism.[14]

The second important factor in the League's history is the attitude toward Israel. Although the setting up of the League predates the creation of the Israeli state, special attention had already been devoted to the question of the Jewish presence. In fact, even the Alexandria Protocol and the League's Pact each contained a special annex referring to the Palestinian issue. The League also gave its support to the military intervention launched in 1948 in reaction to the declaration of the creation of the state of Israel. Again during the various conflicts that would pit together Israel and a member state of the League, the Arab regional organization would give its strong vocal support to that member state, although in many cases the League did not manage to do much more than that. Internal rivalries between the member states and the predominance of their national interests also thwarted any effort to create a coordinated military front to oppose Israel. And whereas the League strongly rejected the possibility of negotiating with Israel, in reality many of its member states were in one way or another entertaining a relationship with Israel. Only in the case of Egypt and the signing of the Camp David Accords in 1978 did a member step over the line by officially recognizing the existence of the state of Israel. However, in 2002 a Saudi-led peace initiative to resolve the conflict in the Middle East offered the possibility of the recognition of Israel by all member states, should Israel withdraw to the 1967 delimitation.

Organizational capacity

The legal mandate of the League to engage with peace and security activities derives from the Pact of the League of the Arab States adopted in 1945. Although article 2, which delineates the purposes of the League, does not encompass security issues, article 5 provides member states with the possibility of having their disputes mediated and settled by the League. It states: "The Council shall mediate in a dispute which may lead to war between two member States or between a member State and another State in order to conciliate them." However, "the Council jurisdiction is limited under that article, both in substance and in form. The Council may arbitrate if, on the one hand, the dispute does not concern a State's independence, sovereignty or territorial integrity, and, on the other, the parties to the dispute agree to have recourse to the Council."[15] Similarly, article 6 also allows the member states to refer to the League's Council in the case of a military aggression by another state including the League's member states. Another important legal landmark came in 2004 with the resolution on Arab Coordination for Combating the Illicit Trade in Small Arms and Light Weapons adopted during a ministerial council of the League in order to control the flow of arms in the Arab world. According to the resolution member states are to coordinate their policies in regard to arms flow and more specifically illicit cross-border arms trade in the region.

The implementation of the program also gives an important role to the multiple national focal points as they need to monitor arm flows and disseminate information on small arms and light weapons to the other member state and to the organization.

However, the League has proven over time to be largely ineffectual in its endeavor to resolve conflicts in the region. This failure is also the result of the provision made in the Pact that the League may only mediate upon the request of the conflicting parties. The League has also suffered from the absence of an elaborate mechanism for the settlement of disputes among its member states.[16] In fact, between 1945 and 1981, only 6 of the 77 inter-Arab conflict situations saw a successful intervention by the League.[17] Overall the League is a very weak institution that suffers from a very low level of implementation of its own resolutions. Since its creation the League has adopted more than 4,000 resolutions, but despite the fact that the great majority of these have been unanimously adopted, only a few have actually been implemented.[18]

In order to address some of its shortcomings the member states agreed in March 2000 on the League of Arab States Mechanism for Conflict Prevention, Management and Resolution Between the Arab States, during the 113th session of the League's Council at the foreign ministerial level. The mechanism opened the way for the adoption of the Statutes of the Arab Peace and Security Council during the 18th ordinary session of the Council of the League at summit level held in Khartoum in March 2006. The Statutes mark a fundamental shift in the League's ability to play a part in peace and security as they ensure that the League will have the capacity to intervene in disputes including those touching on sovereignty, independence, and territorial integrity.[19] With the adoption of this document the League also becomes the organization to which states will have to turn in first resort when a conflict arises among them.

The Statutes entered into force in June 2007 after one third of the member states ratified it, even though it was not until early 2008 that the provisions made in the Statutes started being implemented. The Statutes provide for the establishment of a Peace and Security Council composed of a troika of five member states (the two previous states chairing the League's Council, the current chair and the two states due to chair the following sessions) represented by their foreign ministers. The League's secretary-general also participates in the meetings of the Council. It meets twice a year at ministerial level prior to the meetings of the League's Council or in extraordinary session upon request by a member state or by the secretary-general. It is responsible for proposing collective measures in case of an aggression, developing an early warning system and exerting good offices, and conciliation and mediation to prevent the escalation of disputes. It is also expected to make efforts in regard to post-conflict efforts and reconstruction, humanitarian action, and cooperation; as well as making proposals for the establishment of an Arab peacekeeping force when deemed necessary, in which case it would be responsible for setting up and dispatching civil or military observer missions to conflict areas. The Peace and Security Council, which held its first meeting in May 2008 at the request of Djibouti following a border dispute with Eritrea (see below), makes provision for the following organs:

- The *Data Bank*, which aims to collect information provided by member states and regional and international organizations to help the Council assess a situation.
- An *Early Warning System* to be composed of experts from the staff of the General Secretariat who will analyze the available data and information, monitor the evolution of a situation and submit their report to the Council.
- A *Board of Wise Personalities* composed of prominent Arab personalities. Members of the Board are designated by the chairperson of the Council and then chosen by the secretary-general, to undertake mediation, conciliation or good offices missions between conflicting parties.

As of early 2009, none of these institutions was yet fully established or able to function. So far the only applicable part of the statutes has been the resort to the Council to resolve disputes involving member states. The other instruments such as the Data Bank, the Early Warning System and Board of Wise Personalities will need to be rapidly implemented so as not to transform the Statutes into an ineffective instrument for peace and security in the region. As it currently stands with only the Council properly working, the League has the ability to work on a crisis *a posteriori* and is hampered as to conflict prevention.

Besides the Arab Peace and Security Council, other LAS organs deal with security issues. The League is organized following a very strict inter-governmental framework as it includes many safeguards to prevent the organization from imposing particular decisions upon unwilling states. The Council of the League convenes the representatives of the member states. It can meet at the summit level, when it brings together the heads of states and government, or at ministerial level. However, initially the League's charter makes no clear distinction between the summit and ministerial levels. As a result, the Charter only requires ordinary sessions, i.e. ministerial level sessions, to be held twice a year (in March and in October), while there are no provisions made for summit level meetings. The mandate of the Council is to realize the purposes of the League and supervise the execution of the agreements concluded between the member states. During the meetings, decisions are adopted by a simple majority vote (in which case the decision is only binding on the states who vote in favor) or unanimously (in which case the decision is binding for all member states). However, member states have tended to demonstrate a low level of interest in the work of the League and attendance at the summit is usually low. It is only occasionally, when important topics are discussed, that the League manages to bring together a large number of heads of state and government.

The Special Committees are responsible for establishing the basis and scope of cooperation by drafting agreements that will subsequently be submitted to the Council. The Pact of the League of Arab States makes provision for the establishment of special committees on a series of matters to be dealt by the League. These include the Political Committee, the Social Committee, the Permanent Committee for Administrative and Financial Affairs, and the Legal Committee.

The General Secretariat is composed of a secretary-general and assistant secretaries. The secretariat is the administrative body of the League and has its headquarters in Cairo. It provides support for the councils (summit and ministerial level) and for the special committees. The General Secretariat is subdivided between the conference secretariat, responsible for protocol affairs related to the councils meeting, and seven other departments. In reality the post of secretary-general is one with very little power and its occupant has mainly served as a public figure representing the League and portraying a commitment to the cause of Arabism. This has nevertheless allowed the secretary-general to express some severe criticism of the functioning and inefficiency of the League.[20] Such was for example the case when Amre Moussa declared in an interview that the League ought "to reform or to disappear."[21] Moreover, in his proposal for a reform of the Arab League presented to the ministers of foreign affairs, Moussa also pinpointed several problems hindering the work of the League, including the reluctance of member states to adopt regional instruments, a disinterest in the actions undertaken by the League, and the lack of a precise framework for the Joint Arab Action.[22]

Operational experience

On different occasions the League of Arab States has been involved in peace and security issues. Even though the mandate to deploy peacekeeping forces was only given by the Statutes of the Peace and Security Council, the League has already deployed troops under its umbrella. These peacekeeping operations are:

- Palestine (1948–49)—the refusal by Arab states to accept the partition of Palestine led them to consider the deployment of their armies in Palestine. The Israeli declaration of independence sparked an intervention under the League's aegis. Contingents from Egypt, Iraq, (then) Transjordan, Lebanon, and Syria, as well as a small number of troops from Saudi Arabia and Yemen, fought under the League's umbrella. The intervening forces peaked at around 25,000 troops with the majority being drawn from the Egyptian army (around 10,000). The Arab League also sponsored and supported the Arab Liberation Army, a military corps made up of volunteers from different Arab countries. In a cablegram sent by the secretary-general of the Arab League to the UN secretary-general it was stated that the aim of the intervention was the creation of a united Palestinian state. However, the intervention was marred by inter-Arab rivalries and failed to reach the goal set by the League. In 1949, Israel signed a set of armistices with the Arab states in which they agreed to withdraw their forces behind the armistice demarcation line.
- Kuwait (1961–63)—an Arab League Force was deployed following the departure of the British troops, who had been present in Kuwait until it gained independence. The League deployed its force following concerns expressed by the Kuwaiti head of state that Iraq would try to annex the former British protectorate. Three thousand men consisting of troops from Saudi Arabia, Sudan, the United Arab Republic, Tunisia, and Jordan were deployed to protect the independence of Kuwait until 1963, following Iraq's recognition of its sovereignty and territorial integrity.
- Lebanon (1976–82)—originally known as the Arab Security Force, it became the Arab Deterrent Force (ADF) after a change in its mandate. The decision to deploy an Arab Force followed the Syrian intervention in Lebanon in June 1976. The League's Council at ministerial level adopted a resolution to establish an Arab Force responsible for enforcing a ceasefire and promoting national reconciliation. Later on, a resolution was passed to transform the ongoing operation into a deterrent force. According to the resolution the ADF was to be composed of 30,000 men mainly drawn from Syria, Saudi Arabia, the United Arab Emirates, Libya, North and South Yemen, and Sudan.

Additionally the League of Arab States also set up a military commission in 1980 specifically to supervise and monitor the ceasefire between North and South Yemen that it had helped establish in 1979. A similar commission had already been established earlier (in 1972) for the same conflict. A joint military commission set up by the League also worked in Yemen following the intra-state conflict in 1994.

The League of Arab States also has experience in peacemaking and conflict prevention in its undertaking of mediation attempts to stop conflicts involving some of its member states. The League was thus involved in mediation efforts on several occasions between Kuwait and Iraq (1961, 1973, and 1990) as well as between the warring factions in Somalia (the most notable efforts being in 1997 and 2006–7). The League of Arab States has also attempted to carry out a disarmament program in Somalia. However, the capacity of the League to intervene as a mediator has also on several occasions been hindered by the reluctance of its member states to see the involvement of the regional organization. As the League can only act upon the request of a member state, it has easily been prevented from mediating in several conflicts in the Arab region where member states have refused to call for its intervention.[23]

Since 1948, the Israeli–Palestinian conflict has also ranked high among the League's priorities. In March 2002, the League endorsed the Beirut Declaration, based on a proposal by Saudi Arabia. According to the declaration, the League's member states would offer Israel formal recognition, normalization of relations and peace agreements should Israel withdraw from all territories occupied since 1967, solve the Palestinian refugee problem, and recognize the establishment of an independent Palestinian state. This so-called Arab Peace Initiative was again endorsed by the League and its member states during the Riyadh summit in March 2007. In July 2007 a delegation from the League visited Israel for the very first time. UN secretary-general Ban Ki-moon has declared that "the Arab peace initiative is one of the pillars of the peace process ... [it] sends a signal that the Arabs are serious about achieving peace,"[24] but in practice the Initiative has been marred by the fracture of the Palestinian leadership and lack of stern support by the United States.

The League also involved itself in the political crisis in Lebanon. During their extraordinary League ministerial council at the beginning of January 2008, the Arab ministers of foreign affairs charged the League's secretary-general to activate the Arab initiative to end the dangerous crisis in Lebanon resulting from the dispute over the nomination of the president of the republic. The League's secretary-general, Amr Moussa, also visited Beirut and Damascus on several occasions before reporting back to the Arab delegations to the League in order to find a solution to the crisis.

Finally, as mentioned earlier, the Arab Peace and Security Council has also started involving itself in crisis situations. The Council convened its first ever meeting in May 2008 to discuss the border dispute between Djibouti and Eritrea, and agreed to send a fact-finding mission on the ground. Again, following the conviction of the Sudanese president, Omar El-Bashir, by the International Criminal Court in July 2008, the Arab League reacted strongly against the conviction through its Peace and Security Council.

Before the adoption of the Statutes in 2006, the actions of the League in the field of peace and security were greatly hindered on the one hand by the restrictions put in its founding treaty and and on the other hand by the actions of its own member states. Since its capacity to intervene was limited to cases that were not touching on issues of independence, state sovereignty or territorial integrity, the League had to bypass a given number of conflict and crisis arising in the region.[25] Similarly, member states have on numerous occasions been reluctant to involve the Council in their disputes, and have sometimes even resorted to extra-regional allegiances. The institutional design of the League also made it unable to enforce decisions on its member states. It therefore managed to impose its decisions in only 6 of 77 inter-Arab conflicts[26] and has tended to largely favor conciliation over arbitration or adjudication of claims.[27]

One of the main reasons for the adoption of the Statutes has been to overcome the League's dismal results in ensuring peace and security in the region. The fact that the League is no longer prevented from intervening in internal conflicts opens up the way for a greater role for this regional organization. Nevertheless, for the League to become a credible actor in peace and security it is crucial that the organization ensures the proper implementation of its decisions by the conflicting parties.

Conclusion

Throughout the history of the League, members' strong attachment to state sovereignty and bitter internal disputes have rendered the organization largely ineffectual. On several occasions, the League has been heavily criticized for failing to defend the interests of Arab states. One particularly vocal critic has been the leader of Libya, Moammar al-Ghadafi, who has repetitively threatened to withdraw from the League and has accused the other member states of being mainly driven by personal interests. In 2004 Ghadafi declared in a press conference after having walked out of a League summit, that "unfortunately Libya is forced to boycott the summit because it does not agree to the agenda of the Arab governments. Libya wants the agenda of the Arab peoples."[28]

The organization itself is also structurally weak. The secretariat has a low budget of approximately US$46 million (2009). Some of the institutions affiliated to the League of Arab States have an autonomous budget resting on the voluntary contributions of member states. However, the Statutes of the Arab Peace and Security Council clearly indicate that the Council's budget is to be drawn from the already strained budget of the General Secretariat. Even though the provisions made by the Statutes have yet to be implemented, it is quite clear that they will become a burden for the functioning of the Secretariat as they could divert an important percentage of the budget. The League's budget also suffers from payment arrears, as some member states do not pay their full share to the organization.

The organization is also weak in human resources. With a staff of around 500, the League has to rely heavily on work carried out by external consultants. And since the staff of the Peace and Security Council is expected to be drawn from the staff of the Secretariat, it remains to be seen how the League's personnel will be able to cope with the new tasks entrusted to them. Moreover, the staff that will be employed by the League for some of the technical aspects of the Peace and Security Council, such as the early warning system, will need to be adequately equipped and trained in order to effectively carry out their mission.

The adoption of the Statutes of the Arab Peace and Security Council offers a promising future for the League of Arab States and its involvement in the settling of disputes. The Statutes also show that the League's members are now increasingly confident that the regional organization can become a credible actor in the areas of conflict prevention, mediation, and dispute settlement. This is particularly clear through the introduction of a provision making the League the first organization to which the member states will have to turn once a dispute or a crisis arises. The fact that the League's capacity to intervene is no longer constrained to conflicts that do not concern sovereignty, political independence or territorial integrity, also goes a long way in empowering the regional organization. Institutionally as well, there have been attempts to facilitate the work of the League, notably in regard to the adoption of resolutions. Nevertheless, the history of the League of Arab States calls for some caution, as previous reform attempts have failed or could not be fully implemented. The danger that the provisions made by the Statutes may end up not being implemented still exists. Another issue that is still to be resolved by the League concerns the way it can apprehend and respond to destabilizing external or non-member-state interventions (including military ones) in the region. Therefore the risk exists that the League could remain largely ineffectual in its capacity to act for the promotion of peace and security in the Arab region.

10 Pacific Islands Forum (PIF)

Of all the sub-regions in Asia, the South Pacific[1] is one of the largest in area, the smallest in populations and territory, and the least examined as an autonomous regional entity. The reasons for this are primarily geographical. The island nations are scattered about the vast expanses of Oceania, and until some decades ago they had little contact with each other, with the other sub-regions in Asia or with the world beyond—except through the Western powers that controlled most of them until independence. Unsurprisingly, the early attempts at regional cooperation were instigated by outside powers.

The first product of regional engineering was the South Pacific Commission (SPC). Created in 1947, it is a paradigmatic case of an international organization originally formed by external powers with possessions in the region (France, The Netherlands, the United Kingdom, and the United States) in cooperation with New Zealand and Australia. The main purposes of the SPC as laid out in the Canberra Agreement were comprehensive and designed to mitigate some opposition from Pacific members who wanted to expel rather than join the former colonial powers. It includes the objective "to advise and assist the participating governments and territorial administrations in promoting the economic, medical, and social development of the peoples of Oceania." In 1997 the organization's name was changed to the Pacific Community, to reflect the expansion of its membership to include also northern Pacific neighbors. The community presently encompasses 22 Pacific island countries and territories and is tasked to provide technical assistance in areas such as health, human development, agriculture, forestry, and fisheries. It is headquartered in Noumea, New Caledonia.

Despite these efforts at regional cooperation the region experienced several security problems that hampered further cooperation. Palmer describes the security situation in Oceania after the Second World War as follows:

After World War II, when it was a major combat theater, Oceania became one of the most peaceful as well as one of the least known of the world's regions; but in recent years, because of the distressful conditions and political instabilities in many of the islands, the increasing activities in the region of outside powers, and disputes with these powers over such important concerns as development assistance, fisheries rights and policies, and nuclear issues, the region has been anything but peaceful.[2]

The greatest instability has been concentrated in Fiji, New Caledonia, Papua New Guinea, Solomon Islands, and Vanuatu. Despite these intra-regional disturbances, the two major regional powers, Australia and New Zealand, were more concerned about deterring outside attacks than addressing intra-regional disputes. In the follow-up of the close cooperation between the USA, Australia, and New Zealand during World War II—during which time Australia came under attack by a foreign power (Japan) for the first time in its history—these countries signed in 1951 the Australia, New Zealand, United States Security Treaty (ANZUS) which bound the signatories to recognize that an armed attack in the Pacific area on any of them would endanger the peace and safety of the others. In the 1980s a major crisis hit ANZUS when New Zealand banned visits by nuclear-powered and nuclear-capable naval vessels, even those of its allies, which led the United States to suspend its security commitments to New Zealand under the ANZUS pact. New Zealand's policy became law in 1987 with the passing of the New Zealand Nuclear Free Zone, Disarmament, and Arms Control Act. Australia and the United States have, however, retained their cooperation. Recently, the ANZUS treaty's provisions were officially invoked for the first time by Australia, to justify the Australian commitment in Afghanistan.

Within this unstable security environment, frustration grew over the non-political orientation of the South Pacific Commission.[3] This led Australia, the Cook Islands, Fiji, Nauru, New Zealand, Tonga, and Western Samoa to form in 1971 the South Pacific Forum, where fundamental issues of common concern such as trade, shipping, tourism, and education, could be amply discussed. Even if political disputes between or among members were usually kept off the agenda of the annual meetings, the Forum "became a central agency for taking positions and exerting pressure on political and security issues on which there is fairly widespread agreement. This is particularly true of nuclear issues."[4] One of the most significant products of the Forum discussions was the South Pacific Nuclear Free Zone Treaty (Treaty of

Rarotonga), which formalized a nuclear-weapon-free zone in the South Pacific. The treaty bans the use, testing, and possession of nuclear weapons within the borders of the zone. Interestingly, the treaty does not restrict port visits by nuclear-powered or armed ships, which is left for individual nations to decide.

In 2000 the South Pacific Forum changed its name to Pacific Islands Forum to better reflect the geographic location of its 16 member states[5] and to convey a truly regional posture. The change was more than cosmetic. It presupposed creating an organization based on an international treaty with specific permanent institutions. These legal and institutional changes are fundamental if the PIF aspires to serve as an effective regional security actor—either at supranational level or through intergovernmentalism. As pointed out by Graham, "the Pacific is perhaps the most vulnerable of all regions to human security threats through the sheer fact of micro-size and macro-distance."[6] The vulnerability to climate change-induced sea level rise and the very large, and often unpatrolled, exclusive economic zones are two security problems which PIF needs to address. For that it would be necessary to have a strong organizational capacity (legal and institutional).

Organizational capacity

The constitutive treaty for the Pacific Islands Forum secretariat currently in force is the Agreement Establishing the Pacific Islands Forum Secretariat, signed at Tarawa on 30 October 2000. Apart from endowing PIF with international legal personality, the Agreement is somewhat vague in terms of equipping the Forum with a legal capacity to operate in the security field. But in the same year the Forum adopted the Biketawa Declaration, which unequivocally converted the PIF into a security organization. By adopting the declaration member states committed themselves to a common vision on good governance, democracy, land, ethnic tensions, socio-economic disparities, and regional crisis-reaction. The shift was triggered by the 2000 Fijian coup d'état and ethnic tensions in the Solomon Islands. Following the crisis in these two countries, a special Forum Foreign Ministers Meeting was held in August 2000 in Apia, Samoa, to discuss these events and to examine how the Forum could respond to similar problems in the future. At the Tarawa Summit in October 2000, PIF leaders announced that the declaration was a mechanism to address "some of the fundamental causes of political instability in the region associated with ethnic tensions, socio-economic disparity, lack of good governance, land disputes, and erosion of cultural values."[7] In fact the declaration was pushed by New Zealand and Australia, who wanted PIF to have a more audible voice in international issues.[8] Canberra and Wellington were indeed preoccupied with the growing problems of the South Pacific and PIF could serve as an apposite forum to project their own regional security interests. From the micro-states' point of view, however, there was reluctance and anxiety over giving a more active interventionist mandate to Biketawa. The document proclaimed that a conflict in any member state was now a regional responsibility, which could be a window of opportunity for political and military interventions. The interim Fijian prime minister, Laisenia Qarase, lobbied heavily to have the proposal thrown out. He received strong support from Melanesian and Micronesian countries but not enough to prevent the declaration from being adopted. New Zealand and Australia relied on Samoa, Kiribati and other smaller countries to get it through.[9] Biketawa has been invoked twice since its promulgation in 2000, in the Solomon Islands (RAMSI) and in Nauru (PRAN) (see below). Three election observer missions in the region—Bougainville, Solomon Islands, and Fiji—have also been undertaken under this framework.

The landmark Biketawa Declaration was preceded by the Honiara Declaration on Law Enforcement Cooperation, which recognized that an adverse law enforcement environment could threaten the sovereignty, security, and economic integrity of the Forum's members and jeopardize economic and social development; and by the Aitutaki Declaration, which established—at least on paper—mechanisms for preventive diplomacy, including use of the Forum Regional Security Committee, the good offices of the Forum's secretary-general, eminent persons, fact finding missions and third-party mediation. This latter declaration also adopted a comprehensive idea of security which included natural disasters, transnational crime including drug trafficking, and economic, social, and environmental policies. In 2002, the Forum decided also to adopt the Nasonini Declaration on Regional Security, which reaffirms the provisions included in the previous declarations and recognizes "the need for immediate and sustained regional action in response to the current regional security environment." In fact the Nasonini Declaration did not bring much novelty in the form of juridical or functional measures, and served simply to highlight further the region's concerns over, and response to, transnational crime and terrorism.

Three years after the establishment of PIF, the 34th summit tasked an Eminent Persons Group to carry out a review of the organization and to propose a new mandate and a new vision. The following year, PIF leaders met at a special retreat in Auckland where they formally adopted the new vision which declared that "leaders believe the Pacific region can, should and will be a region of peace, harmony, security and economic prosperity." It also identified good governance and security as two of the four key goals of the forum (Auckland Declaration). To give effect to the new vision it was agreed to draw up a plan for future action, and a Pacific Plan Task Force was created. In 2005 the Task Force issued the document Pacific Plan for Strengthening Regional Cooperation and Integration, which was accepted at the Port Moresby Meeting in 2005 as the blueprint for future cooperation in the region. In the Pacific Plan, the "pursuit of security" was included as one of the major goals of the organization and called for the implementation of the Pacific Islands Regional Security Technical Cooperation Strategy in border security, including for transnational crime, bio-security, and mentoring for national financial intelligence units.

This process of internal overhauling was to take another major step when at the same Port Moresby meeting leaders reached a consensus on the need to adopt a *new* Agreement Establishing the Pacific Islands Forum, which clearly established the PIF as an intergovernmental organization in accordance with international law. The new agreement again identified security as one of the goals of the organization (article II)—in line with the Auckland Declaration and the Pacific Plan. This agreement will, however, only be in force when it is ratified by all 16 members of the Forum—a process that is still pending. Until then the Forum's constitutional documentation will remain weak. As noted by Angelo regarding the first agreement, "its level of detail is minimal and the phraseology general."[10]

If there is no doubt about the strong legal mandate of PIF to engage in peace and security-related activities, its institutional capacity to exercise the mandate is less salient. Presently, the pre-eminent decision-making body of the Forum is the annual Forum Leader's Meeting, where heads of state gather to define guiding principles and strategies. The PIF's administrative arm is, however, the PIF Secretariat (headed by the secretary-general), based in Suva, Fiji. It is comprised of four main sections, including one on "political, legal and international" issues (it may also deal with security topics). The institutional capacity of PIF also includes the Forum's Official Committee, which gives general policy directions to the secretariat.

The Forum has also attained some progress in developing a natural disaster Regional Early Warning Strategy through a process of comprehensive multi-party consultation and integration of national and regional early warning systems. Given the geographically vulnerable situation of most of the Pacific Islands, the establishment of an early warning mechanism of this nature is of paramount importance. It is therefore justified that PIF has adopted a "human" element in its definition of security. Apart from the Aitutaki Declaration, at the 2007 PIF summit in Nuku'Alofa, member states have endorsed the "applicability of the human security concept to the region"[11] with a view to developing a regional human security framework that will provide a set of tools for preventing and addressing crises and conflicts. Along the same lines, the Pacific Plan Annual Progress Report of 2007 also puts the stress on the desire to secure "human" conditions, "not neglecting the importance of state or government security."[12]

But despite its conceptual freshness, the early warning mechanism's capacity to monitor political and military conflicts (and not only natural disasters) is underdeveloped. Often the Forum has to rely on the weak national capacity of its members to produce some data and is hence not able to ensure its quality nor inter-state coordination and harmonization. The lack of institutional capacity in monitoring, reporting, and policy formulation, and the difficulties in closing the early warning–response gap obliges the PIF to rely frequently on Australia and New Zealand, which risk being regarded as "interventionist" or "neo-colonial."[13] In fact, the 2005 report on Strengthening Regional Management: A Review of the Architecture for Regional Cooperation in the Pacific (the Hughes Report), commissioned by the PIF Secretariat, identified various institutional limitations. It was pointed out that PIF represented a collection of institutions that had evolved over time in an uncoordinated and ineffective fashion.[14] Indeed, the Secretariat has no standing crisis management organ to enable agile responses to impending crises. Nor is there any institution responsible for the crafting of long-term initiatives aimed at the structural prevention of conflict. The role of the secretary-general is essentially reactive, as he can only act after consultation with the PIF's leaders or in the implementation of a decision agreed by all of the Forum's leaders.[15] Even if the Secretariat has developed a Human Security Framework for Conflict Prevention (2009–2011) it will operate under the already existing (weak) mechanisms.

Moreover, the Forum has no formal rules governing its operations or the conduct of its meetings. The agenda is based on reports from the Secretariat and decisions by the leaders are reached by consensus and are outlined in a Forum communiqué, from which policies are developed and a work program is prepared. Hence, similarly to ASEAN (see Chapter 3), the decision-making process in PIF is also inspired by the "Pacific Way," a particular code of dealing with conflicts by means of negotiation, consensus, and non-interference.[16] Some authors even argue that the survival and the vitality of regional cooperation in the South Pacific is pivoted on this peculiar cultural affinity.[17] In practice, however, this is a much-debated concept. Some authors argue that the "Pacific Way" is an elite ideology that has served as a smokescreen for the defense of elite privileges and the smothering of popular discontent.[18] Moreover, PIF's recent interventions violate the traditional posture of non-intervention, consensus building, and sovereignty protection. As an illustration, former Australian prime minister John Howard used terms such as cooperative intervention to describe Australia's response to threatening situations in the Pacific, and did not rule out preventive and pre-emptive deployments. By the same token, the dispatching in 1997 of the New Zealand-led Truce Monitoring Group (not a PIF intervention) aimed at keeping the fragile peace in Bougainville, epitomizes the same willingness to intervene whenever regional stability is in jeopardy. Finally, in contrast to the "Pacific Way," PIF is gradually stepping back from its early preference for a lack of formality and legal structures. As the Forum broadens its mandate and engages in more complex security operations, the need to adopt a more substantial juridical architecture is accentuated.[19]

Operational experience

Despite the constant reiteration of the Forum's purpose to pursue regional security, its overall operational experience is low. PIF's operational experience cannot be disassociated from Australia and New Zealand's growing activism in the region. While their initiatives are formally discussed with PIF leaders, it is clear that the pace of conflict resolution in the region is set by these two countries. This is particularly evident in the dynamics behind the two major Pacific interventions, in Bougainville and in the Solomon Islands. In the former, New Zealand and Australia provided transport, supplies, aid, troops, police, security, and encouragement to the negotiators, without which the talks could not have been held at all.[20] In the latter, a PIF intervention, Australia's support was fundamental. Apart from the intervention in the Solomon Islands, PIF operational experience has been confined to election observation (e.g. Papua New Guinea, Nauru, Republic of Marshall Islands in 2007, and Nauru in 2008) and minor peacebuilding and peacemaking operations.

Regional Assistance Mission to the Solomon Islands (RAMSI)

The prevailing atmosphere of lawlessness and widespread extortion in the Solomon Islands prompted a formal request by the government for outside help.[21] The civil unrest was propelled by ethnic tensions and was mainly characterized by fighting between the Isatabu Freedom Movement (also known as the Guadalcanal Revolutionary Army) and the Malaita Eagle Force.[22] With the country bankrupt and the capital in chaos, the parliament passed the Facilitation of International Assistance Act 2003, which paved the way for RAMSI's deployment.[23] In August 2003 PIF leaders "endorsed" this "package of assistance" and noted that it was being provided under the framework of the Biketawa Declaration. The Forum further stressed:

> Recalling the *Outcome Statement* issued by Forum Foreign Affairs Ministers at their meeting in Sidney on 30 June 2003, Leaders warmly commended the swift and cooperative response of Forum members in deploying the agreed policing operation to help restore law and order, supported by armed peacekeepers, and a programme of assistance to strengthen the justice system and restore the economy and basic services.
>
> (Italics as original)[24]

In July 2003, Australian and Pacific Island police and troops arrived in the Solomon Islands under the auspices of the Australian-led Regional Assistance Mission to the Solomon Islands. A sizable international security contingent of 2,250 police and troops, led by Australia and New Zealand, and with representatives from about 20 other Pacific nations, began arriving the following month under Operation Helpem Fren ("Helping Friend" in Pidgin English).[25] Australia decided to intervene, first of all, because it took conscience of how weak and failing states can destabilize the region. The conflict is to some extent a product of the negative consequences of the instability in Bougainville. In the 1990s refugees, weapons, and a militaristic gun culture had flooded into the Solomon Islands and contributed to the deteriorating security situation.[26] Second, Australia was also concerned that the porousness of the Solomon Islands could also serve as an invitation card for transnational criminal operations such as identity fraud, money laundering, and drug trafficking. And since the Islands were financially bankrupt and vulnerable to external funds, there was a possibility that foreign powers with interests contrary to Australia would become involved with the governance of the country. The intervention was above all a product of the so-called "Howard Doctrine" which suggests that Australia should act in a deputy peacekeeping capacity to the global policing role of the United States. The Bali bombings and the "war on terror" encouraged the Australian government to intervene, if necessary by military means, to eliminate the threat of terrorism in the region.[27]

Currently RAMSI has a broad peacekeeping mandate. After the security situation in the country was stabilized, the focus turned to longerterm issues, such as economic reform, public sector restructuring, strengthening the machinery of government, and improving accountability and rebuilding the Solomon Islands Police Force. In PIF's view RAMSI is an operation carried out under article 52 (peacekeeping) and not 53 (peace enforcement) of the UN Charter.[28]

At the 2006 PIF summit in Nadi, the Forum decided to establish a task force to review RAMSI. The compelling report of the task force, submitted in June 2007, underlined that RAMSI had strong and widespread support throughout the Solomon Islands, highlighted the "excellent work" being done to strengthen key government institutions, and complimented its efforts on recovering the national economy and in ensuring external investments. However, the task force was also of the view that additional measures should be put in place to strengthen the regional character of RAMSI. Australia's predominance should be avoided.[29]

Peacebuilding and peacemaking

The major peacebuilding operation was carried out in Nauru. In 2004, at the PIF summit in Apia, the Forum "strongly supported Nauru's request for Forum assistance under the Biketawa Declaration recognizing Nauru's economic crisis and the threats this posed to its security and national stability"[30] and established the Pacific Regional Assistance for Nauru, covering many aspects of governance, economy and finance, social development, and environment and population. Under the Pacific Regional Assistance to Nauru (PRAN), Nauru has developed its own National Sustainable Development Strategy (NSDS) with the assistance of the PIF and the Asian Development Bank. This operation was unprecedented because the intervention was justified, and Biketawa was invoked, on the ground that the development and economic policies of Nauru were doing harm to its citizens. It is a palpable example of human security.

Other regional peacebuilding operations include, for instance, the 2003 Australia and Papua New Guinea (PNG) Enhanced Cooperation

Program (ECP) to help address PNG's development challenges in the areas of law and order, justice, economic management, public sector reform, border control, and transport security and safety; and the 1999 small New Zealand police mission in Bougainville as part of the Bougainville Community Policing Project (BCPP) to formally establish community-based policing. Despite the unequivocal regional nature of these missions, they have been established on a bilateral basis and not through PIF.

Besides peacebuilding, PIF also has some experience with peacemaking. The good offices function has been employed on many occasions, mainly through the establishment of ad hoc eminent persons groups (to undertake situation analyses) and ministerial missions. Examples of the first include the Eminent Persons Group visit to the Solomon Islands in 2002 to report on possible areas of assistance to the Forum. Examples of the latter include the PIF's ministerial mission to New Caledonia (ongoing since 1993) and the Ministerial Contact Group mission to Fiji (2008), established to further monitor the progress of Fiji's preparations for the elections and the return to democracy. The mission was not successful, however, and in May 2009 PIF took the decision to suspend Fiji given the poor democratic credentials of the military regime led by Frank Bainimarama.

Conclusion

Interventions by the major PIF powers, Australia and New Zealand, to put an end to conflicts or to assist in post-war reconstruction, are not new. But impelled perhaps by the terrorist attacks of 2001 and the Bali bombings of 2002, these two powers have re-invented their security approaches in the Pacific region.[31] This new orientation is what former Australian foreign minister Alexander Downer named "cooperative intervention"[32] and is triggered by the recognition that major instability in one country has the potential to affect the whole region. Arguing also for the relevance of the regional setting in the South Pacific, Wallensteen notes that, "similarities and parallels are more easily made within a regional setting. One [rebel] group may observe the actions of another and draw its own lessons for its own situation. There does not need to be an organizational link for this type of diffusion of conflict behavior." He adds that "the May 2000 hostages-taking in Fiji is likely to have been a direct inspiration to the MEF (Malatia Eagle Force) in Solomon Islands to try a similar tactic in June 2000."[33]

As this context is not likely to change in the near future, the PIF will remain as a strictly inter-governmental organization whose major achievements in peace and security are to offer political legitimacy to the regional interests of its major states. The preponderance of the major powers is not totally welcomed by the other member states. Papua New Guinea, the Solomon Islands, Vanuatu, and Fiji have strengthened their own links through the Melanesian Spearhead Group with headquarters in Port Vila, Vanuatu. But the security situation is very inviting. While regional stability is still an issue—ethnic strife in Papua New Guinea, Nauru's near-bankruptcy, Fiji's discrimination against Indians or Tonga's authoritarian monarchy—New Zealand and Australia will remain vigilant and predisposed to intervene.

In this context true regionalism will remain constrained. As enumerated by Graham, the major obstacles include the continual stress on national sovereignty which curbs the process of integration, or the still undefined idea of what the Pacific regional identity and purpose is.[34] This lack of robust regional institutional capacity is reflected in the low resource capacity of PIF. It comprises approximately 100 employees and its 2009 running budget is roughly only US$16.1 million (FJ$30.2 million).

Part IV
Europe

11 European Union (EU)[1]

With the end of the Second World War, the international political scenario favored the progressive integration of Europe. At its inception it was a project of political engineering aimed at fostering peace and resolving European conflicts. The Schuman Declaration of 1950 laid out a plan to build a peaceful and united Europe one step at a time. According to the French foreign minister, the pooling of coal and steel production should first create a "de facto solidarity" that would ultimately make war between France and Germany "materially impossible." This was the basis for the creation of the European Coal and Steel Community (ECSC) in 1951. In the early 1950s there was also an attempt to establish a European Defense Community (EDC), which entailed the symbolic formation of a European army only five years after the end of the Second World War. However, defense was considered a fundamental part of national sovereignty and few countries were prepared to give it up.

This wave of support for a united Europe led to the signature by "the Six"[2] of the Treaties of Rome in 1957 which resulted in the creation of the European Economic Community (EEC) and of the European Atomic Energy Community (EURATOM). Western Europe had clearly set itself on the path of economic integration.

The foreign policy of Europe was born of what was felt to be a need on the part of the member states of the European Economic Community to consult each other more effectively on foreign policy issues. In 1969, the six founding members issued a declaration (Hague Summit) which called for a "united Europe capable of assuming its responsibilities in the world of tomorrow and of making a contribution commensurate with its tradition and mission."[3] This paved the way for the emergence of the External Policy Cooperation (EPC) in the 1970s, a consultation structure based on periodic meetings between diplomats and ministers, which grew more complex as time progressed. The central objective of EPC was to create a forum where the regular exchange of information and periodic meetings between foreign ministers and senior officials was enabled in order to increase the weight of the EU (then EEC) in international affairs. EPC was, however, akin to "a private club, operated by diplomats, for diplomats."[4] Nevertheless, in 1986 the Single Act gave EPC a treaty base (article 30), codified procedures, created a secretariat in Brussels, and provided for better preparation of meetings.

The Treaty on European Union (adopted at Maastricht in 1992) was the logical outcome of 20 years of European political cooperation and a decisively new step. Its preamble declares the resolve of member states to implement a common foreign and security policy and the progressive framing of a common defense policy. In 1996, the Treaty of Amsterdam established a High Representative for the CFSP and the Policy Planning and Early Warning Unit (now called the Policy Unit), a small structure comprising some 20 people who help to pinpoint strategic options, flesh them out and implement them. It also paved the way for the incorporation in the frame of the EU of the "Petersberg Tasks," which included humanitarian and rescue tasks, peacekeeping, and tasks of combat forces in crisis management, including peacemaking.

At the end of the 1990s, the uneasiness with which the EU handled the Balkan wars served both to unveil the weaknesses of the CFSP and to persuade European leaders to further foreign policy cooperation.[5] This set the stage for the famous Saint-Malo meeting in 1998, where France and the UK agreed on a fundamental point: the EU should intervene in international affairs not only economically and commercially, but also in terms of security and defense.

At the June 1999 European Council in Cologne, member states agreed hence that "the European Union shall play its full role on the international stage" and should "assume its responsibilities regarding a common European policy on security and defense." This new European Security and Defense Policy (ESDP), a policy tool within the CFSP, was further refined in the Council summits in Helsinki (1999) and Feira (2000). It comprises both a civil and a military part—the civil part enables intervention in four domains: policing, civil protection, civil administration, and judicial administration. The military part is based on an instrument that enables the Union to constitute a combined force of 60,000 men from the member states' respective national armed forces and deploy them within 60 days for a period of up to a year.

Another major step was taken when the European Security Strategy (ESS) was adopted by the member states at the Brussels European Council of December 2003. It identifies the global challenges and key threats to the security of the Union and clarifies its strategic objectives in dealing with them, such as building security in the EU's neighborhood and promoting an international order based on effective multilateralism (Box 11.1). Biscop notes that "it is crucial for the success of the Strategy to recognize that it does not just concern security policy in the narrow sense, that is in the politico-military dimension, but that because of its distinctive and ambitious comprehensive approach it directly covers *all* dimensions of EU external action."[6] In December 2008 the European Council adopted a Report on the Implementation of the European Security Strategy—Providing Security in a Changing World, which reinforces (does not replace) the European Security Strategy. Adjusting to an ever-mutating global context, the report adds energy security and climate change to the list of key threats to Europe previously included in the European Security Strategy.

Box 11.1   The European Security Strategy (excerpts)

Key threats

Large-scale aggression against any Member State is now improbable. Instead, Europe faces new threats which are more diverse, less visible and less predictable:

Terrorism

Terrorism puts lives at risk; it imposes large costs; it seeks to undermine the openness and tolerance of our societies, and it poses a growing strategic threat to the whole of Europe. Increasingly, terrorist movements are well-resourced, connected by electronic networks, and are willing to use unlimited violence to cause massive casualties.

Proliferation of weapons of mass destruction

is potentially the greatest threat to our security. The international treaty regimes and export control arrangements have slowed the spread of WMD and delivery systems. We are now, however, entering a new and dangerous period that raises the possibility of

(*Box continued on next page*)

a WMD arms race, especially in the Middle East. Advances in the biological sciences may increase the potency of biological weapons in the coming years; attacks with chemical and radiological materials are also a serious possibility.

Regional conflicts

Problems such as those in Kashmir, the Great Lakes Region and the Korean Peninsula impact on European interests directly and indirectly, as do conflicts nearer to home, above all in the Middle East. Violent or frozen conflicts, which also persist on our borders, threaten regional stability.

State failure

Bad governance—corruption, abuse of power, weak institutions and lack of accountability—and civil conflict corrode States from within. In some cases, this has brought about the collapse of State institutions.

Organized crime

Europe is a prime target for organized crime. This internal threat to our security has an important external dimension: cross-border trafficking in drugs, women, illegal migrants, and weapons accounts for a large part of the activities of criminal gangs. It can have links with terrorism.

Source: Council of the EU website, www.consilium.europa.eu/

In 2004, European leaders adopted the Headline Goal 2010 where they made the commitment that by the year 2010 they would be capable of responding "with swift and decisive action applying a fully coherent approach" to the whole spectrum of crisis management operations covered by the Treaty of the EU and the European Security Strategy. These include humanitarian and rescue tasks, disarmament operations, support to third countries in combating terrorism, peacekeeping tasks and tasks of combat forces in crisis management, and peacemaking. These forces are generated on the basis of EU Battlegroups, a high readiness military force consisting of at least 1,500 combat soldiers which may be deployed within 5–10 days of approval by the Council.

In recent years the broadening and deepening of EU foreign policy has been punctuated by some political clashes between member states, inter-agency competition and, not seldom, policy incoherence. To address some of these aspects, European leaders signed the Lisbon Treaty in 2007. If ratified (not likely after rejection by Ireland in June 2008) the Treaty would ensure the establishment of the External Action Service—a foreign office or diplomatic corps. The Treaty would also create the post of EU Foreign Minister, which the document coined as "The High Representative of the Union for Foreign Affairs and Security Policy." The title might be too long to be used, but some EU countries were too reluctant to accept a title that could suggest a federalist track. Another EU example of political correctness.

Over the last 30 years the EU has, thus, been shaping its capacity to express its voice abroad. According to Habermas, Europe has a "second chance" to influence world history—this time through a "non imperial process of reaching understanding with, and learning from, the world."[7]

Organizational capacity

The EU has a strong legal capacity to operate in the domain of peace and security. The Treaty of the European Union states that "The Union shall define and implement a common foreign and security policy covering all areas of foreign and security policy" (art. 11), the objectives of which include safeguarding the common values, fundamental interests, independence, and integrity of the union, preserving peace, and strengthening international security. The legal mandate is therefore intra-regional and extra-regional. Similarly, for instance, to NATO or the CIS, the EU has the legal capacity to operate outside the juridical area comprised by its member states. And as the mandate and operational capacity of the EU have indeed been applied *abroad*, the EU does not regard itself as a Chapter VIII regional organization.

To exercise its mandate, all major EU organs are involved at various degrees of responsibility. As Keukeleire and MacNaughtan describe: "single by name, dual by regime, multiple by nature—this is the Union's institutional framework in a nutshell."[8] At the top of the decision-making process stands the European Council, which brings together the heads of state or government of the member states, along with the president of the Commission and the high representative for CFSP. It is a core institution for the CFSP since it notably defines its "principles and general guidelines." The Amsterdam Treaty also conferred on it an enhanced guiding role. For example, it is the European Council that adopts strategy documents such as the European Security Strategy.

Second, the European Commission, as the key collegial body, is to be "fully associated with the work carried out in the common foreign and security policy field" (Treaty of European Union, article 27). Analogously to member states, it is empowered to take initiatives in the CFSP field—but does not have, unlike the situation for the first pillar, a quasi-monopoly over initiatives. Represented in over 120 countries, the Commission has available to it very considerable human and financial resources: about 22,000 staff, the majority of which deals with issues with a soft security dimension, and a budget of €133.8 billion (2009).

The Commission has long experience in post-conflict institution-building, election observation, civil protection, and support to the UN, OSCE, and NGO operations in the field of rule of law, police, and civilian administration. It has also been long engaged in pre-crisis and conflict prevention, dealing with human rights monitoring, democracy programs, security sector reform, and good governance.[9] Within the Commission's structure, the European Humanitarian Aid Office (ECHO) coordinates humanitarian aid, funding of emergency and disaster relief; the European Agency for Reconstruction is responsible for managing the main EU assistance programs in the Western Balkans; the Directorate General for Development (DG DEV) formulates the development policy applicable to all developing countries, the Directorate-General for External Relations (DG RELEX) contributes to the formulation of an external relations policy, and the EuropeAid Co-operation Office is tasked to implement the external aid instruments of the European Commission and is responsible for the management of election observation missions.

Third, the Council of the European Union comprises the representatives of the member states. It plays an essential part in the domain of the CFSP and takes "the decisions necessary for defining and implementing the common foreign and security policy." It is the body that adopts all CFSP instruments and actions. Within the Council of the European Union, the CFSP falls within the remit of the General Affairs and External Relations Council (GAERC), composed of ministers of foreign affairs, and which in principle meets once a month. But the expansion of the EU's foreign policy competences means that foreign ministers now face an "impossibly overloaded agenda."[10] For instance at the GAERC meeting of 10–11 November 2008,[11] EU foreign ministers have debated the Congo, the EU–Russia summit, the Western Balkans, Afghanistan, Iraq, the Financing for Development Conference, regional integration and the European partnership agreements, and the food crisis!

The most important implementation arm is, nevertheless, the Political and Security Committee (PSC—commonly referred to by the French acronym COPS). The COPS is the linchpin of the CFSP and the ESDP and deals with management and policy-making on political and security issues on a daily basis. But the person who embodies the foreign policy of the EU and prepares most decisions before they are presented for decision is the high representative for CFSP (SG/HR). He may also appoint special representatives to pursue CFSP and ESDP policies in clearly designated matters, such as the Middle East or Kosovo. Other relevant institutions include the Policy Planning and Early Warning Unit (Policy Unit), the Joint Situation Centre (SITCEN), the Committee of Permanent Representatives (COREPER), the EU Military Committee (EUMC), the EU Military Staff (EUMS), the Committee of Civilian Aspects of Crisis Management (CIVCOM), and the European Union Monitoring Mission (EUMM). Finally, although it does not have co-decision powers, the European Parliament nevertheless exercises significant influence over the CFSP on the basis of the opinions and policy focuses it ex-presses and by exercising its budgetary powers. Its Committee on Foreign Affairs, Human Rights, Common Security and Defense Policy and its Sub-Committee on Security and Defense represent important fora for debating foreign policy.[12]

The major shortcoming in the institutional capacity of the EU is internal coordination. Article 3 of the TEU stipulates that "the Union shall in particular ensure the consistency of its external activities as a whole in the context of its external relations, security, economic and development policies. The Council and the Commission shall be responsible for ensuring such consistency and shall cooperate to this end." In practice this has been very difficult to attain. It often happens that both the Commission and the member states intervene in a crisis with different instruments, and this generates confusion at the European level as well as with third parties. The multiplicity of projects, missions, and initiatives available to manage a crisis jeopardizes EU's influence, instead of strengthening it.

Operational experience

The EU is the regional organization with the greatest experience in peace and security, whether measured in terms of financial resources or in the quantity of missions deployed. Its areas of intervention are wide. In conflict prevention the EU operates through various channels that include development cooperation and external assistance, trade policy instruments, humanitarian aid, social and environmental policies, diplomatic instruments and political dialogue, cooperation with international partners and NGOs, and crisis management instruments. Indeed, *structural prevention* is a key facet of EU external action. More than half of the official development assistance (ODA) worldwide comes from the EU or its individual member states, making the EU the world's biggest aid donor, paying out more than €30 billion a year in official aid. The EU is also involved in *preventive diplomacy* in various theaters. Particularly important in this regard is the work of the high representative of CFSP (and its special representatives) virtually on the whole range of political and security crises occurring worldwide. Preventive diplomacy is also undertaken within specifically designed policy frameworks, such as the European Neighborhood Policy, which provides financial assistance to countries on the fringes of Europe so long as they meet the conditions of government and economic reform.

The most visible facet of EU foreign policy is, however, its military operations outside the EU's territorial area. Although it is not within the scope of this book to go into the detail of each operation, the list below provides a useful overview of the missions launched by the EU since 2003. These cover three continents with different objectives across the whole conflict cycle (conflict prevention, peacemaking, and peacebuilding) and differing dimensions in terms of budget and personnel. As of late 2008 the EU had launched over 20 ESDP operations around the globe, although mostly in Africa and the Balkans. As was shown above, this increase in activity was accompanied by a considerable build-up in terms of institutional capacity in Brussels and policy coordination among member states. While this process refers mainly to the intergovernmental pillar of CFSP (managed by the Council), the European Commission continues to play a crucial role in security terms. The new financial "Instrument for Stability"[13] is a clear demonstration of the activeness of the Commission in this field.

EU's peacekeeping, peace enforcement, and peacebuilding operations include: EU Military Operation in the Former Yugoslav Republic of Macedonia (Concordia) (2003); EU Military Operation in Bosnia and Herzegovina (EUFOR-Althea) (since 2004); Aceh Monitoring Mission (AMM) (2005–6); EU Military Operation in Chad/Central African Republic (EUFOR TCHAD/RCA) (2008–9); EU Police Mission in Bosnia-Herzegovina (EUPM) (since 2003); EU Border Assistance Mission at Rafah Crossing Point in the Palestinian Territories (EU BAM Rafah) (since 2005); EU Integrated Rule of Law Mission for Iraq (Eujust Lex) (since 2005); EU Police Mission in Kinshasa (DRC) (EUPOL Kinshasa) (since 2005); EU Security Sector Reform Mission in the Democratic Republic of the Congo (EUSEC DR Congo) (since

2005); EU Support to AMIS II (since 2005); EU Planning Team in Kosovo (since 2006); EU Police Mission in the Palestinian Territories (EUPOL COPPS) (since 2006); EU Police mission in Afghanistan (EUPOL AFGHANISTAN) (since 2007); EU Rule of Law Mission in Kosovo (EULEX Kosovo) (since February 2008); EU mission in support of security sector reform in the Republic of Guinea-Bissau (EU SSR GUINEA-BISSAU) (since June 2008); EU Police Mission in the Former Yugoslav Republic of Macedonia (Proxima) (2003–5); EU Military Operation in the Democratic Republic of Congo (Artemis) (2003); EU Rule of Law Mission in Georgia (Eujust Themis) (2004–5); EU Police Advisory Team in the Former Yugoslav Republic of Macedonia (EUPAT) (2005–6); EUFOR RD Congo (2006); the European Union Monitoring Mission in Georgia (EUMM) (since October 2008); and the EU military operation in Somalia (EU NAVFOR Atalanta) (since December 2008).

At first glance this is impressive, and the image established in the past of the EC/EU being a payer more than a player in security, seems to no longer stand. Politically, diplomatically, and economically the EU is already present in all the most relevant areas of crisis, including Afghanistan, Iraq, Palestine, and Kosovo. Increasingly it is becoming involved also through military and civilian operations.

Following the disaster of the Balkans in the 1990s, it became evident that the post-Cold War security environment would all but ease Europe of responsibilities and that the purely "civilian power"[14] profile of the EC could not be maintained. Gradually, this principle became largely accepted also by the "neutral" member states (the Nordic countries, Ireland, Austria). This strategic concept emerges quite clearly from the European Security Strategy and permeates the whole evolution of CFSP/ESDP.

This process is far from being concluded and a number of dilemmas remain open, and are reflected in the operational experience itself. The first dilemma lies between the ambition to transform the EU into a fully fledged global player in security and the budgetary and capability constraints coming from the member states. Although EU member states have officially a combined 2 million personnel in their armed forces, only a meager 10–15 percent is estimated to be deployable.[15] The situation in terms of equipment is quite similar. There are plenty of redundancies, inefficiencies, and lack of basic equipment (particularly logistics, airlift, and intelligence gathering) that is crucial to today's operations. Considering the current economic downturn in Europe and the fact that European societies are largely unwilling to accept high spending on defense, some consider it inevitable for member states to accelerate the process of reorganization of their defense sector, through cooperation, integration, and more interoperability and rationalization. ➤ The second dilemma points to the need for effectiveness and rapid reaction mechanisms in the security field on the one hand, and to the member states' commitment to maintaining a strong control, namely, through unanimity. While this is not an absolute impediment to the EU when designing long-term strategies, it can often create stalemate in crisis situations. Further, it leads to the adoption of package deals also in this field, which makes it more difficult to prioritize a particular area or theme. All in all, this is particularly damaging to a common foreign and security policy (and, indirectly, to ESDP) and hampers the EU from projecting its political authority towards the outside world.

The third dilemma is linked to the identity of the EU as a new type of international actor. This opposes, on the one hand, the need for military power, and on the other hand, the precious capital in terms of the soft power of attraction accumulated during the organization's years as a civilian actor.[16] The solution seems to lie in a combination of various instruments, in a "policy mix" between structural and traditional foreign policy approaches[17] which remains the trademark of the EU's external relations. The complex institutional structure set up in Brussels to govern the civilian and military dimensions of the operations is revealing of this tension. This, however, reverberates also in the relationship between EU institutions across pillars—namely the Commission and the Council secretariat—also in the context of the pending institutional reforms (the Lisbon Treaty).

Finally, one last dilemma concerns the autonomy of ESDP vis-à-vis external actors. The United States and NATO are the classic examples of this problem, where the EU builds up independent structures while at the same time maintaining strong links with the former (also in operations and headquarters, for instance through the so-called Berlin Plus agreements with NATO). The UN is also a very good case in point. Within the rhetoric of effective multilateralism, cooperation is certainly improving (UN–EU joint declaration on crisis management, 2003) but coordination with the UN operationally and strategically is not always easy. Being a regional organization with the ambition to act not only within its territory or neighborhood, but also out of area, the EU struggles to fit into the UN Charter's framework for regional agreements, and particularly refuses, as mentioned earlier, to be categorized as a "Chapter VIII organization."

These four dilemmas are not bereft of consequences on the ground. First, most ESDP operations are limited in mandate, personnel, and timeframe, and tend to be rather "safe" in military terms. The EU has so far only sent peacebuilding civilian operations to the difficult theaters of Afghanistan, Iraq, and Palestine. These missions are largely symbolic, serving the purpose of showing the activity of the EU on those fronts, but do not always provide an actual solution to the security problem. In short, the "effectiveness" question becomes cogent. An exception to this is the ambitious mission of EUFOR Chad/RCA, deploying about 3,700 peacekeeping troops with the participation of 22 member states, in a very difficult operational theater. Importantly though, most of the troops are French and the operation's headquarters is also based in France. One can expect that further experience of the new institutional structures (not least the EU Operations Centre, set up in 2007 in Brussels within the EU military staff) will pave the way for even more ambitious missions. However, the budget and personnel constraints among member states remain.

Second, EU member states also use frameworks other than ESDP to deploy their troops abroad, e.g. NATO or the UN directly. This is particularly true for high-risk operations such as in Afghanistan and Lebanon. On the one hand, the EU is still not considered to be always the ideal tool and, on the other hand, member states try to maintain a degree of autonomy over their defense policies. While it is good that various options are available for engaging in security operations, this complex situation creates the potential for overlaps, competition among organizations, and confusion.

Finally, unanimity is burdensome, both in terms of decision-making and implementation. A clear tendency exists in ESDP to proceed under the leadership of one or more member states (taking responsibility for costs, personnel, headquarters), rather than having everybody joining. The idea of "core groups" brought forward by Keukeleire[18] seems relevant here regarding CFSP as well as ESDP. The insertion in the Lisbon Treaty of the idea of permanent structured cooperation, which would encourage the cooperation in defense of the willing and able member states, is another demonstration of this problem

Conclusion

The history of the ESDP process has been a *reactive* one that developed in the context of a certain set of circumstances, instead of a *proactive* one, promoted for internal European strategies.[19] Wars and crises in the EU's back yard have been the real catalysts for the development of autonomous instruments to address international threats and challenges. Since the first ESDP mission in FYROM in 2003, there have been five military missions, three military support missions, seven police missions, two border control missions, three rule of law missions and one peace monitoring mission. Of the twenty, only five have been purely military and most of the remaining have been Civilian Crisis Management (CCM) missions, taking place in three different continents.[20] Despite this large extension of missions, the EU has been able to develop its security capabilities without "losing its soul" as a new type of "civilian" foreign policy actor.

A number of challenges lie ahead in the establishment of a more coherent and defined defense identity. The problem of the reorganization by the member states of their defense spending, the problem of the unanimity rule in ESDP, the problem of the balance between civilian and military means, the problem of the relations of ESDP with other security actors and organizations: all these questions are intrinsically linked with the problem of the nature and of the future of the EU as a regional organization and as a global player, and on the commitment of member states to invest in it. The debate on institutional reform, which has been almost continuous following the Maastricht Treaty, has somewhat concealed the enormous advances achieved in the foreign policy, security, and defense field, and the strong commitment that most member states have, particularly towards ESDP. As the case of the European Defense Agency, set up before the ratification of the Constitutional Treaty, shows, this is an area where European states want to cooperate. The 2008 French presidency's prioritization of progress in this field is quite indicative in this sense.

Unlike the general orientation of most scholars[21] it is pointless to use the United States as a benchmark for evaluating the ESDP. Rather, the EU contribution to the world order should be considered within a broad conception of security that comprises a vast array of old and new threats, where the military is only one among many policy tools. To be more effective, the EU needs to use its military and civilian resources for crisis management and the whole spectrum of civilian issues, aiming at promoting economic reform, development, good governance, stabilization, and conflict prevention.[22] Thereby, the political will of the member states and the quality of their commitment in providing peace and security represent the most challenging requirements to fulfill, if the EU wants to play a coherent and effective role in crisis management. The elaboration of a new European Security Strategy and the development of a European Strategic Culture are essential to this end.

12 North Atlantic Treaty Organization (NATO)[1]

The roots of the Atlantic Alliance can be traced back to the Treaty of Dunkirk (1947) and the Brussels Treaty (1948). Whereas through the first the UK and France agreed to give mutual support to each other should the event of a renewed German aggression occur, the Brussels Treaty, signed by Britain, France, Belgium, The Netherlands, and Luxembourg, created a collective-defense Alliance that was also aimed at "strengthening of economic, social and cultural ties between the signatories." Although both made reference to Germany, underneath the formal letter of the treaties, "the German threat" was used, in fact, to cloud the real intention of the signatories, which was to create a defense system against the Soviet Union.[2]

In 1948, encouraged by this new context, President Harry Truman and Secretary of State Dean Acheson decided to reverse America's former isolationism in favor of a policy of active economic and military combat against communism throughout the world. The North Atlantic Treaty Organization (NATO) was the military embodiment of this doctrine. It encompassed 10 European states (Belgium, Denmark, France, Iceland, Italy, Luxembourg, The Netherlands, Norway, Portugal, and the UK) plus Canada and the United States in a deliberate endeavor to protect Europe against the Soviet Union and the expansion of communism.[3] As the first NATO secretary-general, Hastings Lionel Ismay, stated, famously the Alliance's mandate was "to keep the Russians out, the Americans in, and the Germans down."

However, NATO was more of a political than a military organization until the Korean War (1950–53), when the military threat started to be concrete and the Europeans began to be persuaded that the time for a stronger Alliance had arrived. An integrated military structure controlled by two American supreme commanders was thereby established at the beginning of the 1950s. Unsurprisingly, the organization was initially equipped mainly with American assets until the Lisbon conference in 1952, when the Allies decided that it was time to provide the necessary forces for long-term missions and to extend their military capacities to better fulfill their mandate. During the Cold War NATO's policy was hence based on two principles. The first was to maintain adequate military strength and political unity to deter aggression and other forms of military or political pressure. The second was to pursue a policy aimed at a relaxation of tensions between East and West—a policy based to a large extent on general military strength.

After the end of the Cold War, NATO had to adjust its mandate, missions, and scope to the changed international environment, as its original raison d'être of defending Europe from the Soviet threat was no longer valid. The first step came in the early 1990s, when NATO started to cooperate with states from the former Soviet sphere. Most of the former Soviet bloc countries signed the Partnership for Peace and showed interest in joining NATO later on. The second step was taken at the Washington summit in April 1999, where a new strategic concept commensurate with the twenty-first century security challenges, and aiming at rethinking and strengthening NATO's presence on the international scene, was approved.

The new NATO Strategic Concept reaffirmed the traditional purpose of providing "security and freedom" for its members through both political and military means, but it innovated by enlarging its concept of security and its area of potential operation. The Concept notes that

> The security of the Alliance remains subject to a wide variety of military and non-military risks which are multi-directional and often difficult to predict. These risks include uncertainty and instability in and around the Euro-Atlantic area and the possibility of regional crises at the periphery of the Alliance, which could evolve rapidly. Some countries in and around the Euro-Atlantic area face serious economic, social and political difficulties.[4]

It further dissociates NATO from a Chapter VIII organization as its mandate was enlarged to operate out-of-area. NATO still is a European organization, but its scope became global. The Strategic Concept provides also for the establishment of a European Security and Defense Identity (ESDI) within the Alliance, "by being prepared to make available assets and capabilities for operations." At the Washington summit it was also agreed that terrorism and the proliferation of weapons of mass destruction (WMD) were key challenges for the Alliance. NATO acted in this framework in September 2001, when, for the first time, the article 5 mutual defense clause was invoked, following the terrorist attacks on

American territory. Ever since, NATO has not halted the process of political and military transformation. As a result, at the Bucharest summit of April 2008, member states decided to continue their efforts to deploy and sustain more forces, to review the peacetime establishment of the NATO command structure, and to increase defense spendings.

At present, NATO provides a crucial forum of consultation between North America and Europe on security and defense issues, and it serves as a regional and strategic stabilizer.[5] The cooperation and commitment of the member states is based on the common values of democracy, rule of law, peaceful resolution of disputes and, of course, the indivisibility of security for all its member states. However, despite the image of solidarity and strong internal cohesion, there have been internal divisions and diverging strategies among the member states, namely on Bosnia, Kosovo, Iraq, and Afghanistan.

Organizational capacity

The legal capacity of NATO derives primarily from the North Atlantic Treaty of 1949, where member states agreed that, "an armed attack against one or more of them in Europe or North America shall be considered an attack against them all" (art. 5). Thus the guiding principle by which NATO works is the common commitment and mutual cooperation among sovereign states in support of the indivisibility of security for all its members. Inspired by the end of the Cold War, the adoption of the Strategic Concept in 1999 enlarged the legal mandate of the Alliance. The Concept is an authoritative statement of the objectives of the organization, and provides the highest level of guidance on the political and military means to be used in achieving them. The Alliance is committed to a broad approach to security, recognizing the importance of political, economic, social, and environmental factors in addition to the indispensable defense dimension. In pursuit of its policy of preserving peace and enhancing security and stability as set out in the Strategic Concept, NATO may also conduct non-article 5 crisis response operations.

In 2006, NATO has also adopted the Comprehensive Political Guidance (CPG) aimed at outlining a framework and political direction for NATO's continuing transformation. The CPG was produced to support the Strategic Concept, but it does little to settle the debate about NATO's overarching purpose. Hence, energy is being put in preparing a new Strategic Concept which was commissioned at the April 2009 Strasbourg and Kehl summit. As the British secretary of state for defense puts its to justify the revised Concept, "the 1999 Strategic

Concept has served NATO well, but the security environment has changed significantly and NATO has changed with it."[6] It will hence be a critical opportunity for member states to discuss reform in a number of important areas including enlargement, capabilities, and partnerships. The armed conflict in Georgia in the summer of 2008 has also sparked internal debate over the political reverberation of NATO's keenness in inviting Georgia and Ukraine to join the Alliance, countries which Russia sees as within its sphere of influence.

To exercise its legal mandate NATO has a double-layered structure, consisting of civilian and military bodies. However, the key political decision-making body and the only body established by the North Atlantic Treaty is the North Atlantic Council (NAC). The Council brings together representatives of all member countries to discuss policy or operational issues. It provides a forum for wide-ranging consultation between members on all issues affecting their security. The NAC is supported by several specialized committees such as the Policy Coordination Group, the Political Committee, the Military Committee and the Senior Civil Emergency Planning Committee. Yet, the most relevant civilian is the secretary-general, elected for four years and endowed with an ample mandate. He is the chairman of the NAC and the Defence Planning Committee (DAC) and takes overall responsibility for the executive capacity of NATO. On the military side, the highest authority is the Military Committee, which brings together member states' military representatives. It provides recommendations and strategic orientation over the overall military conduct of the organization. It advises NATO's two Strategic Commanders: the Supreme Allied Commander Transformation (SACT) and the Supreme Allied Commander Europe (SACEUR).

By adopting the 1999 Strategic Concept, crisis management is considered to be a fundamental security task of NATO. It can involve both military and non-military measures of response to a threat. In addition to the ones mentioned above, NATO has different mechanisms in place to deal with crises. For example the NATO Crisis Management Process represents a number of systems and structures which are available to deal with crises. The process consists of four principal elements: the NATO Crisis Response System (NCRS), the NATO Intelligence Warning System (NIWS), NATO's Operational Planning System and NATO Civil Emergency Planning Crisis Management Agreements.

The most fundamental recent innovation in NATO's military organizational capacity is the establishment of the NATO Response Force (NRF). The NRF is a force of 25,000 troops—involving air, land, and sea components—and special forces that could be deployed upon five

days' notice for up to one month. The force was considered fully functional at the 2006 Riga summit but so far it is not getting the capabilities
that it needs to carry out the full range of missions. Yet, as pointed out
in Chapter 1, the readiness to deploy is one of the major assets of
international organizations, when compared to more stagnant bodies
such as the UN.

For this complex organizational architecture to work with agility, a
swift decision-making structure is essential. However, NATO's decisions are taken by consensus. The process does not require a government to vote in favor of a particularly complex decision, but rather to
object explicitly if it opposes such a decision. Though consensus is an
important tool for maintaining political solidarity for controversial
measures that are often related to armed conflict and state-survival, at
the same time there can be political costs "due to the sparring and the
time involved in reaching consensus."[7] This has inspired the Alliance
to use a degree of subterfuge. Often states may invoke the so-called
"silence procedure," under which any member state objecting to a
measure might send the secretary-general a letter stating its opposition.
There is also a procedure where the Supreme Allied Commander
Europe (SACEUR) and other commanders can draft informal defense
plans without the official authorization of the NAC. To overcome this
hindrances some authors argue that NAC decisions should be taken by
qualified majority voting instead.[8] In practice, however, this remains
illusive as the veto power is the only procedure through which the
United States controls decision-making at NAC and small states
ensure that their interests are safeguarded.

NATO's comprehensiveness is both its asset and its liability. The
extension of its mandate and membership produced a multiplicity of
committees and advisory bodies, and raised the level of bureaucracy.
There are approximately 4,200 people working at NATO headquarters:
2,100 members of national delegations and staff of national military
representatives, 400 members of missions of NATO partners, 1,200
civilians of the international staff or agencies located in the headquarters
and 500 members of the international military staff. But despite its heavy
machinery NATO still plays a fundamental role in international relations, as it represents a "community of values" related to the security of
its members.[9]

Operational experience

During the Cold War, as a collective security organization NATO was
successful at containing the perceived Soviet threat without intervening

militarily. In the early 1990s, however, the new and more comprehensive mandate presupposed a new international responsibility. NATO has hence been involved in various military operations, namely peacekeeping and peace enforcement. It has extended both its geographic reach and the range of its operations. In Bosnia it has deployed Operation Deliberate Force (1992–95), and Implementation Force (IFOR) (December 1995–December 1996), which was followed by Stabilization Force (SFOR) (December 1996–December 2004). But the most visible mission in the Balkans was Operation Allied Force (March–June 1999), tasked to force Serbia to withdraw its troops from Kosovo. This mission incurred high humanitarian and social costs, which together with the absence of a UNSC authorization generated a strong reaction around the world. Since June 1999, NATO has put in place the Kosovo Force (KFOR) with some 15,000 international troops. In Macedonia, the Alliance has deployed three missions: Task Force Harvest (August–September 2001), Operation Amber Fox (September 2001–December 2002), and Operation Allied Harmony (December 2002–March 2003), aimed at minimizing the risk of destabilization in the country.

These initial efforts in Europe have been complemented over the last years with muscular operations "out of area." Article 6 of the NATO Treaty limited the Alliance's geographic reach to being "on the territory of any of the parties in Europe or North America, on the Algerian Departments of France, on the territory of or on the Islands under the jurisdiction of any of the parties in the North Atlantic area north of the Tropic of Cancer." Nevertheless, the end of the Cold War compelled NATO to overhaul these geographic parameters.

In Iraq, NATO trains and supports the development of security institutions, which includes help building effective armed forces and providing them with equipment and technical assistance. In Darfur, NATO provided training and technical assistance to the African Union Mission in Sudan. In Pakistan, NATO airlifted supplies donated by Alliance members and other countries into the earthquake-stricken region of Kashmir and provided medical relief. In Somalia NATO assists the AU mission by providing airlift support to African states willing to deploy in Somalia under AMISOM and is involved in an anti-piracy naval operation in the Gulf of Aden. NATO is also providing capacity-building support to the AU's long-term peacekeeping capabilities, in particular the African Standby Force. The most important mission is, however, the International Security Assistance Force (ISAF) in Afghanistan which has been under NATO command and control since 2003. ISAF was launched to enable the Afghan Transitional Administration and the UN Assistance Mission in Afghanistan to operate in the area around Kabul. Later on, the operation was expanded, covering other parts of the country via Provincial Reconstruction Teams (PRT). The mission, with approximately 50,000 troops, is the "most challenging mission since the Alliance was formed."[10] Given the distance from Europe, the technical complexity and the operational environment, ISAF would have been an unimaginable mission just 15 years ago. But currently it is marred with problems: insurgency is spreading, the country is still politically fragmented, and the opium production has reached alarming and unprecedented levels. There is still resentment among European leaders that the United States has abandoned its commitments in Afghanistan to focus on an unpopular war in Iraq, leaving to the Europeans the difficult task of pacifying the thorny political situation.

NATO has a substantial operational record for an organization that some considered defunct and purposeless after the Cold War.[11] Given that the Soviet Union never invaded any of the NATO allies, the Alliance can be considered a successful military pact. Presently, it is unequivocally the largest military and security organization in the world. Yet, the recent extension of the range of its operations has raised important questions.

The first concerns the development of civilian conflict management skills. Although NATO is still perceived as a purely military organization, in fact it serves as a valuable asset in the framework of humanitarian assistance, as showcased in Pakistan. But this mission unveiled also a pressing need for greater coordination with various actors in the field of civilian management. Analogously, the Comprehensive Political Guidance recommended that the Alliance focus on civilian–military relations. This would involve increasing NATO's technical capacity in drafting and implementing peace accords; demobilizing and reintegrating combatants; designing and enforcing civil and criminal legal systems; training local police; fashioning, staffing and training for civil services; and reconstructing and operating public utilities.

The second important question is the interaction with other intergovernmental organizations, namely the United Nations. In September 2005, the NATO secretary-general proposed a framework agreement regarding NATO–UN cooperation, but the UN has shown some hesitation in adopting the document. In fact a Joint Declaration on UN/NATO Secretariat Cooperation was adopted in September 2008 by the secretaries-general of both organizations but its circulation was surprisingly (and apparently purposefully) limited. The central question remains whether the cooperation should be highly institutionalized or be confined to selective cooperation.[12] In the future there may even be a problem of overlap between the two organizations. In recent years, but more emphatically since the Riga summit of 2006, NATO has debated how to deepen relations with countries beyond the transatlantic community, starting with partners such as Australia, Japan, and New Zealand. The Alliance's secretary-general has often conveyed the idea that NATO's needs "global partners" to face global threats such as terrorism and WMD.[13] It has even been suggested that the Alliance should offer membership "to any democratic state in the world that is willing and able to contribute to the fulfillment of NATO's responsibilities."[14] If NATO goes global it will likely clash with the aspirations of the only global authority which might legitimize the use of military force: the United Nations.

Third, although NATO's operational and organizational capacities are not directly dependent on EU resources, the fact that both organizations overlap in terms of mandate (peacekeeping and peace enforcement) and membership (21 member states in common) makes the EU an important agent for the Alliance. Albeit the EU and NATO were able to negotiate successfully the "Berlin Plus" agreement in 2002, which allowed the EU to draw on some of NATO's military assets for its own peacekeeping operations, the relationship between both organizations "is plagued by mistrust, unhealthy competition, and information sharing problems."[15] On several occasions Turkey, Cyprus, and Greece—for their own political reasons—have blocked greater cooperation between both organizations. There is plenty of room for maneuver at this level, however. The EU and NATO could, for instance, strengthen the relationship between the NATO Response Force and the EU Battlegroups. Both could also adopt a "reverse Berlin Plus" which would allow NATO access to the EU's civilian capacities. At the Riga summit the Alliance indeed decided that a comprehensive approach engaging military and civilian international actors was required to meet new international challenges. At the Bucharest summit in 2008, NATO agreed on an action plan to take this forward, but at the time of writing no major breakthrough has been attained.

Conclusion

Since its creation, NATO has faced, and been able to survive, various crises by engaging in successful (and often arduous) adjustment processes. Even if recent events—such as the crisis over whether to provide defensive measures to protect Turkey in the event that Iraq decided to attack, or George W. Bush's decision to act without NATO to retaliate over the 9/11 strikes—have laid a cloud of suspicion over the value of the Alliance, the past is also prolific in crises of transatlanticism. These include the 1956 Suez Canal crisis, the French withdrawal from NATO integrated military command in 1966, and President Ronald Reagan's decision to bomb Libya in 1986. The Vietnam War, the Soviet invasion of Afghanistan, Germany's Ostpolitik, or the US military interventions in Grenada and Panama, have also reflected serious political differences. But NATO has revealed a vital capacity to survive and remain relevant. The current challenge is to shift from being a twentieth-century collective security provider in Europe, to becoming one of the twenty-first century's peace and security providers in the wider world.

But in the process NATO has to address some important matters. The case of Yugoslavia has shown that NATO has underestimated the potential consequences of its non-authorized actions. The civilian casualties, the destruction of fundamental infrastructures, and the humanitarian consequences of this operation have been amplified by the fact that the missions were not authorized by the UN Security Council. As long as public opinion and other international actors are persuaded that NATO epitomizes the unilateral will of US strategies, NATO will continue to be regarded with some unease by some agents.

This, together with the disparity between American and European contributions in terms of financial resources[16] and military equipment, represents one of the most difficult problems to overcome. From the European perspective, the United States concentrates too much on strictly military resources, instead of tilting the budget more in favor of civilian capabilities. From the American point of view, Europe expects more and pays less. In fact the EU has 27 different military systems, budgets, and internal structures dealing with defense. This means that the European resources are often used in a dispersive way and the internal fragmentation remains a difficult obstacle to overcome. As pointed out by Jaap De Hoop Scheffer, "Europe's defense sector remains fragmented, which leads to duplication, unhelpful competition from too many rival systems, and, significant capability gaps or incompatibilities."[17] Albeit the Prague summit produced an informal pledge from the member states to meet a 2 percent gross national product spending level for national defense, increasing the European budget for defense is not an optimal solution if it is not parallel to an effort to standardize the expenditures and the systems of those states that are both NATO and EU members.[18]

Despite all the challenges it has to face, a retrospective look at the Alliance detects major accomplishments. Apart from the attainment of the yearned-for objective of deterring the Soviet Union, the eastern expansion of NATO's membership has played an important part in stabilizing democratic civil–military relations in the new member states.[19] But NATO is at a crossroads and its future is not yet clear.

13 Conclusions

It is unquestionable that international organizations have become prominent agents in regional security. It is difficult today to foresee a situation where a violent conflict will not result in some form of conflict management initiative by an international organization. From a quantitative perspective, we have witnessed over the last decade an exponential increase in the number of such organizations; today there is virtually no region in the world which is not covered by some kind of institutional arrangement tailored to promote economic cooperation, development, or peace and security. From a qualitative perspective, these organizations are gradually extending their mandates and their operational experience in political and security matters, engaging not only with soft security issues but also with robust and traditional peacekeeping and even supranational political representation. For instance, the EU represents European interests in WTO negotiations and the AU participated in the 2008 G8 summit in Hokkaido. But despite their potential, these regional bodies are not flawless. In Chapter 1 we brought to light the existence of conundrums that warranted reflection and critical analysis. These included (i) capacity, (ii) partiality, (iii) hegemony, (iv) priority, (v) overlapping, (vi) absence of institutions or mandate in peace and security, (vii) inter-organizational information-sharing, and (viii) mandate. The critical analysis in the book corroborated that these puzzles are likely to set the policy and academic agenda in the future.

Capacity

The organizational capacity of an organization to undertake peace and security depends on two aspects: first, the constitutional provisions according it the mandate to become active; and second, the institutional mechanisms through which it can function and exercise that mandate. Presently, most regional organizations operate in peace and security under a clear legal mandate. In most cases the mandate is given explicitly by the founding document (e.g. the Constitutive Act of the AU or the Treaty of the EU), whereas in others legal provisions have been adopted at a later stage through the signature of specific protocols and other legally binding documents (e.g. ECOWAS' Protocol for Conflict Prevention, Management, Resolution, Peacekeeping and Security; PIF's Biketawa Declaration; or LAS' Mechanism for Conflict Prevention, Management and Resolution Between Arab States). These specific conventions are predominantly adopted to ensure or legitimize a mandate extension or to provide clear benchmarks and administrative guidance over the operational capacity of an organization. Yet, some other organizations—not covered in the book—lack a legal mandate altogether. The Community of Portuguese Speaking Countries (CPLP) and the Caribbean Community (CARICOM), although they have considerable experience in peace and security, have neglected the need to adopt constitutional provisions that would endow them with an unambiguous mandate. There are no indications that they will rectify the situation soon.

In terms of institutional capacity most organizations today have adopted a fairly functional administrative architecture. But apart from the general organic structure of the organizations, it is important to assess their organizational capacities and the operational experience in the specific areas of conflict prevention, peacekeeping, peace enforcement, and peacebuilding (see below). The case of peacekeeping is illustrative of the discrepancies between the different organizations. Out of the 11 organizations included in this book, all except ASEAN have a mandate to conduct either traditional or robust peacekeeping operations. Nevertheless, only two of them, NATO and the EU, have a robust military structure that permits them to engage in large-scale peace operations. Others, such as the AU, PIF, LAS, and the CIS have peacekeeping experience but it is mostly dependent on the capacity of a major player (e.g. Nigeria/South Africa, Australia, Egypt, or Russia) to pay the financial toll and supply the logistical and military assets for the operation. Another set of organizations, ECOWAS and SADC, are in the process of setting up standby forces, but their endeavor has been dogged by lack of resources and organizational capacity. Finally, IGAD and OAS have a legal mandate to engage in peacekeeping, but due to either lack of political will (OAS) or lack of resources (IGAD) they are not likely to pursue the peacekeeping way.

Partiality

Most interventions by regional bodies are not impartial, as member states generally have close ethnic, economic, personal or political relations with the conflicting parties. Often these personal or national interests tend to hold sway over the more substantial issues of conflict resolution or prevention.[1] Regional organizations are thus often hijacked by leaders to augment their own stature and to legitimize national interests, rather than to promote regional and international peace and prosperity. For example in East Timor, the interests of Indonesia and its behind-the-doors pressure led ASEAN member countries, with the exception of Singapore which initially abstained, to always vote with Indonesia in UN resolutions on East Timor.[2] In Sudan, although President Omar El-Bashir claimed at the annual summit that he had invited IGAD to intervene and mediate in the North/South conflict because he believed that the regional organization would be neutral "without loopholes through which colonialism could penetrate on the pretext of humanitarianism,"[3] in practice he expected that his best friends would dominate the deliberations in the mediation committee.[4] But it is peacekeeping—mostly due to its anticipated capacity to bring about instant change—that is more vulnerable to be hijacked by member states to advance their national interests. In fact, it is difficult to identify one single regional peacekeeping intervention where a partaking country did not promote in some degree its national interests. The case of Africa is paradigmatic. As we saw, in all interventions carried out by ECOWAS, SADC or the AU, the contributing countries aimed at projecting their national agendas. As the director of the AU Peace and Security Department noted, "national interests play a role in the regional game and we have to know how to articulate them."[5] In the political field, countries are interested in demonstrating to the broader community that they are a meaningful player. Nigeria and South Africa achieve this goal by pursuing regional hegemonic strategies, whereas other countries such as Mozambique (in Burundi), or Ethiopia and Uganda (in Somalia) use the AU to market their political image. Often, however, the main national political trigger is connected to ethnic relations and blood ties. Given the inconsistency of African borders, conflicts affecting communities in one country often spill over to the same ethnic community in the other side of the border. This was, for example, the context for Senegal's intervention in Guinea-Bissau. The spillover is not only instigated on ethnic lines but also by regional migratory factors. Nigeria (in Liberia), Senegal (in Côte d'Ivoire), Guinea-Conakry (in Guinea-Bissau), and South Africa (in Lesotho) partially justified their interventions by the need to curb the regional spillover effects expressed in refugee flux or diffusion of small arms. Besides these political issues, economic interests also inform the decision to intervene. Armed conflicts lead to the disruption of markets and the decrease of profits. Ethiopia and

South Africa's intervention in Burundi, or Nigeria's role in Liberia, have been partially led by economic partisanship. Some countries are also interested in the business of peacekeeping and in the fact that higher earnings and exposure to better technology will appease the military. Moreover, African leaders often adopt a strategy of the personalization of politics, and strong relationships between heads of state—based either on empathy or animosity—are recurrent. It would be difficult to understand Angola and Zimbabwe's military deployment in Congo if we did not account for the personal bond between Eduardo dos Santos and Robert Mugabe. The same holds for the good relations between President Babangida and Samuel Doe of Liberia or President Diouf of Senegal and Joao Vieira of Guinea-Bissau. In addition to these personal factors, some leaders have also decided to intervene in order to boost their own personal image abroad. Ugandan president Yoweri Museveni's decision to intervene in Somalia or Nigerian president Abacha's role in Sierra Leone are cases in point. Even more neutral organizations, such as the European Union, have been used to camouflage national agendas, as was the case with the intervention in Chad/Central African Republic, prompted and led by French energy and political interests. At NATO, it would be difficult to envision a military intervention in Cyprus, as the decision-making process would be marked by acrimonious debates between Turkey and Greece. National interests in this situation would overshadow the regional interest.

Hegemony

The issue of partiality is more striking when a region is dominated by a hegemonic power, as Nigeria's role in ECOWAS, Russia's in CIS, or South Africa's in SADC, stand as testimony. The issue of hegemony is a double-edged sword. On the one hand, there is indeed the danger that hegemonic powers will seize the decision-making apparatus of the organizations and render them paralyzed or play them out to convey national agendas. The likelihood of a regional body intervening militarily is exponentially increased if the national interests of the sub-regional hegemonic power are favorable to the intervention. South Africa, Nigeria, Ethiopia, the United States, and Australia have all capitalized on their membership of sub-regional organizations to cynically pursue their national interests under the cover of international altruism. In fact, as reinforced by another AU official "if there is no national interest involved it is difficult for a regional or sub-regional organization to intervene."[6] Some of these interventions are primarily national operations and become "regional" only after an organization "acknowledges," "supports," or "approves" the intervention (often even retroactively). South African intervention in Lesotho (SADC), Russian interventions in Abkhazia and Tajikistan (CIS), or the Australian mission to the Solomon Islands (PIF) were not strategically planned and monitored in the headquarters of an organization but rather in the corridors of power in Pretoria, Moscow or Canberra. National operations only become "regional" due to administrative and political astuteness. As Coleman pointed out about the South African intervention in Lesotho:

> South Africa made very little effort to make Operation Boleas a truly regional military effort. It did not consult fully with its regional neighbours before launching its intervention. It did not seek regional approval for its intervention at the SADC Summit in Mauritius just days prior to the launching of Operation Boleas. And with the exception of Botswana's infantry company, South Africa operated alone in Lesotho.[7]

On the other hand, the weight of a hegemon can be positively used to bring about consensus and to provide resolute leadership. Egypt, South Africa, and Nigeria are informally consulted during the deliberations of the Peace and Security Council of the AU (even when not members of the PSC). As pointed out by an AU official responsible for the management of the PSC, "these countries are the most important states within the AU. Their views normally have significant weight. They are the leaders in their respective regions and, normally, the other sub-regional countries gravitate around them."[8] Moreover, given the financial and military difficulties in deploying a military force, it would be difficult for a sub-region to act effectively with no support from a sub-regional great power.[9] This was evident in Guinea-Bissau and Somalia.

Priority

The analysis in the book also showed evidence that there is no coordination mechanism in place between the UN and regional organizations. When a conflict erupts, who takes the initiative to intervene? And on what basis? It is often the case where the intervention of a regional organization is preferable vis-à-vis the UN (and vice-versa). For example, in the Balkans, those designing the post-Dayton political system viewed the UN as a discredited organization and turned to regional organizations for the implementation of the Agreement: NATO for security,

OSCE for elections and democratization, and the Council of Europe for building legal institutions.[10] But this is not always the case.

The UN Charter foresees that regional bodies might take the initiative to intervene in the "pacific settlement of local disputes" (art. 52) before referring them to the Security Council. In the case of enforcement, no mission should be carried out without the authorization of the Security Council (art. 53). Hence Chapter VIII gives us some indications in terms of priority and authority. But there are important questions that need to be addressed. For instance, the Charter says that the interventions have to be "consistent with the Purposes and Principles of the United Nations" (art. 52), but this motto remains so vague that regional organizations may try to play it out. For example, in 1948 LAS claimed that it was acting to uphold the principles of the UN when it intervened in an attempt to reverse Israel's declaration of independence. In 1999, US secretary of state Madeleine Albright strongly refuted the idea that NATO intervention in Kosovo had no legitimacy on the grounds that the North Atlantic Council was a more legitimate voice on the use of force than the Security Council, which included many non-democracies (and thus included countries that defended principles inconsistent with the purposes and principles of the UN). Second, as we saw in Chapter 1, not all organizations may be considered Chapter VIII agencies or arrangements, accentuating the difficulty in identifying who might take precedence over the others. But even in the case of a Chapter VIII organization intervening to mitigate a local conflict (pacific settlement), as this does not need to be authorized by the Security Council, who assures that the intervention is legitimate, the conduct is fair, and that its objectives are morally sound? As we saw, sometimes an intervention opens a Pandora's box that permits states to use military means to tackle security problems not related to the initial purposes of the intervention, as was the case with a Senegalese campaign against Casamance forces in northern Guinea-Bissau (under ECOWAS) and with Angola's firm determination to cut off supply lines to rebel UNITA members in Congo (under SADC). Therefore, greater participation by regional organizations "cannot be an excuse for the Security Council to shirk its responsibility,"[11] because only the Council has the competence to provide a regional operation with legitimacy.

Overlapping

This issue of priority is even more conspicuous when there are too many organizations willing to intervene. In some regions in the world, such as Europe, Central Asia, the Caribbean, and in all sub-regions in Africa, there is a proliferation of organizations with a security mandate (Table 13.1). The issue of overlapping would not be problematic if there were a clear division of labor between them, but this is seldom the case. At the initial steps of European institutionalization a sharing of responsibilities did exist between the COE (conflict prevention and human rights protection), NATO (collective defense and counter-insurgency), OSCE (peacebuilding and election monitoring) and the EU (soft security and civilian crisis management), but this is hardly the case now: NATO is involved with peacebuilding in Afghanistan and with civilian crisis management in Iraq, whereas the EU has embraced post-war reconstruction in the Balkans and robust peacekeeping in Africa. Ironically, there is an ongoing inter-regional dialogue between these organizations illustrated by the existence of joint programs, high-level meetings, and MoUs. But the dialogue is mostly about establishing close cooperation based on their shared priorities rather than on a true division of labor. The EU and the OSCE might have an old and active collaboration based on experience-sharing in the field of human rights and the rule of law, but if the EU's interests prompt it to deploy a peacebuilding mission, for example in the Balkans or the Caucasus, that decision will not take OSCE's interests, capacities, or willingness to intervene into major consideration. At best they would establish some type of field collaboration. In Central Asia regional security bodies have mushroomed over the last years, not due to a need to fulfill a niche but to create yet another organization to satisfy the temporary objectives of a lead nation. In Eastern Africa, the overlapping of early warning mechanisms has reached an almost anecdotal level: although IGAD has established a well functioning early warning mechanism (Conflict Early Warning and Response Mechanism—CEWARN), the East African Community has also developed a draft Protocol on Early

Table 13.1 Regional overlapping

	Possible contributing organizations
Europe	COE, OSCE, EU, NATO
Central Asia	BSECC, CSTO, CIS, CICA, GUAM, CDC
Caribbean	CARICOM, OAS, OECS, ACP
North Africa	AU, AMU, CEN-SAD, LAS, OIC
Southern Africa	AU, COMESA, SADC, ACP
West Africa	AU, ECOWAS, MRU, ACP
East Africa	AU, COMESA, EAC, IGAD, IC/GLR, ACP
Central Africa	AU, CEMAC, ECCAS, IC/GLR, ACP

Warning and Response Mechanism. Perversely, as Kenya and Uganda are members of both organizations, what regional body shall they report to? And how should they proceed if they receive contradictory instructions from the regional organizations on how to respond to the imminent conflict? The problem of overlapping leads to unaccountability, resource ineffectiveness, and political competition.

Absence of institutions or mandate in peace and security

In some regions there is no, or no suitable, regional body to which a requisite intervention might be delegated. Despite the proliferation of integration and cooperation arrangements, there are indeed some parts of the world which are devoid of any kind of regional agency with a mandate to conduct security operations. For instance, if a conflict breaks out in Mongolia or if a regional intervention is requested to tackle the Israeli–Palestinian conflict, no local regional organization would be able to intervene.[12] In some other regions the problem is not so much the lack of an organization but the lack of a legal mandate to carry out peace operations. This is the case of the South Asian Association on Regional Cooperation. With the UN playing a negligible role in South Asia or in the Middle East, the provision of security in these regions is contingent on the capacity of the state to do so. But if in theory the state is still the most prominent political actor and the bedrock of social organization and social protection, there is a long list of states that can no longer perform their basic security and development functions and that have no effective control over their territory and borders. This raises the question of the "fairness" of the ongoing process of devolution, and of expecting regional bodies to complement the work of the UN. With states, regional organizations, and the United Nations hiccupping in their capacity of providing security in some regions, how are development and protection ensured? Decentralization and delegation are only acceptable if they are paralleled by an equal dedication on the part of the UN to promote the formation and strengthening of institutions where they are currently non-existent or weak. Geography should not define people's security.

Inter-organizational information-sharing

With the termination of the high-level meetings between the UN and regional bodies, coordination will likely be more problematic. The cocktail of different bodies active in regional security—which includes, as mentioned, not only institutions with a Chapter VIII mandate, but also agencies that operate outside their own regions, collective defense organizations, and bodies that are not contained by any regional proximity parameter—is more pernicious than advantageous. Even if all of them have a role to play under different chapters of the UN Charter, the present lack of understanding will likely lead to lack of accountability. The EU and the AU have taken an important step forward by signing an Africa–EU Joint Strategy and its Action Plan (2008–10), which have at their core the need to strengthen cooperation in peace and security. European and African actors are also expected to live up to their commitments to enhance contacts, coordination, and cooperation in the UN and other international bodies, and set up efficient consultative and coordination structures. In fact, the EU seems to be keen on not letting the joint strategy slide into another good-wishes document and has established an implementation team, chaired by General P. M. Joana, special adviser to the high representative for the CFSP on African capabilities, to monitor progress. Although this is a step in the right direction, global inter-organizational cooperation should be more ambitious and comprehensive than mere bilateral regionalism. Presently there is no forum where the majority of regional institutions may exchange experiences and debate issues of common concern.

Mandate

Although all organizations covered in the book (and all present in Table 1.2) have competences in peace and security, they vary widely in terms of *where* and *how* they can operate. There is indeed an acute need for the UN to provide guidelines on who should be empowered to do what and under what circumstances. Aware that the global institution cannot remove itself from its responsibility to provide a clear framework of security provision, Kofi Annan in his report *A Regional-Global Security Partnership* pledged to take the partnership "to a new level of clarity, practicality and seriousness."[13] But this is far from being accomplished and the Security Council itself often authorizes Chapter VIII organizations to operate under Chapter VII (e.g. AMISOM), disarranging further what it is already malfunctioning.

The book has shown the importance of identifying with some rigor who qualifies as a Chapter VIII organization and what are the principles that define the exact area of possible intervention of a Chapter VIII agency. The UN Charter declares that regional agencies and arrangements can only intervene in "local disputes," but what counts as a local dispute? Is it both inter-state and intra-state? Does it only encompass the total area covered by member states? Or is an organization entitled to intervene in a state even if it might not be a member of that organization although it is clearly situated in the region and therefore it meets the requirements for "local"? As we saw, the League of Arab States intervened in Israel in 1948 and today it is an active player in the Israeli–Palestinian peace process. But Israel is not one of its 22 members. In another striking example of lack of juridical clarity, the CIS has tagged itself as a Chapter VIII agency and has intervened in Tajikistan and Abkhazia in that capacity. But the CIS's homegrown definition of peace operation (*mirotvorchestvo*) is at odds with current UN doctrine and practice. If according to the Charter, the Security Council ought to authorize peace enforcement but not pacific settlement/traditional peacekeeping, the Russian idea of peace operations bewilders this distinction, which certainly allows for unaccountability to flourish. In another case of a malfunctioning regional intervention, ECOWAS in Liberia, the Security Council disregarded the legal basis for the establishment and deployment of ECOMOG. While atrocities were being committed, the Security Council's statements or resolutions did not shed any light upon the mandate of the operation.[14]

Comparing the performance of international organizations

Despite these conundrums, the organizational capacity and operational experience of international organizations in regional security is so pronounced and diverse that a comparative analysis is warranted. The summary will focus on conflict prevention, peacemaking, peacekeeping and enforcement, and peacebuilding.

Conflict prevention

Almost all organizations undertake conflict prevention activities. The AU, IGAD, and ECOWAS in Africa, and the EU in Europe, maintain conflict prevention centers with early warning systems in place, including in the field in some cases. The EU, specifically, has developed a sophisticated conflict prevention mechanism for early warning of potential conflict areas on a global basis. However, it lacks a mechanism for its own member states. This is based on the political assumption, borne of experience, that its unique integration movement has successfully rendered the prospect of conflict among its own member states unthinkable. Other organizations, such as the SADC, OAS, PIF, or the LAS, have a legal mandate to establish early warning measures, but they are either still non-existent or dysfunctional. Indeed, the LAS has been mandated by its 2006 Statutes of the Arab Peace and Security Council to set up an early warning mechanism, which has not yet materialized. The OAS does not have a specialized early warning unit, but it is working to enhance its capacity in this area under its new preventive strategy through political analysis, data banks, and the development of indicators. The early warning mechanisms of the SADC, on the other hand, suffer from grave financial and human limitations resulting in operational paralysis.

All in all, the book has shown that progress in institutionalizing an effective conflict prevention and early warning function in the organizations under consideration has been hampered for some time by various sensitivities, namely: (i) the use of official intelligence in an otherwise transparent forum; (ii) the sanctity of the principle of state sovereignty; and (iii) concern that an explicit and shared identification of a potential crisis situation may be a negative instrumental factor in worsening the situation.

Despite the fairly robust capacities in operational conflict prevention, only a few organizations are involved in structural conflict prevention (i.e. addressing the root causes of conflicts). So far, only the EU, OAS, and to a smaller extent the PIF, have developed programs that target baseline issues such as democratization, human rights protection, environmental security, and economic welfare. For instance, the EU (and its member states) is the largest aid donor in the world. Through partnerships signed with ACP countries and also with its neighbors in Northern Africa and Central Europe, the EU has established development programs that aim to prevent the outbreak of conflict. On the other hand, the OAS has, for instance, established a Special Program for the Promotion of Dialogue and Conflict Resolution.

Peacemaking

The capacity for peacemaking varies widely from organization to organization. Even if regional organizations are primarily regarded as peacekeepers (under Chapter VIII or VII of the UN Charter), in fact most of them have in place an adequate organic peacemaking structure. A first set of organizations have established panels of eminent people (e.g. AU, ECOWAS, LAS, ASEAN/ARF) composed of personalities nominated by the member states. The book has demonstrated however, that in some organizations the criteria to nominate such personalities is purely political and most of them lack negotiation or mediation skills. Their political weight alone could warrant their nomination only if the organizations had the technical capacity to train these individuals, but that seldom happens. The establishment of panels of wise people is an effective conflict management mechanism, but none of the organizations has set up any robust secretariat to assist them in conflict analysis, data collection, information sharing, or best practice learning.

Another set of organizations, which have no panels of the wise, have nonetheless established other internal peacemaking organs. This is, for example, the case with the OAS Department of Sustainable Democracy and Special Missions, or SADC's Organ on Defense, Politics, and Security Cooperation. Another set of organizations carries out peacemaking primarily through the dispatch of special envoys: either the secretary-general in person, their representatives, or the head of any internal body (e.g. AU, ECOWAS, SADC, OAS, LAS, PIF, EU). As an illustration, PIF's ministerial missions to New Caledonia and to Fiji have been instrumental in collecting empirical data and inciting the Forum to remain engaged in these countries.

Other organizations, such as ASEAN, operate under a more informal and consensus-building framework, as Southeast Asian regional cultural practice is not sympathetic toward legal and institutional peacemaking practices. ASEAN's mediation of the South China Sea dispute, and its role in Cambodia and Myanmar, are illustrative of peacemaking activities carried out with minimum organizational and legal support.

Peacekeeping and peace enforcement

Only a limited number of organizations engage in peacekeeping activities. Some lack the juridical competence, whereas others possess the competence but make the political judgment against undertaking such responsibilities. Some, however, have acquired the juridical competence and exercised the political will to engage in peacekeeping measures within their jurisdictional zones. Since the first military intervention (LAS in Palestine, 1948), intergovernmental organizations have deployed approximately 20 missions. These include the LAS (Palestine, Kuwait, Lebanon, Yemen); ECOWAS (Liberia (twice), Côte d'Ivoire, Guinea-Bissau, Sierra Leone); the AU (Burundi, Somalia, Sudan, Comoros); PIF (Solomon Islands); CIS (Tajikistan; Georgia, South Ossetia; Georgia, Abkhazia; and Moldova); the SADC (Lesotho and the Democratic Republic of Congo); NATO (Bosnia, Kosovo, Afghanistan, and the FYROM); and the EU's peacekeeping missions (Bosnia, FYROM, and Chad/CAR). These deployments vary widely in terms of type and ambition. As we saw, the trigger of the intervention has often more to do with the interests of the intervener than with the need on the ground to intervene.

Presently, only the EU, NATO, and the CIS have the mandate to undertake peacekeeping and enforcement missions outside their jurisdictional zones, on a potentially global basis, on behalf of the United Nations. For the EU and NATO, the extra-jurisdictional mandate is exclusive, whereas the CIS may operate both intra-territorially and extra-territorially. Some organizations which do not have a peacekeeping nor an enforcement capacity have been encouraged to establish such a mechanism. In the case of ASEAN, numerous proposals have been put forward to provide the organization with a military role. However, ASEAN leaders have rejected the proposals and contended that bilateral arrangements are the most viable strategy instead.

In the case of Africa, a note of alert should be given to the organizational framework between the AU and the sub-regional organizations (i.e. ECOWAS, SADC, IGAD, ECCAS). Despite the adoption of a MoU in 2008, the relationship still needs to be strengthened by clarifying the precise role of each organ. The AU has established its African Standby Force on the basis of the existing Regional Economic Communities; nevertheless, some of these sub-regional organizations still have the potential to develop their own independent peace and security agenda. For example, it will be possible for the ECOWAS military component to deploy even without an AU mandate, whereas in the Horn, IGAD's CEWARN is independent of the EASBRIG framework. Problems may also arise because of the overlapping memberships of some African countries. Angola, for example, is a member of both ECCAS and the SADC, and it is therefore technically permitted to take part in the process of establishing a standby force in Central Africa and in Southern Africa.

Peacebuilding

All organizations play a role, of some type and magnitude, in peacebuilding. However, even if they have some operational experience, their organizational capacity is low, and this is reflected in their legal mandate and the organizational structure. The only two organizations worldwide with a strong peacebuilding capacity are the EU and the OSCE. Both have deployed missions as a way to pacify, democratize, humanize, and improve life in societies emerging from crisis or violence. The OSCE's work in peacebuilding is coordinated by the Permanent Council and implemented, primarily, by the field missions. In the EU, the DG RELEX (European Commission) is tasked to supervise and guide the work of the organization in peacebuilding, even if there is a strong inclination to transfer responsibility to the EC delegations. Interestingly, the EU has recently created a Peacebuilding Partnership portal, intended to allow interested organizations and entities working in the fields of conflict prevention, crisis management, and peacebuilding to provide to the Commission, on a voluntary basis, information regarding their areas of activity. Beyond the OSCE and the EU, to a smaller extent also the AU, OAS, and PIF have been involved with peacebuilding. The African Union for instance has developed a clear program in peacebuilding and post-war reconstruction, and has produced a ground-breaking Handbook on Post-Conflict Reconstruction and Development.

Indeed, the peacebuilding capacity of most organizations (e.g. ECOWAS, SADC) is confined to election observation, and some of them have adopted specific protocols to regulate their observation missions, such as SADC's Principles and Guidelines Governing Democratic Elections. However, election observation is generally not integrated into a comprehensive peacebuilding policy, but simply regarded as a temporary and self-contained political exercise.

The future

Unlike the critics of regional interventions, this book has highlighted that regional organizations have a bank of accumulated knowledge that should be capitalized and provide unquestionable comparative advantages vis-à-vis other actors. But in contrast to the fervent apologists of regionalism, the comparative analysis of the book has brought to light some of the shortcomings of these organizations and highlighted the need to mend some of the limitations of global–regional security cooperation. The solution is not to sanctify the monopoly of the United Nations and demean the contribution of regional organizations, nor to advocate regional solutions for all the problems. It would be difficult to conceive the idea that the inhabitants of a region should only receive the level of peace operations that their own regional organization is able to provide. Instead, the next step should be to reiterate the fact that the UN and regional organizations both have a fundamental role to play and that their cooperation ought to be more agile and outcome-oriented. But how? A few examples include:

- By delegating competences to regional actors, the UN should stand on track in the objective to develop more solid standby arrangements and the eventual establishment of a standby peacekeeping force. Regional interventions are, to some extent, a product of the limitations of the global body, and the UN should never decelerate the process of internal reform.

- The high-level meeting process should not wane and the role of each organization—whether it has the mandate and capacity in the various aspects of international peace and security (early warning, conflict prevention, peacemaking, peacekeeping, enforcement and peacebuilding)—could be declared at the eighth high-level meeting. This would be a precursor to proceeding toward the introduction of more formalized agreements between the United Nations and regional organizations.
- The UN should form a Capacity Working Group with the task of developing a 10-year capacity-building program for ensuring uniform strength of the partnership, across both thematic and geographical lines.
- In parallel, the UN should be more proactive in monitoring the activities of regional organizations as called for by article 54 of the UN Charter. Reporting and information sharing should be made mandatory and regular. Regional actions must be entirely accountable to the UN.

Notes

Foreword by the series editors

1 See Edward Luck, *The UN Security Council: Practice and Promise* (London: Routledge, 2006) and Julian Lindley-French, *The North Atlantic Treaty Organization: The Enduring Alliance* (London: Routledge, 2007).
2 For a discussion of the problem of UN overstretch, see Edward Newman, *A Crisis of Global Institutions? Multilateralism and International Security* (London: Routledge, 2007).
3 See, for example, Samuel M. Makinda and Wafula Okumu, *The African Union: Challenges of Globalization, Security and Governance* (London: Routledge, 2008).
4 Rodrigo Tavares, Maximilian B. Rasch, Emmanuel Fanta, Francis Baert, and Tânia FelÚcio, *Capacity Survey: Regional and Other Intergovernmental Organizations in the Maintenance of Peace and Security* (Brussels, Belgium: United Nations University (UNU-CRIS), 2008).

1 International organizations in regional security

1 See Rodrigo Tavares, "Understanding Regional Peace and Security: A Framework for Analysis," *Contemporary Politics* 14, no. 2 (2008): 107–27; Barry Buzan and Ole Wæver, *Regions and Powers: The Structure of International Security* (Cambridge: Cambridge University Press, 2003).
2 Joseph Lepgold, "Regionalism in the Post-Cold War Era: Incentives for Conflict Management," in *Regional Conflict Management*, ed. Paul F. Diehl and Joseph Lepgold (Lanham, Md.: Rowman and Littlefield, 2003), 10.
3 Christine Gray, *International Law and the Use of Force* (Oxford: Oxford University Press, 2004), 282. Research conducted in the late 1980s on Security Council resolutions noted that references to regional organizations were rare—it detected only two such references since the foundation of the UN. See Renata Sonnenfeld, *Resolutions of the United Nations Security Council* (Leiden, The Netherlands, and Boston, Mass.: Martinus Nijhoff, 1988); Hilaire McCoubrey and Justin Morris, *Regional Peacekeeping in the Post-Cold War Era* (The Hague, The Netherlands: Kluwer Law International, 2000), 213.
4 McCoubrey and Morris, *Regional Peacekeeping in the Post-Cold War Era*, 48.

5 *The Causes of Conflict and the Promotion of Durable Peace and Sustainable Development in Africa, Report of the Secretary-General* (General Assembly Security Council document A/52/871-S/1998/318), 13 April 1998, para. 41.

6 Michael Haas, *The Pacific Way: Regional Cooperation in the South Pacific* (New York: Praeger, 1989), 93.

7 See Norma J. Padelford, "Regional Organizations and the United Nations," *International Organization* 8, no. 2 (1954): 203–16; Francis O. Wilcox, "Regionalism and the United Nations," *International Organization* 19, no. 3 (1965): 789–811; Inis L. Claude, *Swords into Plowshares; the Problems and Progress of International Organization* (New York: Random House, 1988), 143; Kennedy Graham and Tânia Felício, *Regional Security and Global Governance: A Study of Interaction Between Regional Agencies and the UN Security Council with a Proposal for a Regional-Global Security Mechanism* (Brussels, Belgium: VUB University Press, 2006).

8 For a historical overview see Louise Fawcett, "Regional Institutions," in *Security Studies: An Introduction*, ed. Paul Williams (London and New York: Routledge, 2008), 307–24.

9 Michael Pugh and Waheguru Pal Singh Sidhu, "Introduction: The United Nations and Regionl Actors," in *The United Nations and Regional Security: Europe and Beyond*, ed. Michael Pugh and Waheguru Pal Singh Sidhu (Boulder, Colo. and London: Lynne Rienner, 2003), 1.

10 In February 1993, the president of the Security Council reacted to the *Agenda for Peace* by stating, inter alia, that "the SC notes the ongoing and constructive collaboration between the UN and various regional arrangements and organizations, within their respective areas of competence, in identifying and addressing humanitarian emergencies, in order to solve crises in a matter appropriate to each specific situation" (S/25344). In May 1993, the Security Council added some extra observations on the *Agenda for Peace* and reaffirmed "the importance that it attaches to the role of regional arrangements and organizations." It also called upon the regional organizations and arrangements to consider new ways to contribute to the maintenance of international peace and security, under Chapter VIII of the Charter (S-25859).

11 The *Supplement to an Agenda for Peace* (1995) outlined some forms of cooperation, which includes: consultation, diplomatic support, operational support, co-deployment, and joint operations. They remain tentative, however.

12 "Comprehensive Review of the Whole Question of Peace-Keeping Operations in all Their Aspects," UN General Assembly resolution A/RES/48/42, para. 63, 14 March 1994.

13 In March 1994 Russia put forward a Draft Declaration on the Improvement of Cooperation Between the United Nations and Regional Organizations (A/AC.182/L.72/REV.2). In 1995, the General Assembly adopted a Declaration on the Enhancement of Cooperation Between the United Nations and Regional Arrangements or Agencies in the Maintenance of International Peace and Security, which recognized that "regional arrangements or agencies can play an important role in preventive diplomacy and in enhancing regional and international cooperation" (A/RES/49/57). The declaration was, however, more a statement of intentions rather than a working plan.

14 UN Secretary-General's Opening Address to 5th High-Level Meeting, New York, July 2003.

15 Joint Statement by Participants in the Sixth High-Level Meeting between the United Nations and Regional and other Intergovernmental Organizations, held at United Nations Headquarters in New York on 25–26 July 2005.

16 S/2008/813 of 31 December 2008. The Panel was chaired by Romano Prodi (Italy).

17 *In Larger Freedom: Towards Development, Security and Human Rights for All, Report of the Secretary-General* (General Assembly document A/59/2005), 6, 21 March 2005.

18 *A Regional-Global Security Partnership: Challenges and Opportunities, Report of the Secretary-General* (General Assembly Security Council document A/61/204-S/2006/590), 28 July 2006. Following this report, the UN has issued another two reports: the *Report of the Secretary-General on the Relationship between the United Nations and Regional Organizations, in particular the African Union, in the Maintenance of International Peace and Security,* in March 2008 (S/2008/186); and the *Report of the Secretary-General on Cooperation Between Regional and Other Organizations,* in August 2008 (A/63/228, S/2008/531).

19 Kwesi Anning (2008), "The UN and the Africa Union's Security Architecture: Defining an Emerging Partnership?" in Dag Hammarskjöld Foundation Occasional Paper Series, *The United Nations, Security and Peacekeeping in Africa: Lessons and Prospects.* Uppsala, Dag Hammarskjöld Foundation, 17.

20 The UN Mission in Kosovo (UNMIK) and the Kosovo Force (KFOR) were the first multidimensional peace operation where non-UN bodies (EU and OSCE) had an operational role under a UN umbrella.

21 *An Agenda for Peace Preventive Diplomacy, Peacemaking and Peacekeeping, Report of the Secretary-General Pursuant to the Statement Adopted by The Summit Meeting of the Security Council on 31 January 1992* (General Assembly Security Council document A/47/277—S/24111), para. 61, 17 June 1992.

22 Bruno Simma, Hermann Mosler, and Helmut Brokelmann, *The Charter of the United Nations: A Commentary* (Oxford: Oxford University Press, 1994), 694.

23 *In Larger Freedom: Towards Development, Security and Human Rights for All, Report of the Secretary-General* (General Assembly document A/59/2005), para. 213, 21 March 2005.

24 *A More Secured World: Our Shared Responsibility, Report of the Secretary-General's High Level Panel Report on Threats, Challenges and Change* (General Assembly document A/59/565), para. 273, 2 December 2004.

25 On Yugoslavia, the Security Council passed resolution 713 (September 1991) that said "recalling the provisions of Chapter VIII of the Charter of the United Nations, commending the efforts undertaken by the European Community and its Member States, with the support of the States participating in the CSCE, to restore peace and dialogue in Yugoslavia." On peace operations, the US Presidential Decision Directive 25 noted that, "any large scale participation of US forces in a major peace enforcement operation that is likely to involve combat should ordinarily be conducted under U.S. command and operational control or through competent *regional organizations* such as NATO or ad hoc coalitions" (italics added).

26 Kennedy Graham, "Towards a Coherent Regional Institutional Landscape in the United Nations? Implications for Europe," *Bruges Regional Integration and Global Governance Papers,* Bruges, 1/2008, July 2008, 15.

27 Thierry Tardy, "The European Union and the United Nations: Global versus Regional Multilateralism," *Studia Diplomatica* 60, no. 1 (2007): 191–209.

28 "Security Council Welcomes Strengthened Collaboration Between UN, Regional Organizations in Conflict Prevention, Stabilizing War-Torn States. Presidential Statement Follows Day-Long Public Meeting: Secretary-General Calls for 'Strategic Partnerships' to Meet Future Challenges" (Security Council press release 8153), 20 July 2004.

29 Statement by Ban-Ki Moon to the Security Council debate (document SC/9163), 6 November 2007.

30 See Communiqué of the 175th Meeting of the Peace and Security Council (5 March 2009).

31 See Eastern African Standby Brigade Coordination Mechanism, *Report of the Workshop of the Experts Working Group on the Concept of Cooperation in Peace and Security in the Eastern Africa Region*, Victoria, Seychelles, 24–26 September 2007.

32 Lepgold, "Regionalism in the Post-Cold War Era: Incentives for Conflict Management," 10; Connie Peck, *Sustainable Peace: The Role of the UN and Regional Organizations in Preventing Conflict* (Lanham, Md.: Rowman and Littlefield, 1998), 220.

33 Francis O. Wilcox, "Regionalism and the United Nations," *International Organization* 19, no. 3 (1965): 807.

34 Lepgold, "Regionalism in the Post-Cold War Era: Incentives for Conflict Management," 13.

35 Lepgold, "Regionalism in the Post-Cold War Era: Incentives for Conflict Management," 10.

36 Paul F. Diehl, "Regional Conflict Management: Strategies, Necessary Conditions, and Comparative Effectiveness," in *Regional Conflict Management*, ed. Paul F. Diehl and Joseph Lepgold (Lanham, Md.: Rowman and Littlefield, 2003), 74.

37 Marrack Goulding, *Peacemonger* (Washington, D.C.: Johns Hopkins University Press, 2003), 217.

38 David A. Lake and Patrick M. Morgan, *Regional Orders: Building Security in a New World* (Pennsylvania: Pennsylvania State University Press, 1997), 5.

39 Muthiah Alagapa, "Regional Arrangements, the UN, and International Security: a Framework for Analysis," in *Beyond Subcontracting: Task-Sharing With Regional Security Arrangements and Service Providing NGOs*, ed. Thomas G. Weiss (Houndmills, UK and London: Macmillan Press, 1998), 23; Connie Peck, *Sustainable Peace: The Role of the UN and Regional Organizations in Preventing Conflict*.

40 Lepgold, "Regionalism in the Post-Cold War Era: Incentives for Conflict Management," 10.

41 Christine Gray, *International Law and the Use of Force* (Oxford: Oxford University Press, 2004), 327.

42 *Identical Letters Dated 21 August 2000 from the Secretary-General to the President of the General Assembly and the President of the Security Council* (General Assembly Security Council document A/55/305-S/2000/809), para. 32, 21 August 2000.

43 Hilaire McCoubrey and Justin Morris, *Regional Peacekeeping in the Post-Cold War Era* (The Hague, The Netherlands: Kluwer Law International, 2000), 54.

44 See Alan K. Henrikson, "The Growth of Regional Organizations and the Role of the United Nations," in *Regionalism in World Politics: Regional Organization and International Order*, ed. Louise Fawcett and Andrew Hurrell (Oxford and New York: Oxford University Press 1995), 135.

45 Jane Boulden, "United Nations Security Council Policy on Africa," in *Dealing with Conflict in Africa: The United Nations and Regional Organizations*, ed. Jane Boulden (Basingstoke, UK and New York: Palgrave Macmillan, 2003), 30.

46 Jeffrey Herbst, "Crafting Regional Cooperation in Africa," in *Crafting Cooperation. Regional International Institutions in Comparative Perspective*, ed. Amitav Acharya and Alastair Iain Johnston (Cambridge and New York: Cambridge University Press 2007), 129.

47 See Judy Dempsey, "EU and NATO Bound in a Perilous Rivalry: Competition Cutting into Effectiveness," *International Herald Tribune*, 4 October 2006.

48 Security Council resolution 1809, 16 April 2008, para. 6.

49 Fredrik Söderbaum and Luk Van Langenhove, *The EU as a Global Player: The Politics of Interregionalism* (New York and London: Routledge, 2007).

50 *A Regional-Global Security Partnership: Challenges and Opportunities: Report of the Secretary-General* (General Assembly and Security Council documents A/61/204-S/2006/590), 28 July 2006, para. 99.

51 "Actions, policies, procedures or institutions undertaken in particularly vulnerable places and times in order to avoid the threat or use of armed force and related forms of coercion by states or groups, as the way to settle the political disputes that can arise from destabilizing effects of economic, social, political and international change" (Michael Lund, *Preventing and Mitigating Violent Conflicts: A Revised Guide for Practitioners* (Washington, D.C.: Creative Associates International, 1997), 3. It includes: (a) preventive diplomacy: mediation, conciliation, negotiation; (b) preventive deployment: the fielding of peacekeepers to forestall probable conflict; (c) preventive disarmament: destroying old weapons and reducing small arms in conflict areas; and (d) structural prevention: political, institutional, and developmental efforts at root causes.

52 Peacemaking refers to the use of diplomatic means to persuade parties in conflict to cease hostilities and negotiate a pacific settlement of their dispute. It involves negotiation, enquiry, mediation, conciliation, arbitration, judicial settlement, good offices—applied after a dispute has crossed the threshold into armed conflict.

53 Peacekeeping is distinguished from peace enforcement in two fundamental ways: first, the mission is dependent on the consent of the host member state; and second the mission has a mandate to use force only in self-defense. Peacekeeping may be seen as of two types: *traditional* includes the stabilization of conflict situations after a ceasefire, and the creation of an environment for the parties to reach a lasting peace agreement, whereas *modern* is broader and comprises assistance in democratization, good governance and economic development

54 Peace enforcement signifies the use of force by a UN or UN partner against one of the parties to enforce an end to hostilities or maintain stability once hostilities have ended. On several occasions the Security Council has authorized member states to use "all necessary means," including force, to achieve a stated objective (within the mission's mandate contained in the

Security Council resolution under Chapter VII) in situations where consent of the parties is not required. Peace enforcement is often referred to as "robust peacekeeping" but it is suggested here that, for the sake of clarity, the term "peacekeeping" should be confined to missions with a Chapter VI (or "six-and-a-half") mandate as described in the preceding footnote.

55 Peacebuilding refers to "post-hostility actions, military and civilian, taken to forestall future eruptions by strengthening structures capable of consolidating a political settlement" (Alex P. Schmid, *Thesaurus and Glossary of Early Warning and Conflict Prevention Terms* (London: FEWER, 1998). This term pertains to assistance to countries and regions in the transition from war to peace.

56 See Robert O. Keohane and Lisa L. Martin, "The Promise of Institutional Theory," *International Security* 20, no. 1 (1995): 39–51; Jean-Marc F. Blanchard, Edward Mansfield, and Norrin M. Ripsman, *Power and the Purse: Economic Statecraft, Interdependence and National Security* (London: Frank Cass, 2000); Martha Finnemore and Kathryn Sikkink, "International Norm Dynamics and Political Change," *International Organization* 52 (Autumn 1998): 887–917.

57 Jolley E. Hansen, Sara McLaughlin Mitchell, and Stephen C. Nemeth, "IO Mediation of Interstate Conflicts: Moving Beyond the Global Versus Regional Dichotomy," *Journal of Conflict Resolution* 52, no. 2 (2008): 295–325.

2 African Union (AU)

1 See Mammo Muchie, ed., *The Making of The African-Nation: Pan-Africanism and the African Renaissance* (London: Adonis and Abbey Publishers, 2003); Christopher Landsberg, "The Fifth Wave of Pan-Africanism," in *West Africa's Security Challenges: Building Peace in a Troubled Region*, ed. Adekeye Adebajo and Ismail Rashid (Boulder, Colo.: Lynne Rienner, 2004), 117–43; Timothy Murithi, *The African Union: Pan-Africanism, Peacebuilding and Development* (Aldershot, UK: Ashgate, 2005).

2 Statament by Kwame Nkrumah's at Ghana's independence, 6 March 1957. www.bbc.co.uk/worldservice/focusonafrica/news/story/2007/02/070129_ghana50 _independence_speech.shtml.

3 The Monrovia Group, a group of moderate-to-conservative pro-Western states, advocated African cooperation in non-sensitive and functional areas such as the economic. It consisted of states that attended a conference in Monrovia, Liberia in May 1961 and approved, later, the Lagos Charter of the Organization of African and Malagasy States (in January 1962).

4 Kwame Akonor, "Stuffing Old Wine in New Bottles: The Case of the Africa Union," in *Africa in the 21st Century*, ed. Ama Mazama (New York and London: Routledge, 2007), 192.

5 Kwane Nkurumah warned OAU members of the problems associated with maintaining colonial borders. While addressing the African Heads of State Summit in Ethiopia in May 1963, he observed that, "there is hardly any African state without a frontier problem with its adjacent neighbors. But let me suggest that this fatal relic of colonialism will drive us to war against one another unless we succeed in arresting the danger through mutual understanding on fundamental issues and through African unity" (cited in Timothy Murithi, "The Responsibility to Protect as Enshrined in Article 4

of the Constitutive Act of the African Union," *African Security Review* 16, no. 3 (2007): 13.

6 Isaias Afeworki, "OAU Summit Opens to Criticism from Newest Member Eritrea," Agence France-Presse—English, 28 June 1993.

7 Murithi, "The Responsibility to Protect as Enshrined in Article 4 of the Constitutive Act of the African Union," 23.

8 See Tanui Kipkoech, "African Political Union Is Premature," *The Nation* (Nairobi), 13 September 1999. Akonor, "Stuffing Old Wine in New Bottles: The Case of the Africa Union."

9 African Union, *Audit of the African Union* (Addis Ababa, Ethiopia: African Union, 2007), 13

10 Cited in Murithi, *The African Union: Pan-Africanism, Peacebuilding and Development*, 87.

11 Samuel M. Makinda and F. Wafula Okumu, *The African Union: Challenges of Globalization, Security and Governance* (New York: Routledge, 2008), 50.

12 The Pan-African Parliament (inaugurated in March 2004) could provide some monitoring on this issue. The visit of a delegation from the PAP to the headquarters of the AU in Addis Ababa on 19–22 February 2008 is an illustration of the will of the parliamentarians to exercise some form of oversight power over the African Commission. The delegation headed by Abdelmadjid Azzedine further requested the Commission to send a delegation to the seat of the PAP in South Africa.

13 Interview, official at the Peace and Security Council of African Union (10 October 2007). Anonymity required.

14 Security Council resolution 1809 (2008), para. 7, 16 April 2008.

15 The five members of the Panel, which includes Salim Ahmed Salim, Brigalia Bam, Ahmed Ben Bella, Elisabeth K. Pognon and Miguel Trovoada, have been appointed in January 2007 for a three-year period.

16 The Situation Room uses primarily open media sources and emphasizes potential, actual, and post-conflict situations, elections, and humanitarian problems. It produces two types of report on a daily basis: *Daily News Highlights* (compiled by open media sources and distributed to a large audience), and *Daily Report* (compiled using field mission data and distributed only internally). Periodically, it also issues *Flash Reports* whenever there is breaking news, *Weekly Updates* on Somalia and Sudan, and *Compiled Reports* on particular issues when requested by Commission staff.

17 African Union (Conflict Management Division/Peace and Security Department), *The CEWS Handbook* (Addis Ababa: African Union, 2008).

18 Interview, Shewit Hailu, Situation Room Coordinator, Conflict Management Division, African Union (11 October 2007).

19 Interview, Charles Mwaura, Senior Political Officer, Peace and Security Dept., Conflict Management Division, Early Warning Unit, African Union (23 November 2007).

20 The Framework Document calls for the establishment of the ASF in two phases: in phase one (up to 30 June 2005), the objective was to establish a strategic level management capacity, whereas in phase two (1 July 2005 to 30 June 2010), it is envisaged that the AU will have the capacity to deploy and to manage complex peacekeeping operations.

21 Cilliers, Jakkie, "The African Standby Force. An update on progress," *Institute for Strategic Studies Paper*, no. 160 (2008).

22 African Union, *Audit of the African Union* (Addis Ababa, Ethiopia: African Union, 2007), 101.

23 Cilliers, Jakkie, "The African Standby Force. An update on progress," *Institute for Strategic Studies Paper*, no. 160 (2008), 6.

24 Interview, Naison Ngoma, Peace and Security Department, Conflict Management Division, Expert Post-Conflict Reconstruction and Peace Building, African Union (24 September 2007).

25 Interview, Naison Ngoma, Peace and Security Department, Conflict Management Division, Expert Post-Conflict Reconstruction and Peace Building, African Union (24 September 2007); Interview, El Ghassim Wane, Head, Conflict Management Division, African Union (5 October 2007); Interview, Charles Mwaura, Senior Political Officer, Peace and Security Dept., Conflict Management Division, Early Warning Unit, African Union (23 November 2007).

26 Vanessa Kent and Mark Malan, "The African Standby Force: Progress and Prospects," *African Security Review* 12, no. 3 (2003): 71–81; Murithi, *The African Union: Pan-Africanism, Peacebuilding and Development*; David Francis, *Uniting Africa: Building Regional Peace and Security Systems* (Aldershot, UK and Burlington, Vt.: Ashgate, 2006).

27 See Paul Williams (forthcoming 2009), "The African Union Peace Operations" in *African Security*, 2. no. 2.

28 Makinda and Okumu, *The African Union: Challenges of Globalization, Security and Governance*, 84–85.

29 Interview, Chrysantus (Chris) Ayangafac, Senior Researcher in the Direct Conflict Prevention Programme, Institute for Security Studies, Addis Ababa (18 September 2007); Interview, Tim Murithi, Senior Research Fellow, Institute for Security Studies, Addis Ababa (12 November 2007).

30 Interview, official at the Peace and Security Council of African Union (10 October 2007). Anonymity required.

31 Contributors of military personnel were: Argentina, Australia, Austria, Bangladesh, Bolivia, Botswana, Brazil, Canada, Cape Verde, China, Czech Republic, Egypt, Finland, Ghana, Guinea-Bissau, Guyana, Hungary, India, Indonesia, Ireland, Italy, Japan, Jordan, Malaysia, Nepal, The Netherlands, New Zealand, Nigeria, Norway, Pakistan, Portugal, Russian Federation, Spain, Sri Lanka, Sweden, Switzerland, Togo, United States of America, Uruguay, and Zambia (eight African countries).

32 Interview, General Paulino José Macaringue, Senior Lecturer, Center for Defence and Security Management, University of the Witwatersrand Graduate School of Public and Development Management (2 November 2007); Interview, Zewdineh Haile, President African Institute for Arbitration, Mediation, Conciliation and Research (AIAMCR) (16 September 2007).

33 Mozambique's army was, nonetheless, not prepared and the intervention was somewhat punctuated by embarrassing episodes (similarly to Mozambique's intervention in East Timor in the late 1990s). The army's poor or inexistent equipment, for instance in terms of transportation vehicles, and their lack of peacekeeping training, demonstrates that the decision to intervene seems to have been driven solely by political interests. South African and British military and financial support to Mozambique did not totally repair the problem. The senior ranks of the army reacted to the political decision with vacillation, whereas the lowest combat ranks, alienated from the

problems, were eager to intervene on foreign soil as a peacekeeping force (interview 33).
34 Interview, official at the Peace and Security Council of African Union (10 October 2007). Anonymity required. Interview, official at the Peace and Security Council of African Union (23 November 2007). Anonymity required.
35 The exact number seems to be unknown for all AU officials interviewed. These figures are estimates.
36 African Union, *Audit of the African Union*, 50.
37 Laurent Correau, "Les Députés panafricains gravement mis en cause dans des affaires de per-diem," *Radio France Internationale*, 30 June 2007.
38 Interview, Geofrey Mugumya, Director, Peace and Security Department, African Union (25 September 2007).
39 For instance, the AU commissioner for economic affairs Maxwell Mkwezalamba has declared that "Africa cannot continue to wait for partners to find solutions for her development problems, including mobilizing financial resources for her" (see "The African Union Faces Financial Problems" in *AU Monitor*, 15 January 2009).
40 Murithi, *The African Union: Pan-Africanism, Peacebuilding and Development*, 34.

3 Economic Community of West African States (ECOWAS)

1 ECOWAS member states are: Benin, Burkina Faso, Cape Verde, Côte d'Ivoire, The Gambia, Ghana, Guinea, Guinea-Bissau, Liberia, Mali, Niger, Nigeria, Senegal, Sierra Leone, Togo. Cape Verde was admitted in 1977. Mauritania, a signatory of the Lagos Treaty, withdrew in 2000 since the country decided to prioritize its national Arab identity rather than being integrated in an organization composed essentially by black African states.
2 Clement E. Adibe, "Muddling Through: An Analysis of the ECOWAS Experience in Conflict Management in West Africa," in *Regional Integration for Conflict Prevention and Peacebuilding in Africa: Europe, SADC and ECOWAS*, ed. Liisa Laakso (Helsinki, Finland: University of Helsinki, 2002), 105.
3 Olatunde Ojo, "Nigeria and the Formation of ECOWAS," *International Organization* 34, no. 4 (1980): 584.
4 Cited in David Francis, *Uniting Africa: Building Regional Peace and Security Systems* (Aldershot, UK and Burlington, Vt.: Ashgate, 2006), 148.
5 Pat McGowan and Thomas Johnson, "African Military Coups d'État and Underdevelopment: A Quantitative Historical Analysis," *The Journal of Modern African Studies* 22, no. 4 (1984): 648. See also Issaka Souaré, *Civil Wars and Coups d'Etat in West Africa: An Attempt to Understand the Roots and Prescribe Possible Solutions* (New York, Toronto, and Oxford: University Press of America, 2006).
6 Francis, *Uniting Africa: Building Regional Peace and Security Systems*, 43.
7 Adibe, "Muddling Through: An Analysis of the ECOWAS Experience in Conflict Management in West Africa," 103.
8 See Cyril I. Obi (forthcoming 2009), "ECOWAS on the Ground: Comparing Peacekeeping in Liberia, Sierra Leone, Guinea Bissau and Cote D'Ivoire," *African Security*, 2, no. 2.

9 Adibe, "Muddling Through: An Analysis of the ECOWAS Experience in Conflict Management in West Africa," 157.

10 The OMC is responsible for data collection and analysis, and the drafting of up-to-date reports that identify/outline possible emerging crises, monitor on-going crises and post-crisis transitions.

11 The Council functions de facto with all member states.

12 Issaka Souaré, *Civil Wars and Coups d'Etat in West Africa: An Attempt to Understand the Roots and Prescribe Possible Solutions* (New York, Toronto, and Oxford: University Press of America, 2006), 155.

13 The current members for 2005 are: General Abdulsalami Abubakar, former president of Nigeria; Gactan Nitchama, former minister of Guinea-Bissau; Bitokotipou Yagnimim, former minister of Togo; Elizabeth Alpha-Lavalie, vice-speaker of the Sierra Leone parliament; Bernadine Do-Rego, Benin; Debra Ebenezer Moses, Ghana; Dieudonne Essienne, Côte d'Ivoire; Abdourahmane Sow, Guinea; Mbaye Mbengue, Senegal; Bahou Ousmane Jobe, Gambia; Leopold Andre Ouedrago, Burkina Faso; Emmanuel Gbalaze, Liberia; Sira Diop, Mali; Amirou Garba, Niger.

14 J. Isawa Elaigwu, *Gawon: A Biography* (Ibadan, Nigeria: West Books, 1986).

15 Thelma Ekiyor, "ECOWAS Conflict Prevention Framework (ECPF): A New Approach to an Old Challenge," *West Africa Civil Society Institute OpEd* vol. 1 (June 2008).

16 See Eastern African Standby Brigade Coordination Mechanism, *Report of the Workshop of the Experts Working Group on the Concept of Cooperation in Peace and Security in the Eastern Africa Region*, Victoria, Seychelles, 24–26 September 2007.

17 Cilliers, Jakkie, "The African Standby Force. An update on progress," *Institute for Strategic Studies Paper*, no. 160 (2008): 14.

18 See Catherine Guicherd, *IPA Meeting Note: The United Nations Contribution to African Capacity-Building for Peacekeeping,* April 2006.

19 Adibe, "Muddling Through: An Analysis of the ECOWAS Experience in Conflict Management in West Africa," 157–58. See also Adekeye Adebajo, *Building Peace in West Africa: Liberia, Sierra Leone and Guinea-Bissau.* (Boulder, Colo.: Lynne Rienner, 2002), 147.

20 Comfort Ero, "ECOMOG: A Model for Africa?," in *Building Stability in Africa: Challenges for the New Millennium Monograph 46*, ed. Jakkie Cilliers and Annika Hilding-Norberg (Pretoria, South Africa: Institute for Security Studies, 2000); David Francis, *Uniting Africa: Building Regional Peace and Security Systems* (Aldershot, UK and Burlington, Vt.: Ashgate, 2006), 177.

21 Interview, Chrysantus (Chris) Ayangafac, Senior Researcher in the Direct Conflict Prevention Programme, Institute for Security Studies, Addis Ababa (18 September 2007); Interview, Dr. Alfred Nhema, Executive Director OSSREA (20 September 2007); Fredrik Söderbaum, "Whose Security? Comparing Security Regionalism in West and Southern Africa," in *New and Critical Security and Regionalism, Beyond the Nation State*, ed. James Hentz and Morten Bøås (London: Ashgate, 2003), 172; Adekeye Adebajo and Christopher Landsberg, "South Africa and Nigeria as Regional Hegemons," in *From Cape to Congo: Southern Africa's Evolving Security Challenges*, ed. Baregu Mwesiga and Christopher Landsberg (Boulder, Colo.: Lynne Rienner, 2005), 190.

22 Christopher Tuck, "Every Car Or Moving Object Gone: The ECOMOG Intervention in Liberia," *African Studies Quarterly* 4, no. 1 (2000). http://web.africa.ufl.edu/asq/v4/v4i1a1.htm.
23 Adebajo, *Building Peace in West Africa: Liberia, Sierra Leone and Guinea-Bissau*, 48.
24 Interview, Chrysantus (Chris) Ayangafac, Senior Researcher in the Direct Conflict Prevention Programme, Institute for Security Studies, Addis Ababa (18 September 2007); David Francis, *Uniting Africa: Building Regional Peace and Security Systems* (Aldershot, UK and Burlington, Vt.: Ashgate, 2006), 167.
25 European Union and United Nations, *Report of the Joint EU-UN Assessment Mission to ECOWAS*, March 2004 (internal EU document).
26 Report of the ECOWAS workshop, *Lessons from ECOWAS Peacekeeping Operations: 1990–2004*, Accra, Ghana, 10–11 February 2005.
27 UNDP, UNDPA, UNU-CRIS, *Joint UN Inter-Agency Mission to ECOWAS on Conflict Prevention and Peacebuilding*, 31 March 2006.
28 Echoes of ECOWAS (ECOWAS weekly bulletin), "ECOWAS Council of Ministers Advocates Prioritization of Activities," *Echoes of ECOWAS* 1, no. 8, 3–11 January 2008.

4 Intergovernmental Authority on Development (IGAD)

1 Eritrea joined in 1993.
2 Eric Berman and Katie E. Sams, *Peacekeeping in Africa: Capabilities and Culpabilities* (Geneva, Switzerland and Pretoria, South Africa: United Nations Institute for Disarmament Research and Institute for Security Studies, 2000), 207; Kassu Gebremariam, "Peacebuilding in the Horn of Africa," in *Building Sustainable Peace*, ed. Tom Keating and W. Andy Knight (Tokyo and New York: United Nations University Press, 2004), 199.
3 Interview, Ambassador Dr. H. B. Attalla, Executive Secretary, IGAD (16 October 2007).
4 Sally Healy, *Lost Opportunities in the Horn of Africa: How Conflicts Connect and Peace Agreements Unravel* (London: Chatham House/Royal Institute of International Affairs, 2008).
5 Michael Lund and Wendy Betts, "In Search of Regionalism," in *Searching for Peace in Central and South Asia: Overview of Conflict Prevention and Peacebuilding Activities*, ed. Monique Mekenkamp, Paul Van Tongeren, and Hans Van De Veen (Utrecht, The Netherlands: European Center for Conflict Prevention, 1999), 123.
6 John Markakis, "Ethnic Conflict and the State in the Horn of Africa," in *Ethnicity and Conflict in the Horn of Africa*, ed. John Markakis and Katsuyoshi Fukui (London: James Currey, 1994), 218.
7 Cirû Mwaûra, Günther Baechler, and Bethuel Kiplagat, "Background to Conflicts in the IGAD Region," in *Early Warning and Conflict Management in the Horn of Africa*, ed. Cirû Mwaûra and Susanne Schmeidl (Asmara: The Red Sea Press, 2002), 34; Kassu Gebremariam, "Peacebuilding in the Horn of Africa," in *Building Sustainable Peace*, ed. Tom Keating and W. Andy Knight (Tokyo and New York: United Nations University Press, 2004), 205.
8 Rodrigo Tavares, "Understanding Regional Peace and Security: A Framework for Analysis," *Contemporary Politics* 14, no. 2 (2008): 107–27.

9 Healy, *Lost Opportunities in the Horn of Africa: How Conflicts Connect and Peace Agreements Unravel*; Lionel Cliffe, "The Regional Dimensions of Conflict in the Horn of Africa," *Third World Quarterly* 20, no. 1 (1999): 89–111.

10 CEWARN was developed by the Forum on Early Warning and Early Response (FEWER), a consortium of NGOs, research centers and international agencies. FEWER selected four members from its network to undertake the consultancy (the Africa Peace Forum, the Center for Refugee Studies—York University, the Swiss Peace Foundation, and Saferworld).

11 For a full historical description see Jakkie Cilliers, "Towards a Continental Early Warning System for Africa," *Institute of Security Studies Occasional Paper 102* (Pretoria, South Aftrica: Institute for Security Studies, 2005). www.iss.co.za/pubs/papers/102/Paper102.htm.

12 Eritrea suspended its membership when the IGAD Council of Ministers, which met in Nairobi in April 2007, issued a communiqué highlighting the accomplishments Ethiopia had made in Somalia in its support of the Transitional Federal Government of Somalia (TFG). The communiqué was approved by consensus, but Eritrea later claimed that the communiqué was a demonstration that IGAD was no longer a neutral organization. According to Eritrea, IGAD has been used by the United States and by Ethiopia to advance their interests.

13 Emmanuel Fanta, "Dynamics of Regional (non-)integration in Eastern Africa," UNU-CRIS Working Paper W-2008/2 (Bruges, Belgium: United Nations University, 2008). See also Iyob Ruth, "The Foreign Policies of the Horn: The Clash between the Old and the New," in *African Foreign Policies: Power and Process*, ed. Gilbert M. Khadiagala and Terrence Lyons (London: Lynne Rienner, 2001), 107–30; Gerard Prunier, "Rebel Movements and Proxy Warfare: Uganda, Sudan and the Congo (1986–99)," *African Affairs* 103, no. 412 (2004): 359–83.

14 Kasaija Philip Apuuli, "IGAD's Protocol on Conflict Early Warning and Response Mechanism (CEWARN): A Ray of Hope in Conflict," in *The Quest for Peace in Africa: Transformations, Democracy and Public Policy*, ed. Alfred G. Nhema (Utrecht, The Netherlands: International Books, 2004), 181.

15 Interview, Daniel Yifru, Director, Peace and Security Division, IGAD (15 October 2007).

16 Cirû Mwaûra and Susanne Schmeidl, "Introduction," in *Early Warning and Conflict Management in the Horn of Africa*, ed. Cirû Mwaûra and Susanne Schmeidl (Asmara, Eritrea: The Red Sea Press, 2002), 21.

17 Interview, Raymond M. Kitevu, Conflict Early Warning and Response Mechanism (CEWARN) (22 October).

18 See Eastern African Standby Brigade Coordination Mechanism, *Report of the Workshop of the Experts Working Group on the Concept of Cooperation in Peace and Security in the Eastern Africa Region*, Victoria, Seychelles, 24–26 September 2007.

19 Interview, Hiruy Amanuel, head of IGAD Capacity Building Program Against Terrorism (ICPAT) (24 September 2007).

20 Abdelwahab El-Affendi, "The Impasse in the IGAD Peace Process for Sudan: The Limits of Regional Peacemaking?" *African Affairs* 100, no. 401 (2001): 581–99.

21 Gilbert M. Khadiagala, *Meddlers or Mediators: African Interveners in Civil Conflicts in Eastern Africa* (Leiden, The Netherlands and Boston, Mass.: Martinus Nijhoff, 2007), 246.
22 Edmond J. Keller, "Understanding Conflicts in the Horn of Africa," in *Exploring Subregional Conflict: Opportunities for Conflict Prevention*, ed. Chandra Lekha Sriram and Zoe Nielsen (Boulder, Colo. and London: Lynne Rienner, 2004), 42.

5 Southern African Development Community (SADC)

1 In early 1974, Zambian president Kenneth Kaunda called for the creation of a "transcontinental belt of independent and economically powerful nations, from Dar-es-Salaam and Maputo on the Indian Ocean, to Luanda on the Atlantic." Cited in Ibbo Mandaza and Arne Tostensen, *Southern Africa in Search of a Common Future: From the Conference to a Community* (Gaborone, Botswana: SADC Secretariat, 1994), vii.
2 Naison Ngoma, *Prospects for a Security Community in Southern Africa* (Pretoria, South Africa: Institute for Security Studies, 2005), 5; Mandaza and Tostensen, *Southern Africa in Search of a Common Future: From the Conference to a Community*, 4.
3 The member states of SADC are: Angola, Botswana, DRC, Lesotho, Madagascar, Malawi, Mauritius, Mozambique, Namibia, South Africa, Swaziland, Seychelles (withdrew in 2003 and rejoined in 2008), Tanzania, Zambia, and Zimbabwe.
4 Gabriël H. Oosthuizen, *The Southern African Development Community: The Organization, its Policies and Prospects* (Midrand, South Africa: Institute for Global Dialogue, 2006), 59; Mandaza and Tostensen, *Southern Africa in Search of a Common Future: From the Conference to a Community*, 13.
5 The Namibian, "SADC Adopts Draft Mutual Defence Pact," *The Namibian*, 30 July 2001.
6 Fernando Goncalves, "Southern Africa: in Search of a Common Security," *Southern Africa Political and Economic Monthly* 8, no. 7 (1995): 6.
7 Peter Vale, *Southern Africa: Exploring a Peace Dividend* (London: Catholic Institute for International Relations, 1996), 380.
8 Ngoma, *Prospects for a Security Community in Southern Africa*, 120.
9 Oosthuizen, *The Southern African Development Community: The Organization, its Policies and Prospects*, 224.
10 Ngoma, *Prospects for a Security Community in Southern Africa*, 141.
11 Oosthuizen, *The Southern African Development Community: The Organization, its Policies and Prospects*, 83.
12 For instance, at the SADC Summit in August 1997, South African president Nelson Mandela, then acting chairman of the SADC, threatened to resign if the SADC Organ was not brought under the control of the central SADC Chair. This dispute between Mandela and Zimbabwe's President Robert Mugabe, who headed the SADC Organ, led the SADC Summit to suspend its Organ. See L. M. Fisher and N. Ngoma, "The SADC Organ Challenges in the New Millennium," Institute for Security Studies Occasional Paper 114 (Pretoria, South Africa: Institute for Security Studies); Laurie Nathan, "Organ Failure: A Review of the SADC Organ on Politics,

180   *Notes*

Defence and Security," in *Regional Integration for Conflict Prevention and Peace Building in Africa: Europe, SADC and ECOWAS*, ed. Liisa Laakso (Helsinki, Finland: University of Helsinki, 2002), 62–102.

13 Georges Berghezan and Felix Nkundabagenzi, "La Guerre du Congo-Kinshasa: Analyse d'un conflit et Transferts d'Armes vers l'Afrique Centrale," *Rapport du GRIP* 99, no. 2 (1999): 18; Daniel Compagnon, "Mugabe and Partners (Pvt) Ltd ou l'investissement politique du champ économique," *Politique Africaine* 81 (2001): 114.

14 Oosthuizen, *The Southern African Development Community: The Organization, its Policies and Prospects*, 86.

15 Gilbert M. Khadiagala, "Foreign Policy Decision Making in Southern Africa's Fading Frontline," in *African Foreign Policies: Power and Process*, ed. Gilbert M. Khadiagala and Terrence Lyons (London: Lynne Rienner, 2001), 142.

16 Ngoma, *Prospects for a Security Community in Southern Africa*, 153.

17 See Eastern African Standby Brigade Coordination Mechanism, *Report of the Workshop of the Experts Working Group on the Concept of Cooperation in Peace and Security in the Eastern Africa Region*, Victoria, Seychelles, 24–26 September 2007.

18 Interview, official at Embassy of the United Kingdom in Zimbabwe (24 October 2007). Anonymity required. Interview, official at French Embassy in South Africa (6 November 2007). Anonymity required. Interview, official at French Embassy in South Africa (7 November 2007). Anonymity required. Interview, General Louis Fisher, former chief of Botswana Defense Forces (9 November 2007).

19 Blue Hungwe (1997, in Zimbabwe), Blue Crane (1999, in South Africa), Tulipe (Madagascar, 1999), Tanzanite (2002, in Tanzania); Air-Borne Africa (2002, in Botswana), Exercise Thokgamo (2005, in Botswana).

20 Interview, official at French Embassy in South Africa (6 November 2007). Anonymity required. Interview, official at French Embassy in South Africa (7 November 2007). Anonymity required.

21 Following an instruction from the Ministerial Committee of the Organ meeting in Maputo in July 2003, the ISDSC approved the conceptual principles on which the SADC early warning system is to be based. In July 2004, the 25th meeting of the ISDSC mandated a team of experts from the SADC and Organ troikas to initiate the establishment of the regional early warning system, which has not yet been finalized.

22 Interview, Chrysantus (Chris) Ayangafac, Senior Researcher in the Direct Conflict Prevention Programme, Institute for Security Studies, Addis Ababa (18 September 2007). Interview, John Makumbe, professor, University of Zimbabwe (29 October 2007). Fredrik Söderbaum, "Whose Security? Comparing Security Regionalism in West and Southern Africa," in *New and Critical Security and Regionalism, Beyond the Nation State*, ed. James Hentz and Morten Bøås (London: Ashgate, 2003), 176. Adekeye Adebajo and Christopher Landsberg, "South Africa and Nigeria as Regional Hegemons," in *From Cape to Congo: Southern Africa's Evolving Security Challenges*, ed. Baregu Mwesiga and Christopher Landsberg (Boulder, Colo.: Lynne Rienner, 2005), 186.

23 Interview, General Louis Fisher, former chief of Botswana Defense Forces (9 November 2007).

24 Institute for Security Studies, "Hawks, Doves or Penguins? A Critical Review of the SADC Military Intervention in the DRC" in *Institute for Security Studies Occasional Paper* 88 (Pretoria, South Africa: Institute for Security Studies, 2004), 4; Willie Breytenbach, Dalitso Chilemba, Thomas A. Brown, and Charlotte Plantive, "Conflicts in the Congo: From Kivu to Kabila," in *African Security Review* 8, no. 5 (1999), www.iss.co.za/Pubs/ASR/8No5/ ConflictsInTheCongo.html. Interview, Ibbo Mandaza, SAPES-Southern African Political Economy Series (25 October). Interview, official at European Commission Delegation to Zimbabwe (29 October 2007). Anonymity required. Interview, Tom Wheeler, South African Institute of International Affairs (1 November 2007). Interview, General Paulino José Macaringue, Senior Lecturer, Center for Defence and Security Management, Wits University Graduate School of Public and Development Management (2 November 2007). Interview, official at French Embassy in South Africa (6 November 2007). Anonymity required. Interview, Chris Maroleng, Institute for Security Studies, Pretoria (7 November 2007). Georges Berghezan and Felix Nkundabagenzi, "La Guerre du Congo-Kinshasa: Analyse d'un conflit et Transferts d'Armes vers l'Afrique Centrale," *Rapport du GRIP* 99, no. 2 (1999): 18. Daniel Compagnon, "Mugabe and Partners (Pvt) Ltd ou l'investissement politique du champ économique," *Politique Africaine* 81 (2001): 114.

25 Eric G. Berman and Katie E. Sams, "The Peacekeeping Potential of African Regional Organizations," in *Dealing with Conflict in Africa: The United Nations and Regional Organizations*, ed. Jane Boulden (New York: Palgrave Macmillan, 2003), 50.

26 This idea was conveyed for instance by the representative of the United Kingdom at the second Security Council meeting with regional organizations held in July 2004. *Security Council Welcomes Strengthened Collaboration Between UN, Regional Organizations in Conflict Prevention, Stabilizing War-Torn States. Presidential Statement Follows Day-Long Public Meeting: Secretary-General Calls for 'Strategic Partnerships' to Meet Future Challenges* (Security Council press release 8153), 20 July 2004.

27 Fredrik Söderbaum, "Whose Security? Comparing Security Regionalism in West and Southern Africa," in *New and Critical Security and Regionalism, Beyond the Nation State*, ed. James Hentz and Morten Bøås (London: Ashgate, 2003), 173.

28 Khadiagala, "Foreign Policy Decision Making in Southern Africa's Fading Frontline," 150.

29 The SADC Secretariat is not very forthcoming at making the latest figures public. In fact, a Council Decision on "Categories of Information for Posting on the Website" taken in August 2003 at Dar es Salaam makes some of the info restricted. In our field work SADC staff could not provide a clear figure either. However, a newspaper, citing late Zambian president Levy Mwanawasa, has put the figure for 2007/8 at US$18.9 million (see "Seychelles rejoins SADC," *Times of Zambia*, 19 August 2007).

6 Organization of American States (OAS)

1 Gordon Connell-Smith, *The Inter-American System* (Oxford: Oxford University Press, 1966); Marianne H. Marchand, "North American Regionalisms and Regionalization in the 1990s," in *Regionalization in a Globalizing*

World: A Comparative Perspective on Forms, Actors and Processes, ed. Michael Schulz, Fredrik Söderbaum, and Joakim Öjendal (London and New York: Zed Books, 2001), 199.

2 Connie Peck, *Sustainable Peace: The Role of the UN and Regional Organizations in Preventing Conflict* (Lanham, Md.: Rowman and Littlefield, 1998), 140.

3 James Brown Scott, *The International Conferences of American States, 1889–1928: A Collection of the Conventions, Recommendations, Resolutions, Reports, and Motions Adopted by the First Six International Conferences of the American States, and Documents Relating to the Organization of the Conferences* (Oxford: Oxford University Press, 1931); Gordon Connell-Smith, *The Inter-American System* (Oxford: Oxford University Press, 1966).

4 Robert A. Pastor, "North America and the Americas: Integration Among Unequal Partners," in *Global Politics of Regionalism: Theory and Practice*, ed. Mary Farrell, Björn Hettne, and Luk Van Langenhove (Ann Arbor, Mich. and London: Pluto Press, 2005), 210.

5 Scott, *The International Conferences of American States, 1889–1928: A Collection of the Conventions, Recommendations, Resolutions, Reports, and Motions Adopted by the First Six International Conferences of the American States, and Documents Relating to the Organization of the Conferences*; Joaquín Tacsan, "Searching for OAS/UN Task-Sharing Opportunities in Central America and Haiti," in *Beyond Subcontracting: Task-Sharing With Regional Security Arrangements and Service Providing NGOs*, ed. Thomas G. Weiss (Houndmills, UK and London: Macmillan Press, 1998), 95–97.

6 The OAS member states are: Antigua and Barbuda, Argentina, The Bahamas, Barbados, Belize, Bolivia, Brazil, Canada, Chile, Colombia, Costa Rica, Cuba (excluded from participation since 1962), Dominica, Dominican Republic, Ecuador, El Salvador, Grenada, Guatemala, Guyana, Haiti, Honduras, Jamaica, Mexico, Nicaragua, Panama, Paraguay, Peru, Saint Kitts and Nevis, Saint Lucia, Saint Vincent and the Grenadines, Suriname, Trinidad and Tobago, USA, Uruguay, and Venezuela.

7 Andrew Hurrell, "Regionalism in the Americas," in *Regionalism in World Politics: Regional Organization and International Order*, ed. Louise Fawcett and Andrew Hurrell (Oxford and New York: Oxford University Press 1995), 265; Monica Herz, "Managing Security in the Western Hemisphere: The OAS' New Activism," in *The United Nations and Regional Security: Europe and Beyond*, ed. Michael Pugh and Waheguru Pal Singh Sidhu (Boulder, Colo. and London: Lynne Rienner, 2003), 215; Tacsan, "Searching for OAS/UN Task-Sharing Opportunities in Central America and Haiti," 92–93.

8 Andrew F. Cooper and Thomas Legler, *Intervention Without Intervening? The OAS Defense and Promotion of Democracy in the Americas* (Basingstoke, UK: Palgrave Macmillan, 2006), 24.

9 Pastor, "North America and the Americas: Integration Among Unequal Partners," 210.

10 Herz, "Managing Security in the Western Hemisphere: The OAS' New Activism," 213.

11 Carolyn M. Shaw, "Conflict Management in Latin America," in *Regional Conflict Management*, ed. Paul F. Diehl and Joseph Lepgold (Lanham, Md.: Rowman and Littlefield, 2003): 128.

12 Herz, "Managing Security in the Western Hemisphere: The OAS' New Activism," 216.
13 Peck, *Sustainable Peace: The Role of the UN and Regional Organizations in Preventing Conflict*, 143; Shaw, "Conflict Management in Latin America," 126.
14 The Secretariat for Political Affairs was created in 2006 and the former Department of Crisis Prevention and Special Missions, the Unit/Department for the Promotion of Democracy, the Department for Democratic and Political Affairs and its Office for the Prevention and Resolution of Conflicts were dismantled and their functions harmonized and integrated in the new organizational structure.
15 Shaw, "Conflict Management in Latin America," 144.
16 Herz, "Managing Security in the Western Hemisphere: The OAS' New Activism," 214.
17 Hurrell, "Regionalism in the Americas," 265.
18 AGRES 1080, 5 June 1991. Resolution 1080, on Representative Democracy, stipulates the actions that the organization can take in case of "sudden or irregular interruption of the democratic political institutional process or of the legitimate exercise of power by the democratically elected government in any of the Organization's member states." Available at www.oas.org/juridico/english/agres1080.htm.
19 Peck, *Sustainable Peace: The Role of the UN and Regional Organizations in Preventing Conflict*, 142.
20 The other two units of the Department are the Fund for Peace; and the Special Missions unit, which includes the work of the Mission to Support the Peace Process in Colombia (MAPP-OAS).
21 OAS mediation led to the signing of the Agreement to Establish a Transition Process and Confidence-Building Measures. It defined an Adjacency Line and instructed the General Secretariat to establish an office in the Adjacency Zone (AZ) for the purpose of fostering community-to-community contacts across the Adjacency Line and providing information on the transition process and the measures implemented.
22 After the incursion of Colombian security forces in Ecuadorian territory on 1 March 2008, OAS adopted several decisions to mediate between the two countries and prevent the escalation of the conflict. It is worth noting the 25th meeting of Consultation of Ministers of Foreign Affairs of the OAS, where member states resolved "to instruct the Secretary General to use his good offices to implement a mechanism for observing compliance with this resolution and the restoration of an atmosphere of trust between the two Parties."
23 In October 2008, in Cochabamba, the OAS participated in the dialogue process between the Executive Branch of the government and the regional opposition self-named CONALDE (Governors of the oriental regions of the country). The OAS also participated in November in the Congress dialogue which facilitated the Constitutional referendum held on 25 January 2009.
24 Carolyn M. Shaw, "Limits to Hegemonic Influence in the Organization of American States," *Latin American Politics and Society* 45, no. 3 (2003): 76; Alex J. Bellamy and Paul D. Williams, "Who's Keeping the Peace? Regionalization and Contemporary Peace Operations," *International Security* 29, no. 4 (2005): 162.

25 See Kennedy Graham and Tânia Felício, *Regional Security and Global Governance: A Study of Interaction Between Regional Agencies and the UN Security Council with a Proposal for a Regional-Global Security Mechanism* (Brussels, Belgium: VUB University Press, 2006), 71.

26 Tacsan, "Searching for OAS/UN Task-Sharing Opportunities in Central America and Haiti," 111.

27 Andrew F. Cooper and Thomas Legler, *Intervention Without Intervening? The OAS Defense and Promotion of Democracy in the Americas* (Basingstoke, UK: Palgrave Macmillan, 2006), 27; Yasmine Shamsie, "Moving Beyond Mediation: The OAS Transforming Conflict in Guatemala," *Global Governance* 13, no. 3 (2007): 409–25.

28 Herz, "Managing Security in the Western Hemisphere: The OAS' New Activism," 215.

29 Cooper and Legler, *Intervention Without Intervening? The OAS Defense and Promotion of Democracy in the Americas*, 33.

30 Shaw, "Limits to Hegemonic Influence in the Organization of American States," 88.

31 Cooper and Legler, *Intervention Without Intervening? The OAS Defense and Promotion of Democracy in the Americas*, 31.

32 Herz, "Managing Security in the Western Hemisphere: The OAS' New Activism," 226; Tacsan, "Searching for OAS/UN Task-Sharing Opportunities in Central America and Haiti," 106.

33 John W. Graham, "La OEA se Hunde: Merece ser Salvada?," *Foreign Affairs en Español* 5, no. 2 (April-June 2005), www.foreignaffairs-esp.org/20050401faenespessay050210/john-w-graham/la-oea-se-hunde-merece-ser-salvada.html.

7 Association of Southeast Asian Nations (ASEAN)

1 Amitav Acharya, *The Quest for Identity: International Relations of Southeast Asia* (Oxford and New York: Oxford University Press, 2000).

2 Norman Palmer, *The New Regionalism in Asia and the Pacific* (Lexington, Mass. and Toronto: Lexington Books, 1991), 61.

3 Relations between the Philippines and Malaysia remained cool until the 1990s—when the Filipino president Fidel Ramos paid the first top-level visit to Kuala Lumpur in several decades.

4 Barry Buzan, *People, States and Fear: An Agenda for International Security Studies in the Post-Cold War Era* (Sussex, UK: Harvester Wheatsheaf, 1991).

5 Joakim Öjendal, "Southeast Asia at Constant Crossroads: An Ambiguous 'New Region,'" in *Regionalization in a Globalizing World: A Comparative Perspective on Forms, Actors and Processes*, ed. Michael Schulz, Fredrik Söderbaum, and Joakim Öjendal (London and New York: Zed Books, 2001): 155.

6 Ann Murphy, "From Conflict to Cooperation in Southeast Asia, 1961–1967: The Disputes Arising Out of the Creation of Malaysia and the Establishment of the Association of Southeast Asia (ASEAN)," Ph.D. thesis, Department of Political Science, Columbia University, 2002.

7 Kishore Mahbubani, "Measures for Regional Security and Arms Control in the South-East Asian Area," in *Disarmament and Security Issues in the*

Asia-Pacific Region, ed. United Nations Dept. for Disarmament Affairs (New York: Dept. for Disarmament Affairs, United Nations, 1992), 110 (italics added).

8 Palmer, *The New Regionalism in Asia and the Pacific*, 65.

9 Shaun Narine, "Peacebuilding in Southeast Asia," in *Building Sustainable Peace*, ed. Tom Keating and W. Andy Knight (Tokyo and New York: United Nations University Press, 2004), 232.

10 Brunei Darussalam, Cambodia, Indonesia, Lao PDR, Malaysia, Myanmar, Philippines, Singapore, Thailand, and Vietnam.

11 *ASEAN Vision 2020*, available online at www.aseansec.org/1814.htm.

12 Connie Peck, *Sustainable Peace: The Role of the UN and Regional Organizations in Preventing Conflict* (Lanham, Md.: Rowman and Littlefield, 1998), 176.

13 Johan Saravanamuttu, "ASEAN: a Rejoinder," *Security Dialogue* 25, no. 4 (1994): 469–72.

14 Acharya, *The Quest for Identity: International Relations of Southeast Asia*.

15 R. James Ferguson, "ASEAN Concord II: Policy Prospects for Participant Regional Development," *Contemporary Southeast Asia* 26, no. 3 (2004): 393–416.

16 For a more detailed analysis of ASEAN's informal decision-making process see Mely Caballero Anthony, "Mechanisms of Dispute Settlement: The ASEAN Experience," *Contemporary Southeast Asia* 20, no. 1 (1999): 38–66.

17 Paul J. Davidson, "The ASEAN Way and Role of Law in ASEAN Economic Cooperation," *Singapore Yearbook of International Law* 8 (2004): 165–76.

18 Supposedly the ASEAN Way derives from the Malaysian concepts of *musjawarah* and *mufukat*. *Musjawarah* refers to the process of decision-making through consultation and discussion, while *mufukat* refers to the unanimous decision that is achieved through *musjawarah*. See Richard Robison, "The Politics of Asian Values," *Pacific Review* 9, no. 3 (1996): 309–27.

19 Ralf Emmers, "Southeast Asia's New Security Institutions," in *Asia's New Institutional Architecture: Evolving Structures for Managing Trade, Financial, and Security Relations*, ed. Vinod K. Aggarwal and Min Gyo Koo (Heidelberg, Germany: Springer, 2008), 210.

20 The Vientiane Action Program is a six-year plan (adopted on 29 November 2004), put forward by the ASEAN leaders in order to establish the ASEAN Community, which is the end goal of the organization for 2015.

21 Bertrand Fort, "ASEM's Role for Co-operation on Security in Asia and Europe," *Asia Europe Journal* 2, no. 3 (2004): 355–63.

22 Emmers, "Southeast Asia's New Security Institutions," 182.

23 For a critical overview see Yuen Foong Khong and Helen E. S. Nesadurai, "Hanging Together, Institutional Design, and Cooperation in Southeast Asia: AFTA and ARF," in *Crafting Cooperation: Regional International Institutions in Comparative Perspective*, ed. Amitav Acharya and Alastair Iain Johnston (Cambridge and New York: Cambridge University Press, 2007), 58–66.

24 Khong and Nesadurai, "Hanging Together, Institutional Design, and Cooperation in Southeast Asia: AFTA and ARF," 38.

25 Sheldon W. Simon, "Whither Security Regionalism? ASEAN and the ARF in the Face of New Security," in *Reassessing Security Cooperation in the Asia-Pacific: Competition, Congruence and Transformation*, ed. Amitav

Acharya and Evelyn Goh (Cambridge, Mass. and London: MIT Press, 2007): 113–33.

26 The accepted definition of preventive diplomacy was the following:

> Consensual diplomatic and political action taken by sovereign states with the consent of all directly involved parties to help prevent disputes and conflicts from arising between states that could potentially pose a threat to regional peace and stability; to help prevent such disputes and conflicts from escalating into armed confrontation; and to help minimize the impact of such disputes and conflicts in the region.

It includes the following instruments: confidence building efforts; norms building; enhancing channels of communication; and the role of the ARF chair.

27 Daljit Singh, "The Politics of Peace: Preventive Diplomacy in ASEAN," *Harvard International Review* 16, no. 3 (Spring 1994): 32.

28 Alastair Iain Johnston, "Socialization and International Institutions: The ASEAN Way and International Relations Theory," in *International Relations Theory and the Asia-Pacific*, ed. G. John Ikenberry and Michael Mastanduno (New York: Columbia University Press 2003), 126.

29 Mely Caballero-Anthony, "The Regionalization of Peace in Asia," in *The United Nations and Regional Security: Europe and Beyond*, ed. Michael Pugh and Waheguru Pal Singh Sidhu (Boulder, Colo. and London: Lynne Rienner, 2003), 203.

30 Adam Malik, "Regional Cooperation in International Politics," in *Regionalism in Southeast Asia* (Jakarta, Indonesia: Yayasan Proklamasi/Center for Strategic and International Studies, 1975), 162.

31 See Association of Southeast Asian Nations, "Declaration on the Conduct of Parties in the South China Sea," www.aseansec.org/13163.htm.

32 Shaun Narine, "Peacebuilding in Southeast Asia," in *Building Sustainable Peace*, ed. Tom Keating and W. Andy Knight (Tokyo and New York: United Nations University Press, 2004), 224.

33 Association of Southeast Asian Nations, "ASEAN Urges Restart of Six-Party Talks on North Korea," www.aseansec.org/afp/153.htm

34 Association of Southeast Asian Nations, "ASEAN Chairman Statement on Myanmar," www.aseansec.org/21057.htm.

35 Chairman's Statement of the Thirteenth ASEAN Regional Forum, para. 20 (Kuala Lumpur, 28 July 2006).

36 Human Rights Watch, "Letter to ASEAN Secretary-General Surin Pitsuwan" (25 February 2009).

37 Caballero-Anthony, "The Regionalization of Peace in Asia," 204.

38 See full text, Association of Southeast Asian Nations, press release SG/SM/7303, www.aseansec.org/6910.htm.

39 Association of Southeast Asian Nations, media release "Interesting Changes to the ASEAN Institutional Framework", www.aseansec.org/21087.htm.

40 Cuong Nguyen and Clay Wescott, "Results-Based Monitoring of Regional Integration and Cooperation in ASEAN," in *Governing Regional Integration for Development: Monitoring Experiences, Methods and Prospects*, ed. Philippe de Lombaerde, Antoni Estevadeordal, and Kati Suominen (Aldershot, UK: Ashgate, 2008), 103–24.

41 Simon, "Whither Security Regionalism? ASEAN and the ARF in the Face of New Security," 113–33.

42 Chung-in Moon and Chaesung Chun, "Sovereignty: Dominance of the Westphalian Concept and Implications for Regional Security," in *Asian Security Order: Instrumental and Normative Features*, ed. Muthiah Alagappa (Stanford, Calif.: Stanford University Press, 2003), 106–37.

43 Narine, "Peacebuilding in Southeast Asia," 213–39.

44 Rowan Callick, "Kevin Rudd's Pan-Asian Vision," *The Australian*, 23 August 2008.

45 *Security Council Presidential Statement Recognizes Importance of Regional Organizations in Prevention, Management, Resolution of Conflicts. Secretary-General Says UN Partnerships with Organizations Strong, Active; Enabled More Rapid Response to Crises, More Effective Post-Conflict Peacebuilding* (Security Council document SC/9163), 6 November 2007.

46 Narine, "Peacebuilding in Southeast Asia," 213–39.

8 Commonwealth of Independent States (CIS)

1 Patrick Jotun, "Regionalization in Caucasia and Central Asia," in *Regionalization in a Globalizing World: a Comparative Perspective on Forms, Actors and Processes,* ed. Michael Schulz, Fredrik Söderbaum, and Joakim Öjendal (London and New York: Zed Books 2001), 100.

2 Roger E. Kanet and Alexander V. Kozhemiakin, *The Foreign Policy of the Russian Federation* (London: Macmillan, 1997), 226.

3 S. Neil MacFarlane, "On the Front Lines in the Near Abroad: The CIS and the OSCE in Georgia's Civil Wars," in *Beyond Subcontracting: Task-Sharing With Regional Security Arrangements and Service Providing NGOs,* ed. Thomas G. Weiss (Houndmills, UK and London: Macmillan Press, 1998), 118.

4 Martha Brill Olcott, "Central Asia's Security Challenges," paper presented to the Spring 2001 meetings of the Schlesinger Working Group on Strategic Surprises, Washington, D.C., 10 April 2001; Jotun, "Regionalization in Caucasia and Central Asia," 105.

5 For a historical overview see Gregory Gleason, "The Federal Formula and the Collapse of the USSR," *Publius: The Journal of Federalism* 22, no. 3 (1992): 141–63. In 1993 Georgia decided to join CIS, but following the South Ossetian War of 2008 the Georgian parliament voted unanimously (on 14 August 2008) to withdraw from the regional organization.

6 Sergei A. Voitovich, "The Commonwealth of Independent States: An Emerging Institutional Model," *European Journal of International Law* 4, no. 1 (1994): 403–17.

7 Gregory Gleason, "The Federal Formula and the Collapse of the USSR," *Publius: The Journal of Federalism* 22, no. 3 (1992): 141–63; Voitovich, "The Commonwealth of Independent States: An Emerging Institutional Model," 403–17.

8 Chapter 4 of the Concept states that, "When working to settle conflicts in accordance with Chapter VIII of the Charter of the United Nations, the Commonwealth of Independent States shall interact closely with other international organizations and particularly with the United Nations and OSCE." The full text of the Concept for the Prevention and Settlement of

Conflicts in the Territory of States Members of the Commonwealth of Independent States as attached to the *Letter dated 26 January 1996 from the Permanent Representative of the Russian Federation to the United Nations addressed to the Secretary-General* is available at www.un.org/documents/ga/docs/51/plenary/a51-62.htm.

9 Kristina Jeffers, "Misreading Moscow: Toward a New Interpretation of Russian Peacekeeping in the Early 1990s," M.A. in Law and Diplomacy thesis at the Fletcher School, Tufts University, 2006, 39.

10 Michael Yermolaev, "Russia's International Peacekeeping and Conflict Management in the Post-Soviet Environment," in *Monograph nr 44: Boundaries of Peace Support Operations: The African Dimension*, ed. Mark Malan (Pretoria, South Africa: Institute of Security Studies, 2000), 6.

11 Gail Lapidus, Victor Zaslavsky, and Philip Goldman, *From Union to Commonwealth: Nationalism and Separatism in Soviet Republics* (New York and Cambridge: Cambridge University Press, 1992); Philip G. Roeder, "Soviet Federalism and Ethnic Mobilization," *World Politics* 43 (January 1991): 196–232.

12 Roy Allison, "Peacekeeping in the Soviet Successor States," *EU-ISS Chaillot Paper* 18, (1994): 8; Anna Kreikemeyer and Andrei V. Zagorski, "The Commonwealth of Independent States (CIS)," in *Peacekeeping and the Role of Russia in Eurasia*, ed. Lena Jonson and Clive Archer (Boulder, Colo. and Oxford: Westview Press, 1996), 157.

13 Kreikemeyer and Zagorski, "The Commonwealth of Independent States (CIS)," 160.

14 According to the CIS commander-in-chief there were 25,000 peacekeepers from Russia, Kazakhstan, Kyrgyzstan, and Uzbekistan. Former prime minister Abdullojonov estimated that 30,000 people died in the climax of civil war. See John Mackinlay and Evgenii Sharov, "Russian Peacekeeping Operations in Georgia," in *Regional Peacekeepers: The Paradox of Russian Peacekeeping*, ed. John Mackinlay and Peter Cross (Tokyo and New York: United Nations University Press, 2003), 156.

15 Mackinlay and Cross, "Russian Peacekeeping Operations in Georgia," 63–110; MacFarlane, "On the Front Lines in the Near Abroad: The CIS and the OSCE in Georgia's Civil Wars," 115–36.

16 Kreikemeyer and Zagorski, "The Commonwealth of Independent States (CIS)," 162.

17 Lena Jonson and Clive Archer, "Russia and Peacekeeping in Eurasia," in *Peacekeeping and the Role of Russia in Eurasia*, ed. Lena Jonson and Clive Archer (Boulder, Colo. and Oxford: Westview Press 1996), 9.

18 Trevor Waters, "Russian Peacekeeping in Moldova: Source of Stability or Neo-Imperialist Threat?" in *Regional Peacekeepers: The Paradox of Russian Peacekeeping*, ed. John Mackinlay and Peter Cross (Tokyo: United Nations University Press, 2003), 132–55; Kristina Jeffers, "Misreading Moscow: Toward a New Interpretation of Russian Peacekeeping in the Early 1990s," M.A. in Law and Diplomacy thesis, the Fletcher School, Tufts University, 2006.

19 John Mackinlay, "Conclusion: The Paradox of Russian Peacekeeping," in *Regional Peacekeepers: The Paradox of Russian Peacekeeping*, eds. John Mackinlay and Peter Cross (Tokyo and New York: United Nations University Press, 2003b), 205.

20 Yermolaev, "Russia's International Peacekeeping and Conflict Management in the Post-Soviet Environment," 7.
21 John Mackinlay, "Introduction," in *Regional Peacekeepers: The Paradox of Russian Peacekeeping*, ed. John Mackinlay and Peter Cross (Tokyo and New York: United Nations University Press, 2003a), 6.
22 Yermolaev, "Russia's International Peacekeeping and Conflict Management in the Post-Soviet Environment," 7.
23 Jeffers, "Misreading Moscow: Toward a New Interpretation of Russian Peacekeeping in the Early 1990s."
24 MacFarlane, "On the Front Lines in the Near Abroad: The CIS and the OSCE in Georgia's Civil Wars," 130.
25 MacFarlane, "On the Front Lines in the Near Abroad: The CIS and the OSCE in Georgia's Civil Wars," 30.
26 Gregory Gleason, "Stability and Change in Central Asia," in *Exploring Subregional Conflict: Opportunities for Conflict Prevention*, ed. Chandra Lekha Sriram and Zoe Nielsen (Boulder, Colo. and London: Lynne Rienner, 2004), 83.
27 MacFarlane, "On the Front Lines in the Near Abroad: The CIS and the OSCE in Georgia's Civil Wars," 130.
28 Roger E. Kanet and Alexander V. Kozhemiakin, *The Foreign Policy of the Russian Federation* (London: Macmillan, 1997), 227.
29 Russian Deputy Foreign Minister Sergei Razov at the State Duma (cited in Pavel K. Baev, "Will Putin Pull the Plug on the CIS?," *Eurasia Daily Monitor* 2, no. 50 (2005): 2).
30 Even if the CIS's official website (in Russian) mentions the decision-making process involved in the adoption of the annual budget, the updated budget figure is not provided. The latest figure is from 2001 (237,901,000 rubles).
31 Pavel K. Baev, "Will Putin Pull the Plug on the CIS?," *Eurasia Daily Monitor* 2, no. 50 (2005): 1–2.

9 League of Arab States (LAS)

1 Chapter written by Emmanuel Fanta.
2 Libya, Palestine, Morocco, Saudi Arabia, and Yemen also participated in the Conference as observers.
3 Yehoshua Porath, *In Search of Arab Unity, 1930–1945* (London: Routledge, 1986), 285.
4 Porath, *In Search of Arab Unity, 1930–1945*, 283; Nevertheless, King Faruq of Egypt dismissed his prime minister, Mustafa al-Nahass, the day after the signing of the Alexandria Protocol as he considered that the option laid out in the protocol was still going too far and could threaten Egyptian sovereignty (Israel Gershoni and James P. Jankowski, *Redefining the Egyptian Nation, 1930–1945* (Cambridge: Cambridge University Press, 2002), 203.)
5 Quoted in Porath, *In Search of Arab Unity, 1930–1945*, 285.
6 Israel Gershoni and James P. Jankowski, *Redefining the Egyptian Nation, 1930–1945* (Cambridge: Cambridge University Press, 2002), 206.
7 Gregory L. Aftandilian, *Egypt's Bid for Arab Leadership: Implications for U.S. Policy* (New York: Council on Foreign Relations Press, 1993).
8 Ahmed Gomaa, *The Foundation of the League of Arab States: Wartime Diplomacy and Inter-Arab Politics, 1941 to 1945* (London: Longman, 1977).

9 Michael Barnett and Etel Solingen, "Designed to Fail or Failure of Design? The Origins and Legacy of the Arab League," in *Crafting Cooperation. Regional International Institutions in Comparative Perspective*, ed. Amitav Acharya and Alastair Iain Johnston (Cambridge and New York: Cambridge University Press, 2007), 200.

10 Barnett and Solingen, "Designed to Fail or Failure of Design? The Origins and Legacy of the Arab League," 200–1.

11 Barnett and Solingen, "Designed to Fail or Failure of Design? The Origins and Legacy of the Arab League," 201–3.

12 Israel Gershoni, "Rethinking the Formation of Arab Nationalism in the Middle East, 1920–45: Old and New Narratives," in *Rethinking Nationalism in the Arab Middle East*, ed. James P. Jankowski and Israel Gershoni (New York: Columbia University Press, 1997), 3–25.

13 Barnett and Solingen, "Designed to Fail or Failure of Design? The Origins and Legacy of the Arab League," 207.

14 Emmanuel Sivan, "Arab Nationalism in the Age of Islamic Resurgence," in *Rethinking Nationalism in the Arab Middle East*, ed. James P. Jankowski and Israel Gershoni (New York: Columbia University Press, 1997): 207–28.

15 Hussein A. Hassouna, "The League of Arab States and the United Nations," in *Regionalism and the United Nations*, ed. Berhanykun Andemicael (New York: Oceana Publications, 1979), 309.

16 Hassouna, "The League of Arab States and the United Nations," 315–16.

17 Barnett and Solingen, "Designed to Fail or Failure of Design? The Origins and Legacy of the Arab League," 214.

18 Saïd Ihrai, "Le Maintien de la Paix et de la Sécurité Internationale dans les Projets de Réforme de la Ligue des Etats Arabes," in *La Sécurité Internationale Entre Rupture et Continuité: Mélanges en l'honneur du professeur Jean-François Guilhaudis*, ed. Emile Bruylant (Brussels, Belgium: Editions Bruylant 2007), 302.

19 Ihrai, "Le Maintien de la Paix et de la Sécurité Internationale dans les Projets de Réforme de la Ligue des Etats Arabes," 312.

20 Barnett and Solingen, "Designed to Fail or Failure of Design? The Origins and Legacy of the Arab League," 216.

21 La Lettre du Centre d'Etudes et de Recherche sur le Monde Arabe et Méditerranéen, "Entretien Avec Amre Moussa," *La Lettre du CERMAM* (April 2005).

22 Moussa quoted in Ihrai, "Le Maintien de la Paix et de la Sécurité Internationale dans les Projets de Réforme de la Ligue des Etats Arabes," 303.

23 One explanation for this reluctance to call upon the League to intervene in conflict situations has to do with the various defense agreements that the League's member states have signed with external powers such as the USA, the UK or France (Ihrai, "Le Maintien de la Paix et de la Sécurité Internationale dans les Projets de Réforme de la Ligue des Etats Arabes," 317–318).

24 See "Arab Leaders Relaunch Peace Plan" (BBC News, 28 March 2007).

25 Hassouna, "The League of Arab States and the United Nations," 309.

26 Etel Solingen, "The Genesis, Design and Effect of Regional Institutions: Lessons from East Asia and the Middle East," *International Studies Quarterly* 52, no. 2 (2008): 283; Barnett and Solingen, "Designed to Fail or Failure of Design? The Origins and Legacy of the Arab League," 214.

27 Hussein A. Hassouna, "The League of Arab States and the United Nations," in *Regionalism and the United Nations*, ed. Berhanykun Andemicael (New York: Oceana Publications, 1979), 310–11.

28 Arab News, "Qaddafi Walks Out," *Arab News*, 23 May 2004.

10 Pacific Islands Forum (PIF)

1 Defined as the territory created by two parallel lines where one is drawn northeast of Australia and New Zealand and the other southwest of Hawaii. For a discussion of different definitions of "South Pacific" see Ron Crocombe, *The South Pacific* (Suva, Fiji: University of the South Pacific, 2001), 16–18.

2 Norman Palmer, *The New Regionalism in Asia and the Pacific* (Lexington, Mass. and Toronto: Lexington Books, 1991), 98.

3 One of the founding fathers of the Forum, then prime minister of Fiji Ratu Sir Kamisese Mara, describes the creation of the Forum as follows: "We decided that if we could not talk inside the conference room we would talk outside, and the island leaders talked far into the night ... As a result of all the problems with the South Pacific Commission, the Pacific leaders decided we should have our own forum." Cited in Shennia Spillane, "The Pacific Plan 2006–15: Legal Implications for Regionalism," in *Models of Regional Governance for the Pacific: Sovereignty and the Future Architecture of Regionalism*, ed. Kennedy Graham (Christchurch, New Zealand: University of Canterbury, 2008), 73.

4 Palmer, *The New Regionalism in Asia and the Pacific*, 105.

5 The Forum's member states are: Australia, the Cook Islands, the Federated States of Micronesia, Fiji, Kiribati, the Marshall Islands, Nauru, New Zealand, Niue, Palau, Papua New Guinea, Samoa, the Solomon Islands, Tonga, Tuvalu, and Vanuatu. Since 2006, associate member territories are New Caledonia and French Polynesia.

6 Kennedy Graham, "Models of Regional Governance: Is There a Choice for the Pacific?," in *Models of Regional Governance for the Pacific: Sovereignty and the Future Architecture of Regionalism*, ed. Kennedy Graham (Christchurch, New Zealand: University of Canterbury, 2008), 26.

7 Forum Communiqué, para. 8, 31st Pacific Islands Forum, Tarawa, 29 October 2000.

8 Stephen Hoadley, "Pacific Islands Security Management by New Zealand and Australia: Towards a New Paradigm," Centre for Strategic Studies Working Paper 20/05, Wellington, New Zealand, 2005; Kevin Clements, "Conflict Prevention: Does 'Responsibility to Protect' Fit into Biketawa?," in *Models of Regional Governance for the Pacific: Sovereignty and the Future Architecture of Regionalism*, ed. Kennedy Graham (Christchurch, New Zealand: University of Canterbury, 2008), 141.

9 Ian Frazer and Jenny Bryant-Tokalau, "Introduction: The Uncertain Future of Pacific Regionalism," in *Redefining the Pacific? Regionalism Past, Present and Future*, ed. Jenny Bryant-Tokalau and Ian Frazer (Aldershot, UK: Ashgate, 2006), 1–23.

10 Anthony Angelo, "The UN Charter and Regional Security: Is the PIF a Regional Organization?," in *Models of Regional Governance for the Pacific: Sovereignty and the Future Architecture of Regionalism*, ed. Kennedy Graham (Christchurch, New Zealand: University of Canterbury, 2008), 64.

11 Forum Communiqué, 38th PIF summit, Nuku'Alofa, Tonga, 16–17 October 2007, annex A.
12 PIF Secretariat, *Pacific Plan Annual Progress Report*, 2007, 28.
13 Clements, "Conflict Prevention: Does 'Responsibility to Protect' Fit into Biketawa?," 146.
14 See also Spillane, "The Pacific Plan 2006–15: Legal Implications for Regionalism," 72–82.
15 Clements, "Conflict Prevention: Does 'Responsibility to Protect' Fit into Biketawa?," 145.
16 I. C. Campbell, *A History of the Pacific Islands* (Berkeley: University of California Press, 1996).
17 Michael Haas, *The Pacific Way: Regional Cooperation in the South Pacific* (New York: Praeger Publishers, 1989).
18 William Sutherland, "Regional Governance, Peace and Security in the Pacific: A Case for Give and Take," UNU-CRIS Occasional Paper, O-2004/12, Bruges, 2004.
19 Spillane, "The Pacific Plan 2006–15: Legal Implications for Regionalism," 72–82.
20 Hoadley, "Pacific Islands Security Management by New Zealand and Australia: Towards a New Paradigm."
21 Elsina Wainwright, "Responding to State Failure—The Case of Australia and Solomon Islands," *Australian Journal of International Affairs* 57, no. 3 (2003): 485–98; Clive Moore, *Happy Isles in Crisis: the Historical Causes for a Failing State in Solomon Islands, 1998–2004* (Canberra, ACT: Asia Pacific Press, 2004); Shahar Hameiri, "The Trouble with RAMSI: Reexaming the Roots of Conflict in Solomon Islands," *The Contemporary Pacific* 9, no. 2 (2007): 409–41.
22 Although the conflict is generally portrayed as an ethnic dispute (even by its perpetrators), a more careful analysis reveals that the crisis was in fact triggered by successive governments' poor policies, a flawed political system, poor leadership, and other socio-economic development issues that have not been properly addressed (Tarcisius Tara Kabutaulaka, "Beyond Ethnicity: The Political Economy of the Guadalcanal Crisis in Solomon Islands," in Australian National University, *State, Society and Governance in Melanesia Project*, Working Paper 01/1, 2001).
23 This was not the first occasion for the government of a Pacific country to seek help in this way. Vanuatu brought in troops from Papua New Guinea at independence to help put down the Santo Rebellion (see Frazer and Bryant-Tokalau, "Introduction: The Uncertain Future of Pacific Regionalism" 1–23).
24 *Forum Declaration on Solomon Islands*, Annex 1 to Forum communiqué to 34th PIF summit, Auckland, New Zealand, 14–16 August 2003.
25 Fiji, Tonga, and PNG sent troops and police and Samoa, Vanuatu, Cook Islands, Nauru, Tuvalu, and Kiribati sent police officers. The cost of Operation Helpem Fren was estimated at US$200 million in the first year, most of it met by Australia but with contributions also from New Zealand, the EU, UN, World Bank, IMF and ADB.
26 Wainwright, "Responding to State Failure—The Case of Australia and Solomon Islands," 489.
27 Tarcisius Tara Kabutaulaka, "Australian Foreign Policy and the RAMSI Intervention in Solomon Islands," *The Contemporary Pacific* 17, no. 2 (2005): 283–308.

28 Spillane, "The Pacific Plan 2006–15: Legal Implications for Regionalism," 74.
29 *PIF Review of the Regional Assistance Mission to Solomon Islands (RAMSI)*, April-June 2007.
30 Forum communiqué, 35th PIF Summit, Apia, Samoa, 5–7 August 2004, para. 26.
31 For instance, the *New Zealand Defence Policy Framework 2000* states: "New Zealand has special obligations to Pacific Neighbours to assist in maintaining peace, preserving the environment, promoting good governance and helping achieve economic well being. We want a secure neighbourhood and we must work towards that" (Ministry of Defence of New Zealand, "The Government's Defence Policy Framework," in *Government Defence Statement* (Wellington, New Zealand: Ministry of Defence, 2001), 3).
32 Clive Moore, "The RAMSI Intervention in the Solomon Islands," *The Journal of Pacific Studies* 28, no. 1 (2005): 74.
33 Peter Wallensteen, *Conflict Prevention and the South Pacific: Plenary Address*, delivered to the Conference on Securing a Peaceful Pacific, Christchurch, New Zealand, 16 October 2004, 3.
34 Graham, "Models of Regional Governance: Is There a Choice for the Pacific?," 40.

11 European Union (EU)

1 Chapter written with research assistance from Daniele Marchesi and Tiziana Scaramagli.
2 Belgium, France, Italy, Luxembourg, The Netherlands, and West Germany, became "the Nine" in 1973 with the accession of Ireland, the United Kingdom, and Denmark. In 1981 Greece and in 1986 Spain and Portugal joined the EC. In 1995 the Community enlarged to include Austria, Finland, and Sweden; and in 2004 to include Cyprus, the Czech Republic, Estonia, Hungary, Latvia, Lithuania, Malta, Poland, Slovakia, and Slovenia. The last enlargement, in 2008, included Bulgaria and Romania.
3 See Fraser Cameron, *The Foreign and Security Policy of the European Union: Past, Present and Future* (Sheffield, UK: Sheffield Academic Press, 1999), 16.
4 Simon Nuttall, *European Political Co-Operation* (Oxford: Clarendon Press, 1992), 11.
5 Alyson J. K. Bailes, "The European Security Strategy: an Evolutionary History," *SIPRI Policy Paper*, no. 10, 2005.
6 Sven Biscop, *The European Security Strategy: A Global Agenda for Positive Power* (Aldershot, UK: Ashgate, 2005), 136 (italics as original).
7 Cited in Björn Hettne and Fredrik Söderbaum, "Civilian Power or Soft Imperialism? The EU as a Global Actor and the Role of Interregionalism," *European Foreign Affairs Review* 10, no. 4 (2005): 538
8 Stephen Keukeleire and Jennifer Macnaughtan. *The Foreign Policy of the European Union* (Basingstoke, UK and New York: Palgrave Macmillan, 2008), 66.
9 Catriona Gourlay, "European Union Procedures and Resources for Crisis Management," *International Peacekeeping* 11, no. 3 (2004): 404–21.
10 Keukeleire and Macnaughtan, *The Foreign Policy of the European Union*, 71.

11 Press release, (document 15396/08 (Presse 319), 2903rd External Relations Council meeting, Brussels, Belgium, GAERC, 10–11 November 2008.
12 International Crisis Group, "EU Crisis Response Capability Revisited," *Europe Report*, no. 160, 2005.
13 Adopted in 2006, The Instrument for Stability is, according to the EU, the main thematic tool which provides for development cooperation measures, as well as financial, economic and technical cooperation measures with partner countries in contexts of crisis and emerging crisis on the one hand and of stable conditions for cooperation on the other hand.
14 Hans W. Maull (1990) defines a civilian power as involving three central characteristics: (a) the acceptance of the necessity of cooperation with others in the pursuit of international objectives; (b) focus on non-military, primarily economic, means to secure national goals; and (c) willingness to develop supranational structures to address issues of international management. The idea of "civilian power" was first launched by François Duchêne in 1972 as the ability to promote and encourage stability through economic and political means. Nowadays the debate is centered on the question of whether military integration is compatible with a civilian power agenda. A majority of views suggests that military means are embedded in a civilian power context (Henrik Larsen, "The EU: A Global Military Actor?," *Cooperation and Conflict* 37, no. 3 (2002): 283–302; Stelios Stavridis, "Militarising the EU: The Concept of Civilian Power Europe Revisited," *The International Spectator* 41, no. 4 (2001): 43–50). Others, on the other hand, contend that enhancing the EU's military resources "would close off the path of fully embracing civilian power. And this means giving up far too much for far too little" (Karen Smith, "The End of Civilian Power Europe : A Welcome Demise or Cause for Concern?", *The International Spectator* 35, no. 2 (2000): 11–28).
15 Sven Biscop, *Permanent Structured Cooperation and the Future of ESDP: Transformation and Integration*, paper presented to the 3rd seminar in the EUISS-coordinated series on the European Security Strategy, Helsinki, Finland, 18–19 September 2008.
16 Mario Télo, *Europe: A Civilian Power? European Union, Global Governance, World Order* (Basingstoke, UK: Palgrave Macmillan, 2007); Zaki Laïdi, *EU Foreign Policy in a Globalized World: Normative Power and Social Preferences* (London and New York: Routledge, 2008).
17 Keukeleire and Macnaughtan, *The Foreign Policy of the European Union.*
18 Stephen Keukeleire, "EU Core Groups—Specialization and Division of Labour in European Union Foreign Policy," CEPS Working Document, no. 252, 2006.
19 Adrian Treacher, "From Civilian Power to Military Actor: The EU's Resistable Transformation," *European Foreign Affairs Review* 9, no. 1 (2004): 49–66.
20 Jolyon Howorth, *Security and Defence Policy in the European Union* (Basingstoke, UK and New York: Palgrave Macmillan, 2007).
21 Robert Kagan, *Of Paradise and Power: America and Europe in the New World Order* (New York: Alfred A. Knopf, 2003).
22 Kari Möttölä, "The European Union and Crisis Management," in *European Security and Transatlantic Relations after 9/11 and the Iraq War*, ed. Heinz Gärtner and Ian M. Cuthbertson (Basingstoke, UK and New York: Palgrave Macmillan, 2005), 183–98.

12 North Atlantic Treaty Organization

1 Chapter written with research assistance from Tiziana Scaramagli.
2 For example the foreign affairs minister of the provisional government of France, Georges Bidault, in a meeting with Ernest Bevin (British secretary of state for foreign affairs in the Attlee government) in September 1945 referred to the German threat as a "convenient myth" (cited in Dietmar Hueser, "Charles De Gaulle, George Bidault, Robert Schuman et L'Ale-magne 1944–50: Conceptions-Actions-Perceptions," *Francia* 23, no. 3 (1996): 64). Bevin himself, in 1946, told the cabinet that, "the danger of Russia has become certainly as great as, and possibly even greater than, that of a revived Germany" (cited in Norrin Ripsman, "Two Stages of Tran-sition from a Region of War to a Region of Peace," *International Studies Quarterly* 49, no. 4 (2005): 680). Later in 1948, he pointed out that the Brussels Treaty had to mention Germany because a failure to do so "would be unnecessarily provocative to the Russians (cited in John Baylis, "Britain and the Dunkirk Treaty: The Origins of NATO," *Journal of Strategic Studies* 5, no. 2 (1982): 245.
3 Since April 1, 2009, NATO has 28 member states: Albania, Belgium, Bulgaria, Canada, Croatia, Czech Republic, Denmark, Estonia, France, Germany, Greece, Hungary, Iceland, Italy, Latvia, Lithuania, Luxembourg, Netherlands, Norway, Poland, Portugal, Romania, Slovakia, Slovenia, Spain, Turkey, United Kingdom, United States.
4 NATO Strategic Concept, April 1999 (para. 20). Available at www.nato.int/docu/pr/1999/p99-065e.htm.
5 Julian Lindley-French, *The North Atlantic Treaty Organization: The Enduring Alliance* (New York and London: Routledge, 2007).
6 Speech delivered by the Secretary of State for Defence at Wilton Park on 15 January 2009. Available at www.acronym.org.uk/docs/0901/doc01.htm.
7 Paul Gallis, *NATO's Decision-Making Procedure*, CRS Report for Congress, Washington, D.C., 5 May 2003, 4.
8 Hans Binnendijk and Richard Kugler, "Needed—A NATO Stabilization and Reconstruction Force," *Defense Horizons* 45 (2004): 1–8.
9 Sven Biscop, "NATO, ESDP and the Riga Summit: No Transformation without Reequilibration," *EGMONT Paper*, no. 11, 2006.
10 Renée de Nevers, "NATO's International Security Role in the Terrorist Era," *International Security* 31, no. 4 (2008): 54.
11 John J. Mearsheimer, "Back to the Future: Instability in Europe After the Cold War," *International Security* 15, no. 1 (1990): 52; Kenneth N. Waltz, "The Emerging Structure of International Politics," *International Security* 18, no. 2 (1993): 75–76.
12 Janka Oertel, "The United Nations and NATO," paper presented to the ACNUS 21st Annual Meeting, Bonn, Germany, 5–7 June 2008.
13 Speech by NATO secretary-general Jaap de Hoop Scheffer, Riga, Latvia, 14 July 2006.
14 Ivo Daalder and James Goldgeier, "Global NATO," *Foreign Affairs* 85, no. 5 (2006): 106.
15 Julianne Smith, *Transforming NATO (… again): A Primer for the NATO Summit in Riga 2006* (Washington, D.C.: Center for Strategic and International Studies, 2006).

16 The civil budget for 2007 was $364.18 million and covered operating costs of the international staff at NATO headquarters, the execution of approved civilian programs and activities, and the construction, running and maintenance costs of facilities, including personnel costs. The military budget for 2007 was $2 billion, largely financed from the appropriations of the ministries of defense. The civil and military budgets, however, do not cover the costs of the missions, which are financed under the "costs lie where they fall" principle.

17 Michaele Schreyer, "Comment: Truth about NATO Burden-sharing," *Daily Times*, 9 July 2008.

18 Sven Biscop, "Permanent Structured Cooperation and the Future of ESDP: Transformation and Integration," paper presented to the 3rd Seminar in the EUISS-coordinated series on the European Security Strategy, Helsinki, 18–19 September 2008.

19 Rachel A. Epstein, "When Legacies Meet Policies: NATO and the Refashioning of Polish Military Tradition," *East European Politics and Societies* 20, no. 2 (2006): 219–53.

13 Conclusions

1 Dorn Walter, "Regional Peacekeeping Is Not the Way," *Peacekeeping and International Relations* 27, no. 3/4 (1998): 1–3.

2 Ian Martin, "Is the Regionalization of Peace Operations Desirable?" in *The United Nations and Regional Security: Europe and Beyond*, ed. Michael Pugh and Waheguru Pal Singh Sidhu (Boulder, Colo. and London: Lynne Rienner, 2003), 51.

3 Cited in Tim Murithi, (forthcoming 2009), "IGAD on the Ground: Comparing Interventions in Sudan and Somalia," *African Security*, 2, no. 2.

4 See Steven Wondu and Ann Lesch, *Battle for Peace in Sudan: An Analysis of the Abuja Conferences, 1992–1993* (Lanham, Md.: University Press of America, 2000), 153.

5 Interview, Ambassador Dr. H. B. Attalla, Executive Secretary, IGAD (16 October 2007).

6 Interview, Naison Ngoma, Peace and Security Department, Conflict Management Division, Expert Post-Conflict Reconstruction and Peace Building, African Union (24 September 2007).

7 Katharina P. Coleman, *International Organisations and Peace Enforcement: The Politics of International Legitimacy* (Cambridge and New York: Cambridge University Press, 2007), 181.

8 Interview, official at the Peace and Security Council of African Union (10 October 2007). Anonymity required.

9 Interview, Chrysantus (Chris) Ayangafac, Senior Researcher in the Direct Conflict Prevention Programme, Institute for Security Studies, Addis Ababa (18 September 2007).

10 Ian Martin, "Is the Regionalization of Peace Operations Desirable?" in *The United Nations and Regional Security: Europe and Beyond*, ed. Michael Pugh and Waheguru Pal Singh Sidhu (Boulder, Colo. and London: Lynne Rienner, 2003), 48.

11 Jane Boulden, "United Nations Security Council Policy on Africa," in *Dealing with Conflict in Africa: The United Nations and Regional Organizations*,

ed. Jane Boulden (Basingstoke, UK and New York: Palgrave Macmillan, 2003), 30.

12 For an interesting analysis of the absense of a regional organization suitable to address the Israeli–Palestinian conflict see Hilaire McCoubrey and Justin Morris, *Regional Peacekeeping in the Post-Cold War Era* (The Hague: Kluwer Law International, 2000), 187–99.

13 Statement by the President of the Security Council (Security Council document S/2006/590), para. 79, 20 September 2006.

14 See *Letter Dated 90/08/09 from the Permanent Representative of Nigeria to the United Nations Addressed to the Secretary-General*, S/21485, 10 August 1990; *Letter Dated 90/12/14 from the Permanent Representative of The Gambia to the United Nations Addressed to the Secretary-General*, S/22025, 20 December 1990; *Note by the President of the Security Council*, S/22133, 22 January 1991; *Note by the President of the Security Council*, S/23886, 7 May 1992; Security Council resolution 788, 19 November 1992; Security Council resolution 813, 27 August 1998; Security Council resolution 856, 10 August 1993; Security Council resolution 866, 22 September 1993.

Annotated bibliography

Books

Adekeye Adebajo, *Building Peace in West Africa: Liberia, Sierra Leone and Guinea-Bissau* (Boulder, Colo: Lynne Rienner, 2002). A very detailed analysis of ECOWAS' interventions in Liberia, Sierra Leone, and Guinea-Bissau.

Amitav Acharya and Alastair Iain Johnston, eds., *Crafting Cooperation. Regional International Institutions in Comparative Perspective* (Cambridge and New York: Cambridge University Press, 2007). A much-needed book on the institutional design of organizations such as the EU, NATO, ASEAN, the OAS, the AU and the Arab League.

Andrew Cooper and Thomas Legler, *Intervention Without Intervening: the OAS Defense and Promotion of Democracy in the Americas* (Basingstoke, UK: Palgrave Macmillan, 2006). It looks at the evolution of OAS multilateralism for democracy. Theoretically sound.

Bruno Simma, Hermann Mosler, and Helmut Brokelmann, *The Charter of the United Nations: A Commentary* (Oxford: Oxford University Press, 1994). By far the best legal analysis of Chapter VIII of the UN Charter.

Connie Peck, *Sustainable Peace: The Role of the UN and Regional Organizations in Preventing Conflict* (Lanham, Md.: Rowman and Littlefield, 1998). Although most of the information is no longer up to date, the book is still regarded as a key publication in the field.

Gabriel H. Oosthuizen, *The Southern African Development Community: The Organization, Its Policies and Prospects* (Midrand, South Africa: South Africa: Institute for Global Dialogue, 2006). This is the best introduction to SADC's policies and history. It is not widely available but it is worth searching for.

Hilaire McCoubrey and Justin Morris, *Regional Peacekeeping in the Post-Cold War Era* (The Hague, The Netherlands: Kluwer Law International, 2000). Although important information is no longer up to date, the book provides two interesting chapters on the absence, potential, and danger of regional peace support operations.

Jane Boulden, ed., *Dealing with Conflict in Africa: The United Nations and Regional Organizations* (London: Palgrave Macmillan, 2003). It provides an engaging analysis of six case studies of major conflicts in Africa, and for each case study it looks at what responsibilities and tasks were taken on by different organizations.

John Mackinlay and Peter Cross, eds., *Regional Peacekeepers: The Paradox of Russian Peacekeeping* (Tokyo: United Nations University Press, 2003). Probably the best book on the operational procedures, doctrine and military approach of Russia's peacekeeping. It draws from extensive field work.

Katharina P. Coleman, *International Organisations and Peace Enforcement: The Politics of International Legitimacy* (Cambridge and New York: Cambridge University Press, 2007). A very thorough and well written analysis of some of SADC, ECOWAS and NATO's interventions.

Kennedy Graham and Tânia Felício, *Regional Security and Global Governance: A Study of Interaction Between Regional Agencies and the UN Security Council with a Proposal for a Regional-Global Security Mechanism* (Brussels, Belgium: VUB University Press, 2006). Although it was published by a small university press, it provides an interesting, bold, and prescriptive analysis of cooperation between the UN and regional organizations.

Lena Jonson and Clive Archer, eds., *Peacekeeping and the Role of Russia in Eurasia* (Boulder, Colo. and Oxford: Westview Press, 1996). A very lucid account of Russia's peacekeeping in Eurasia with the focus on interventions in Tajikistan, Transdniestr, Abkhazia and Nagorno-Karabakh. It includes also a chapter with a compelling analysis of the CIS written by Anna Kreikemeyer and Andrei V. Zagorski.

Louise Fawcett, "Regional Institutions," in *Security Studies: An Introduction*, ed. Paul Williams (London and New York: Routledge, 2008), 307–24. Although this book chapter aims to be comprehensive its most relevant section is the initial survey of the history and evolution of regional security institutions since the Second World War.

Michael Pugh and Waheguru Pal Singh Sidhu, *The United Nations and Regional Security: Europe and Beyond* (Boulder, Colo. and London: Lynne Rienner, 2003). It has three initial chapters that provide an interesting description of the UN and regional organizations. But the bulk of the book is devoted to European organizations and operations in Europe, hindering the possibility of a solid comparative approach.

Paul F. Diehl and Joseph Lepgold, eds., *Regional Conflict Management* (Lanham, Md.: Rowman and Littlefield, 2003). It is one of the first books to examine the implications and efficacy of regional conflict management. The analysis is broad and not confined to the role of regional institutions.

Samuel M. Makinda and F. Wafula Okumu, *The African Union: Challenges of Globalization, Security, and Governance* (London and New York: Routledge, 2007). A must read for whoever is interested in the African Union. Interesting focus on globalization, governance, security, and development.

Thomas G. Weiss, ed., *Beyond Subcontracting: Task-Sharing With Regional Security Arrangements and Service Providing NGOs* (Houndmills, UK and London: Macmillan Press, 1998). It puts the focus on the issue of devolution.

Chapter 1 by Muthiah Alagappa provides a good introduction to the role of regional organizations in peace and security.

Timothy Murithi, *The African Union: Pan-Africanism, Peacebuilding and Development* (Aldershot, UK: Ashgate, 2005). Written by a leading expert on the African Union, the most interesting chapter is the one on the history of African regionalism.

Websites

African Union (AU)
Addis Ababa, Ethiopia
www.africa-union.org

Economic Community of West African States (ECOWAS)
Abuja, Nigeria
www.ecowas.int

Intergovernmental Authority on Development (IGAD)
Djibouti City, Djibouti
www.igad.org

Southern African Development Community (SADC)
Gaborone, Botswana
www.sadc.int

Organization of American States (OAS)
Washington, D.C., USA
www.oas.org

Association of Southeast Asian Nations (ASEAN)
Jakarta, Indonesia
www.aseansec.org

Commonwealth of Independent States (CIS)
Minsk, Belarus
www.cis.minsk.by

League of Arab States (LAS)
Cairo, Egypt
www.arableagueonline.org

Pacific Islands Forum (PIF)
Suva, Fiji
www.forumsec.org

European Union (EU)
Brussels, Belgium and Strasbourg, France
http://europa.eu

North Atlantic Treaty Organization (NATO)
Brussels, Belgium
www.nato.int

Index

GLOBAL INSTITUTIONS SERIES

NEW TITLE
Global Institutions and the HIV/AIDS Epidemic
Responding to an international crisis

Franklyn Lisk, University of Warwick, UK

Lisk examines the different perspectives of the global response to HIV/AIDS and the role of the different global institutions (multilateral, public and private) involved, including their impact on outcomes.

Selected contents: 1 The evolution HIV/AIDS as a global epidemic and early global response 2 The rise and fall of the global programme on AIDS (GPA) 3 The birth of the joint United Nations programme on HIV/AIDS (UNAIDS) 4 HIV/AIDS and human rights 5 HIV/AIDS as a security threat 6 HIV/AIDS as a development challenge 7 HIV/AIDS and human resource capacity 8 Financing of the global HIV/AIDS response 9 Global governance and HIV/AIDS response 10 Critical and emerging issues and challenges in HIV/AIDS response

September 2009: 216x138: 160pp
Hb: 978-0-415-44496-5: **£65.00**
Pb: 978-0-415-44497-2: **£14.99**

NEW TITLE
African Economic Institutions

Kwame Akonor, Seton Hall University, USA

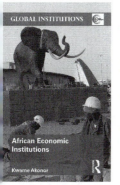

This book examines and assesses the principal international economic organizations (IEO's) based in Africa, analysing how African IEOs have evolved and what contributions they have made to the continents's socio-economic development.

Selected contents: 1 The history of African economic institutions and their development agenda 2 Structure and activities of the African IEOs 3 Towards a heterodox approach 4 African regional economic communities 5 Emerging issues and future direction

November 2009: 216x138: 144pp
Hb: 978-0-415-77637-0: **£65.00**

 **Routledge**
Taylor & Francis Group

To order any of these titles
Call: +44 (0) 1235 400400
Email: book.orders@routledge.co.uk

For further information visit:
www.routledge.com/politics